PSYCHOLOGICAL BASIS OF PHYSICAL EDUCATION

PSYCHOLOGICAL BASIS OF PHYSICAL EDUCATION

Editor
Shamshad Ahmed

ISHA

ISHA BOOKS
Delhi-110033

Psychological Basis of Physical Education

ISBN: 81-8205-245-9

Reprinted in 2012 in India by
Isha Publications
B-69, New Gupta Colony
Near DDA Market
Delhi-110009

Printed at: G. Print Process, Delhi

Contents

1

Meaning and Definition of Psychology

Psychology is the practice of studying, teaching, or applying an understanding of the mind, thought, and behaviour. It is largely concerned with psychology of humans, although the behaviour and thought of non-human animals is also studied; either as a subject in its own right, or more controversially, as a way of gaining an insight into human psychology by means of comparison.

Psychology is conducted both scientifically and non-scientifically. Mainstream psychology is based largely on positivism, using quantitative studies and the scientific method to test and disprove hypotheses, often in an experimental context. Psychology tends to be eclectic, drawing on scientific knowledge from other fields to help explain and understand behaviour. However, not all psychological research methods are scientific, and some may involve qualitative or interpretive techniques more allied to the humanities.

Some psychologists, particularly adherents to humanistic psychology, may go as far as completely rejecting a scientific approach. However, mainstream psychology has a bias towards the scientific method, which is reflected in the dominance of cognitivism as the guiding theoretical framework used by most psychologists to understand thought and behaviour. Psychology does not necessarily refer to the brain or nervous system and can be framed purely in terms of phenomenological or information processing theories of mind. Increasingly though, an understanding of brain function is being included in psychological theory and practice, particularly in areas such as artificial intelligence, neuropsychology, and cognitive neuroscience.

Psychology differs from sociology, anthropology, economics, and political science, in part, by studying the behaviour of individuals (alone or in groups) rather than the behaviour of the groups or aggregates themselves. Although psychological questions were asked in antiquity, psychology emerged as a separate discipline only recently.

History of Psychology

The root of the word psychology (psyche) means "soul" or "spirit" in Greek, and psychology was sometimes considered a study of the soul, though its emergence as a medical discipline can be seen in Thomas Willis' reference to psychology (the "Doctrine of the Soul") in terms of brain function, as part of his 1672 anatomical treatise "De Anima Brutorum".

Until about the end of the 19th century, psychology was regarded as a branch of philosophy. In 1879 Wilhelm Wundt founded a laboratory at the University in Germany in Leipzig specifically to focus on general and basic questions concerning behaviour and mental states. William James later published his 1890 book, Principles of Psychology which laid many of the foundations for the sorts of questions that psychologists would focus on for years to come.

Crucially, the approach of Wundt and James did not involve metaphysics or religious explanations of human thought and behaviour, freeing it from the realms of philosophy and theology, and in many people's eyes, founding the modern science of psychology. Meanwhile, Sigmund Freud had invented and applied a method of psychotherapy known as psychoanalysis. Freud's understanding of the mind was largely based on interpretive methods and introspection, but was particularly focused on resolving mental distress and psychopathology.

Freud's theories were wildly successful, not least because they aimed to be of practical benefit to individual patients, but also because they tackled subjects such as sexuality and repression as general aspects of psychological development. These were largely considered taboo subjects at the time, and Freud provided a catalyst for them to be openly discussed in polite society. Although it has become fashionable to discredit many of Freud's more outlandish theories, his application of psychology to clinical work and his more mainstream work have been massively influential.

Partly as a reaction to the subjective and introspective nature of psychology at the time, behaviourism began to become popular as a guiding psychological theory. Championed by psychologists such as John B. Watson, Edward Thorndike and B. F. Skinner it argued that psychology should be a science of behaviour, not the mind, and rejected the idea of internal mental states such as beliefs, desires or goals, believing all behaviour and learning to be a reaction to the environment. Watson argued that psychology "is a purely objective experimental branch of natural science", "introspection forms no essential part of its methods..." and "The behaviourist... recognizes no dividing line between man and brute".

Behaviourism was the dominant model in psychology for much of the early 20th century, largely due to the creation and successful application (not least of which in advertising) of conditioning theories as scientific models of human behaviour. However, it became increasingly clear that although behaviourism had made some important discoveries, it was deficient as a guiding theory of human behaviour. Noam Chomsky's review of *Skinner's book Verbal Behaviour* (that aimed to explain language acquisition in a behaviourist framework) is considered one of the major factors in the ending of behaviourism's reign. Chomsky demonstrated that language could not purely be learnt from conditioning, as people could produce sentences unique in structure and meaning that couldn't possibly be generated solely through experience of natural language, implying that there must be internal states of mind that behaviourism rejected as illusory. Similarly, work by Albert Bandura showed that children could learn by social observation, without any change in overt behaviour, and so must be accounted for by internal representations.

The rise of computer technology also promoted the metaphor of mental function as information processing. This, combined with a scientific approach to studying the mind, as well as a belief in internal mental states, led to the rise of cognitivism as the dominant model of the mind. Links between brain and nervous system function were also becoming common, partly due to the experimental work of people like Charles Sherrington and Donald Hebb, and partly due to studies of people with brain injury. With the development of technologies for accurately measuring brain function, neuropsychology and cognitive neuroscience have become some of the most active areas in contemporary psychology.

With the increasing involvement of other disciplines (such as philosophy, computer science and neuroscience) in the quest to understand the mind, the umbrella discipline of cognitive science has been created as a means of focusing such efforts in a constructive way. However, not all psychologists have been happy with what they perceive as mechanical models of the mind and human nature.Carl Jung, a one-time follower and contemporary of Freud, was instrumental in introducing notions of spirituality into Freudian psychoanalysis (Freud had rejected religion as a mass delusion).

Humanistic psychology emerged in the 1950s and has continued as a reaction to positivist and scientific approaches to the mind. It stresses a phenomenological view of human experience and seeks to understand human beings and their behaviour by conducting qualitative research. The humanistic approach has its roots in existentialist and phenomenological philosophy and many humanist psychologists completely reject a scientific approach, arguing that trying to turn human experience into measurements strips it of all meaning and relevance to lived existence.

Some of the founding theorists behind this school of thought are Abraham Maslow who formulated a hierarchy of human needs, Carl Rogers who created and developed client centred therapy, and Fritz Perls who helped create and develop Gestalt therapy. Various schools of thought have argued for a particular model to be used as a guiding theory by which all, or the majority, of human behaviour can be explained. The popularity of these has waxed and waned over time.

Some psychologists may think of themselves as adherents to a particular school of thought and reject the others, although most consider each as an approach to understanding the mind, and not necessarily as mutually exclusive theories.

— behaviourism

— cognitivism

— functionalism

— Gestalt psychology

— humanistic psychology and phenomenology

— psychoanalysis

— structuralism

Modern psychology

The majority of mainstream psychology is based on a framework derived from cognitive psychology, although the popularity of this paradigm does not exclude others, which are often applied as necessary. Alternatively, a psychologist may specialise in an area in which cognitive psychology is rarely used.

A psychologist will often attempt to measure or test different aspects of psychological function, using psychometric and statistical methods, including well known standardised tests as well as those created as the situation requires.

Academic psychologists may focus purely on research, aiming to further psychological understanding in a particular area, while other psychologists may work in applied psychology to deploy such knowledge for immediate and practical benefit. However, these approaches are not mutually exclusive and most psychologists will be involved in both researching and applying psychology at some point during their work.

Contemporary psychology is broad-based and consists of a diverse set of approaches, subject areas, and applications. A comprehensive list is given in the Topics and Divisions sections below. Where an area of interest is considered to need specific training and specialist knowledge (especially in applied areas), psychological societies will typically set up a governing body to manage training requirements. Similarly, requirements may be laid down for university degrees in psychology, so that students acquire an adequate knowledge in a number of areas. While the exact divisions may vary from country to country, the following areas are usually considered as core subjects or approaches by psychology societies and universities.

Cognitive psychology

Cognitive psychology is a framework in which to understand the mind more than a subject area, although it has traditionally focused on certain aspects of psychology. Perception, learning, problem solving, memory, attention, language and emotion are all well researched areas. Cognitive psychology is based on a school of thought known as cognitivism, whose adherents argue for an information processing model of mental function, informed by positivism and experimental psychology. Techniques and models from cognitive psychology are widely applied and form the mainstay of psychological theories in many areas of both research and applied psychology.

Clinical and counselling psychology

Clinical psychology is the application of psychology to the understanding, treatment, and assessment of psychopathology, behavioural or mental health issues. It has traditionally been associated with counselling and psychotherapy, although modern clinical psychology may take an eclectic approach, including a number of therapeutic approaches. Typically, although working with many of the same clients as psychiatrists, clinical psychologists do not prescribe psychiatric drugs.

Clinical psychologists largely work within the scientist-practictioner model where clinical problems are formulated as hypotheses to be tested as information is gathered about the patient and his or her mental state. Some clinical psychologists may focus on the clinical management of patients with brain injury. This is known as clinical neuropsychology and typically involves additional training in brain function.

In recent years and particularly in the United States, a major split has been developing between academic research psychologists in universities and some branches of clinical psychology. Many academic psychologists believe that these clinicians use therapies based on discredited theories and unsupported by empirical evidence of their effectiveness. From the other side, these clinicians believe that the academics are ignoring their experience in dealing with actual patients. The disagreement has resulted in the formation of the American Psychological Society by the research psychologists as a new body distinct from the American Psychological Association.

Developmental and educational psychology

Largely focusing on the development of the human mind through childhood (although development through adulthood is also studied), developmental psychology seeks to understand how children come to perceive, understand, and act within the world. This may focus on intellectual, cognitive, neural, social, or moral development and involve a number of unique research methods to engage children in experimental tasks. These tasks often resemble specially designed games and activities that are both enjoyable for the child and scientifically useful.

Educational psychology largely seeks to apply much of this knowledge and understand how learning can best take place in educational situations. Because of this, the work of child psychologists such as Lev Vygotsky, Jean Piaget and Jerome Bruner has been influential in creating teaching methods and educational practices.

Forensic psychology

Forensic psychology is concerned with the psychology of crime, criminals, and law enforcement. A forensic psychologist may be involved in assessment of offenders or interventions to prevent offending behaviour, usually with people who have already come in contact with the legal or penal system. Often this involves working with offenders with mental health problems, or with people who act dangerously or in an antisocial manner (for example, psychopaths). Criminal profiling is another important role fulfilled by forensic psychologists and typically involves building psychological profiles of unknown or at-large offenders from the known evidence.

Health psychology

Whereas clinical psychology focuses on mental health and neurological illness, health psychology is concerned with the psychology of a much wider range of health-related behaviour including healthy eating, the doctor-patient relationship, a patient's understanding of health information, and beliefs about illness. Health psychologists may be involved in public health campaigns, examining the impact of illness or health policy on quality of life or in research into the psychological impact of health and social care.

Industrial and organisational psychology

Involved with the application of psychology to the world of business, commerce and the function of organisations, industrial and organisational psychology focuses to varying degrees on the psychology of the workforce, customer, and consumer, including issues such as the psychology of recruitment, training, appraisal, job satisfaction, stress at work and management. Psychologists may also work on product design, interaction with machines or software, advertising, sales, and marketing, to aid functionality, safety and appeal.

Neuropsychology

Neuropsychology is a branch of psychology that aims to understand how the structure and function of the brain relates to specific psychological processes. Often neuropsychologists are employed as scientists to advance scientific or medical knowledge. Cognitive neuropsychology is particularly concerned with the understanding of brain injury in an attempt to work out normal psychological function. Clinical neuropsychology is the application of neuropsychology for the clinical management of patients with neurocognitive deficits.

Social psychology

Social psychology aims to understand how we make sense of social situations. For example, this could involve the influence of others on an individual's behaviour (e.g., conformity or persuasion), the perception and understanding of social cues, or the formation of attitudes or stereotypes about other people. Social cognition is a common approach and involves a mostly cognitive and scientific approach to understanding social behaviour.

Although in principle, psychology aims to explain all aspects of thought and behaviour, some topics have generated particular interest, either due to their perceived importance, their ease of study or popularity. Many of the concepts studied by professional psychology stem from the day-to-day psychology used by most people and learnt through experience. This is known as folk psychology to distinguish it from psychological knowledge developed through formal study and investigation. The extent to which folk psychology should be used as a basis for understanding human experience is controversial, although theories that are based on everyday notions of the mind have been among some of the most successful.

Divisions and approaches in psychology

Different disciplines in psychology typically signify both a set of practices and an area of interest. The divisions are largely arbitrary and overlapping (although they may have been formalised into areas of interest by psychological societies or regulatory bodies) and most psychologists will use methods from each area as appropriate, even if they mostly focus on one area of interest in their work.

— abnormal psychology

— activity theory

— analytical psychology

— applied psychology

— behavioural medicine

— behavioural psychology

— biobehavioural health

— biological psychology

— cognitive neuropsychology

— cognitive psychology

— cognitive neuroscience

— community psychology

— comparative psychology
— clinical psychology
— counselling psychology
— critical psychology
— developmental psychology
— discursive psychology
— distributed cognition
— dynamic cognition
— ecological psychology
— educational psychology
— embodied cognition
— emotional clearing
— evolutionary psychology
— experimental psychology
— forensic psychology
— health psychology
— humanistic psychology
— individual differences psychology
— industrial and organisational psychology
— medicinal psychology
— medical psychology
— neuropsychology
— personality psychology
— physiological psychology
— popular psychology, self-help, and alternative therapy
— political psychology

— positive psychology
— pre- and perinatal psychology
— problem solving
— psychoanalysis
— psychohistory
— psychometrics
— psychonomics
— psychophysics
— psychophysiology
— psychotherapy a branch of psychiatry as well
— situated cognition
— social psychology
— systemic psychology
— theoretical psychology
— traffic psychology
— transpersonal psychology

Identity Theory and Social Identity Theory

Within social psychology, there are two dominant theory of identity – identity theory and social identity theory. Identity theory is a direct derivation of McCall and Simmons role-identity theory, which suggests that individuals will base their actions on how they like to see themselves and how they like to be seen by others. Therefore, the role-identity requires two components, specifically, the role itself and the identity to be associated with that role.

Social identity theory, however, is based on Festinger's social comparison theory, which suggests that individuals will strive to attach themselves to other individuals who are similar or slightly better. Social identity theory, therefore, focuses on the ways in which individuals perceive and categorize themselves, based on their social and personal identities. Rather than emphasizing role and role behaviors, social identity theory emphasizes group processes and inter-group relations.

Both of these theories posit that, theoretically, the self is multifaceted, dynamic, and is generally responsible for mediating the relationship between social structures and individuals behavior. However, the social identity theory has come to dominate the study of intergroup relations, while identity theory focuses on the concept of role identities. Generally, according to identity theorists, social identity "refers to the ways in which individuals and collectives are distinguished in their social relations with other individuals or collectives".

Social identity is our understanding of "who we are". One of the first things we do when we meet someone is "locate them on our social map" – or identify them. Social identities can also be considered social selves. These social selves are socially constructed and categorized in ways that are accepted by individuals as descriptive of themselves or their peer group. On the other hand, personal identities are "self descriptions referring to unique or highly specific details of [an individual's] biography". Identity theory is derived from the symbolic interactionist perspective of role choice behavior. This theory seeks to understand why people do what they do, or why they make the choices that they do.

Therefore, the most appropriate applications of this theory are ones in which alternative actions are available to the subject, however he/she may only choose one of the alternatives. Identity theory recognizes that social structure and social interaction are both equally constant in limiting, rather than determining, human action. Identity is defined as "a set of meanings applied to the self in a social role or situation defining what it means to be who one is". Choices in roles are seen as a consequence of identity salience, which is a specification of the general category of self. Furthermore, identity salience is a consequence of commitment. Therefore, commitment impacts the identity salience, which impacts role choice.

Identity is based on the categorizations that others have for an individual as well as the individual's acceptance of this categorization. Furthermore, identities exist only insofar as individuals are participants in structured social interaction. It can be suggested that identities are tied to roles, or positions, in organized social relationships. As individual identities are hierarchically organized, these identities will vary in terms of which is the most salient. Consequently, the self is organized based on this salience hierarchy. Therefore, choices are based on the salience of an identity, which is then positioned in the identity hierarchy.

One of the main components of identity theory is the ability of the self to take itself as an object, thereby classifying or categorizing itself in relation to other classifications or categorizations. In identity theory, this is referred to as identification, and "the core of an identity is the categorization of the self as an occupant of a role". It is through the process of identification that an identity is formed. Identification of people and things in the social world, and subsequent definitions of their meanings, is a key component of symbolic interactionism, and for human interactions.

Identification then incorporates the meanings and expectations associated with roles and performances, which ultimately forms a set of guidelines for behavior. Identification encompasses two types of identity. Social identity is identification in terms of broader social categories, while personal identity is defined in terms of categories that are more unique to the individual. In other words, "personal identities serve as the pegs upon which social identities can be hung". The personal identity can also be seen as the set of meanings that are tied to the self and help to sustain it, and these self-meanings carry across roles and situations.

Personal identities also penetrate social identities and carry into the group and into group identities. Furthermore, Strauss noted that identification requires an organized link to others, either formally or symbolically. A concern of identity theorists is the effect of individual position within the larger social structure, in an effort to understand which identity an individual will activate. Identity commitment (or identity salience) is composed of the number of networked ties an individual has as well as the strength of these ties. Stryker, in addressing identity salience, hypothesized that individuals will seek out opportunities to enact a highly salient identity. This hypothesis suggests that identities require more than simply a situational activation, however that the individual must also have the desire to activate them.

Social identity theory suggests that identities are tied to group membership. "Social identity theory is intended to be a social psychological theory of intergroup relations, group processes and the social self". The basic premise of this theory is that identity is formed based on group membership. Tajfel suggests that identity is also a function of the value and emotional attachment placed on a particular group membership. Morrereover, individuals strive to maintain positive social identities, which are primarily derived from favorable comparisons to group members and non-members.

Social identity theory has three primary components – categorization, identification, and comparison. What we referred to as identification under identity theory (the process by which an identity is formed), is known as self-categorization under social identity theory . Social categorization can be seen as a "system of orientation which helps to create and define the individual's place in society". In other words, we categorize individuals to better understand and relate to them. Keeping in mind that an individual can be a member of many different groups, he/she is likely to have a social identity for each group. That is to say that the specific group one is interacting with at any given time will dictate their current social identity.

Social identity theory further suggests that upon joining a group, individuals will think of that group as superior to any other group (or out-group), thereby enhancing their own self-image. Social identity theory suggests that individuals use social groups and group membership to maintain and support their personal and collective identities. As stated earlier, personal identities within identity theory are self-descriptions referring to specific, biographic, personal details. Within social identity theory, personal identities are derived fromo self-classifications, which in turn are based on interpersonal similarities and differences with other group members.

However, similarly to identity theory, these personal identities are private and unique to the individual. The social identities within identity theory are comparable to the collective identities within social identity theory. Collective identities represent self-classification in terms of comparisons with members of certain categories, such as race, class, etc. As Hogg et al note, both theories address the structure and function of a self that is socially constructed, however they do so in very different ways.

Identity theory focuses more explicitly on the structure and function of an individual's identity as they relate to the behavioral roles they play in society. On the other hand, social identity theory focuses on the structure and function of identities as they relate to group membership. Therefore, while the social identity theory perspective is concerned with intergroup relations and group processes, identity theory is more concerned with the roles individuals play in society and the identities that these roles confer.

Within identity theory, the process of identity formation requires the individual to define him/herself in terms of the social relationship. In the creation of a fan identity, the individual will develop either a personal identity, a social identify, or both. Identity theory suggests that individuals have choices and it examines why they make the choices they do. The questions that arises and remain to be answered are, why, and how have they chosen a specific team? Furthermore, if identity is created through interaction, what types of interaction led the individual to make the choices he/she made?

Sports and Sport Fan Research

Recent literature on sport fans has addressed possible reasons as to why individuals find sports to be enjoyable. These reasons include benefits associated with self esteem, an escape from everyday life, entertainment, economic factors, aesthetic or artistic qualities, group affiliation and family needs; however, why one particular team is chosen over another, and how this affiliation forms, is still not adequately addressed. Wann explores this notion to a degree. He focuses on college students and recreational softball players and attempts to determine what motivates people to become fans. Notably, Wann does state that his attempt to understand the motivations of individuals to become sport fans is a preliminary study.

Much of the existing research on sport fans focuses predominantly on college sports, as opposed to professional sports. Wann interviewed university students and recreational softball players regarding their feelings towards sports in general, without distinguishing between professional and college level. Miller used the same methodology and target population. Madrigal focused on fan satisfaction during college basketball games. Finally, Wann, Tucker, and Schrader allowed respondents to freely choose either a professional or amateur team in their interviews.

Focus on professional sports and specifically professional football does exist, but is less common than research on college students. This distinction is necessary in that it can be hypothesized that college students will form natural, although possible temporary allegiances, which are not necessarily seen at the professional level. Although a number of studies have been carried out on sport fans and sports spectators, few of them conceptualize fan or spectator, and any conceptualizations that are provided are not used with any consistency.

This is problematic in that spectators may not necessarily be fans. Furthermore, it is not uncommon for researchers to use the terms interchangeably, as does Smith, for example, which could result in further confusion. Any research that examines sport fans or spectators must first define fan and spectator to avoid any ambiguity and confusion. This is especially important when exploring the reasons for team identification, as there are different degrees of fandom or spectatorship.

To briefly explore some of the existing definitions of sport fans, sports involvement can be seen as revolving around the concept of perceived interest and the personal importance of sports to an individual. Jones suggests that spectators will observe a sport and then forget about it, while fans will have more intensity and will devote parts of every day to the team or the sport itself. Fanship has also been defined as "an affiliation in which a great deal of emotional significance and value are derived from group membership". Spinrad defines a fan as "the person who thinks, talks about and is oriented towards sports even when [the fan] is not actually observing, or reading, or listening to an account of a specific sports event".

Sports and Identity

To better understand sports, sport fandom and identity, it is necessary to understand these factors on two distinct theoretical levels. The first of these levels is an interpersonal or network level and include the influences of friends and family member on identity. Also included in this level are the effects of the community, including the possibility that geographic areas may tend to force local teams on the residents. The second level is a symbolic level. Included in this level are the team specific factors, such as personnel and unique factors, including the team name, logo, colors, and fight song.

Interpersonal/Network Level of Identity

Among the hypothesized factors of identity formation and maintenance is the concept of socialization. It is not at all unreasonable to assume that individuals become fans through socialization, primarily by friends and family . It is possible that this socialization can be traced back to childhood sports socialization. While it once would have been fair to say that sport fans were predominantly male, it is not necessarily true today. However, boys especially are traditionally socialized into sports at a young age. Boys are introduced to athletics at early ages, through both parental influences and marketing means, such as bedding and clothing, which are likely to have athletic themes or emblems on them. Other socialization agents which make a strong contribution to sport socialization include the community, toys, peers and role models.

Dietz-Uhler, Harrick, End and Jacquemotte found that women were more likely to be sport fans because they attended or watched games with friends and family while men were fans because they played sports. Therefore, female fan identity may be, at least in part, dependent on her network of friends and family. In addition to socialization, individuals could become fans as a way to achieve group membership or be a part of a collective unit. Collective behavior can be loosely defined as the behavior of two or more individuals who are acting collectively, whereby each influences the actions of the other. Furthermore, Blumer suggests that there is a need to differentiate between the collectivities in small groups as well as from culturally defined behavior, especially since a group is more than just a collection of individuals. Therefore, collective behavior could be thought of as specific to larger groups with intent.

A primary benefit of collective behavior is the sense of belonging that arises with group identification. Collective identities are known for their ability to give individuals a sense of belonging to a group. One dominant purpose of collective identities is to define borders by differentiating between "us" and "them," thereby creating both opponents and solidarities.

In addition, the sense of the collective supports, reinforces, influences, inhibits, or suppresses actions taken by an individual. Boire reinforces this by noting that the fan considers him/herself to be a part of the team, sharing in its glory and agony of defeat.

Symbolic Level of Identity

In addition to the interpersonal method, fandom can also be created by the desire to be a part of the environment created by a winning team – "jumping on the bandwagon". Stemming from Heider's "balance theory," fans relate to a team using Social Identity Theory processes known as BIRGing (basking in reflected glory) and CORFing (cutting off reflective failures). The primary assumption of this theory is that individuals will seek to resolve attitudes that are not balanced or equitable. Both BIRGing and CORFing stem from Heider's balance theory, which focuses on interattitudinal and interpersonal consistency. This theory suggests that individuals will organize their thoughts about others in a balanced way and that they will strive to restore balance in unbalanced situations.

2

Basic Concepts in Psychology

Behaviour

Behaviour is the way human beings and other organisms act. Many people use the word behaviour to mean conduct—that is, how a person's actions fit society's idea of right and wrong. But in psychology and other behavioural sciences, behaviour is regarded as any activity of a person or other living thing. Most human behaviour results from a combination of many factors. For example, a person might shout in answer to an insult. This response probably results from more than just the insult. It may be caused partly by being tired or hungry or by having been hurt by someone similar to the person now doing the insulting.

Although behaviour has many causes, most scientists seek to isolate single causes. This makes the scientific study of behaviour hard. Many researchers in psychology use controlled experiments in which they can examine the effect of one factor at a time on a particular kind of behaviour. Some investigators design experiments to test the behavioural effects of several factors in various combinations. Still other researchers study behaviour in the "real" world by observing people in their daily activities.

Observing behaviour outside controlled experiments cannot prove that one thing causes another. But studying people in the real world often helps scientists see the ways in which causes identified in experiments actually operate in people's daily lives. Specialists in many fields study behaviour. Psychologists and some biologists study animal behaviour in controlled experiments. Other psychologists study individuals or small groups of people in controlled games or tasks to understand many aspects of behaviour, including the reasons for people's feelings, thoughts, and motives. These studies help establish principles that can be used to explain, predict, and modify behaviour.

Educational researchers study how people behave in the classroom. In sociology, behavioural research focuses mainly on the behaviour of people in large groups and social institutions, such as businesses, churches, governments, and hospitals. An anthropologist may live in an isolated community to study behaviour patterns of a whole group. Scientists from different fields carry out joint studies of specific problems of behaviour. For example, many psychologists, educational researchers, sociologists, and anthropologists are concerned with the ways in which behaviour is connected to physical illness. These scientists work together to learn why people adopt such harmful behaviour patterns as smoking and overeating. The scientists also study how to encourage more healthy behaviour.

Factors that affect behaviour

Human behaviour is determined partly by heredity and partly by environment. In addition, it can be modified through learning.

Heredity

Heredity is determined by genes. Genes are short segments of the cell structures called chromosomes, which parents pass on to their offspring. Genes consist of chemical substances that give the offspring a tendency toward certain physical and behavioural qualities. The extent to which heredity influences behaviour is hard to determine. For example, a person might inherit the genes to be an excellent pianist. But the person may never learn to play the piano well without early and continual training—and a piano on which to practise. In this way, genetic and environmental influences are intertwined in a person's behavioural development. Most scientists agree that genes have some influence over general intelligence and special aptitudes in such activities as athletics, mathematics, music, and science. But heredity is not the only factor involved in producing these characteristics.

Environment

Environment consists of the conditions and forces that surround and influence an organism. The environment can cause certain behaviour. For example, unfamiliar surroundings may arouse curiosity or fear, depending on the circumstances. An intermediate level of arousal tends to have the most favourable effect on behaviour. Extremely high or extremely low levels of arousal may have a negative effect. A slight feeling of anxiety, for example, might help a student's performance on a test. But extreme anxiety could result in a poor performance.

Learning

Learning is the process by which behaviour changes as a result of experience or practice. A person learns a great deal of behaviour through new environments that show examples of new behaviour, give instruction or provide opportunities to practise new behaviour, and reward or punish new behaviour. Learning takes place constantly because people are always being given new problems to solve or are being shown new ways of doing things.

Types of behaviour

Behaviour is often classified as *voluntary* or *involuntary*. Speaking at a meeting, for example, appears to be voluntary, and blushing when spoken to seems involuntary. But both types of behaviour may change with experience. Deciding to speak at a meeting may in fact be determined by a person's previous experience of public speaking. In addition, people may not blush any more once they have gained more self-confidence. Thus, it may be difficult to distinguish between voluntary and involuntary behaviour when such factors are taken into consideration.

Behaviourism

A major aspect of psychology called behaviourism developed from research on learning. It was introduced in 1913 by the American psychologist John B. Watson, who felt psychologists should study only observable behaviour rather than states of consciousness or thought processes. He believed that changes in a subject's behaviour result from conditioning, a learning process in which a new response becomes associated with a certain stimulus.

Watson's approach to behaviourism was strongly influenced by the research of the Russian physiologist Ivan P. Pavlov during the early 1900's. Pavlov's experiments with animals proved that certain reflex actions can become conditioned responses to entirely new stimuli. For example, a dog's mouth begins to water as a reflex when the animal smells meat. Pavlov rang a bell each time he was about to give meat to a dog. Eventually, the dog's mouth began to water when Pavlov merely rang the bell. The flow of saliva had become a conditioned response to the ringing of the bell.

Watson demonstrated that responses of human beings could be conditioned in a similar manner. In one study, he struck a metal bar loudly each time an infant touched a furry animal. The sound scared the child, who in time became frightened by just the sight of the animal. Watson felt that he could produce almost any response in a child if he could control the child's environment.

During the mid-1900's, the American behavioural psychologist B. F. Skinner became known for his studies of how rewards and punishments can influence behaviour. He believed that rewards, or positive reinforcements, cause behaviour to be repeated. Positive reinforcements might include praise, food, or simply a person's satisfaction with his or her own skill. Punishments discourage the behaviour they follow. But punishment also encourages people to avoid situations in which they might be punished. Skinner concluded that positive reinforcement is more effective in teaching new and better behaviour. His work led to the development of teaching machines, which are based on positive reinforcement.

In procedures called behaviour modifications, therapists use positive reinforcers to shape behaviour in desired ways. For example, behaviour modification has been used to help retarded children learn basic school subjects. The children may receive rewards such as smiles, hugs, or food for doing their schoolwork and behaving properly. In other behaviour modification programmes, children work for tokens or points. Later, they can exchange the tokens for sweets, toys, or other rewards. Such programmes have also proved effective in shaping the behaviour of children with normal intelligence and of juvenile delinquents.

Dreams

Dream is a story that a person "watches" or appears to take part in during sleep. Dream events are imaginary, but they are related to real experiences in the dreamer's life. They seem real to the dreamer while they are taking place. Some dreams are pleasant, others are annoying, and still others are frightening. Everyone dreams, but some people never recall dreaming. Others remember only a little about a dream they had just before awakening and nothing about earlier dreams. No one recalls every dream.

The events of a dream usually form a story. In some dreams, the dreamer takes part in the story. In others, the dreamer merely "watches" the tale unfold. In most dreams, the dreamer cannot control what is happening, there is little logical thought, and events occur that could not happen in real life. Occasionally, the dreamer will realize that he or she is dreaming and may be able to alter what happens in the dream. This is known as a lucid dream. People see in most dreams, and they may also hear, smell, touch, and taste in them. Most dreams occur in colour, though the colour is often recalled only vaguely. Dreaming thought seems to put things together in new and unexpected ways. In some cases, this has led to important scientific discoveries or highly creative works.

Dreaming, like all mental processes, is a product of the brain and its activity. Whether a person is awake or asleep, the brain continuously gives off electrical waves. Scientists measure these waves with an instrument called an electroencephalograph. At most times during sleep, the brain waves are large and slow. But at certain times, they become smaller and faster.

During periods of fast brain waves, the eyes move rapidly as though the sleeper were watching a series of events. This stage of sleep, called REM (Rapid Eye Movement) sleep, is when most dreams occur. If awakened during REM sleep, the person is likely to recall details of the dream. Most adults have three to five REM periods each night. They occur every 90 to 100 minutes and last from 5 to 30 minutes each. But some people report dreams from non-REM periods. During REM sleep, the pathways that carry nerve impulses from the brain to the muscles are blocked. Therefore, the body cannot move during dreams. Also, the cerebral cortex—the part of the brain involved in higher mental functions—is much more active during REM sleep than during nondreaming sleep. The cortex is stimulated by neurons (nerve cells) that carry impulses from the part of the brain called the brain stem.

.Many experts who study dreams also feel that they are related to deep wishes and fears of the dreamer, and several theories explaining the meaning of dreams have been developed. During the 1890's, Sigmund Freud, an Austrian doctor who originated psychoanalysis, developed one of the best-known theories of dream interpretation. Freud suggested that dreams are fulfilments of wishes, usually in disguised form. The disguise—or "dream language"—involves condensation (combining several ideas into one image), displacement (shifting a feeling from one idea or person to another), and symbolism (the use of symbols to represent what cannot be pictured directly).

Some scientists have suggested that biological discoveries about dreaming have made psychological theories of dreaming, such as Freud's, unnecessary or false. These scientists argue that a dream is a meaningless response of the cerebral cortex to random stimulation from the brain stem. However, waking thought is also a response of the cerebral cortex to stimulation, often random, from the brain stem.

The function of dreaming is not completely understood. Dreaming sleep may play a role in restoring the brain's ability to handle such tasks as focused attention, memory, and learning. In addition, most psychiatrists and psychologists still believe that a person's hidden feelings often surface in dreams. Psychotherapists therefore analyse patients' dreams in an effort to help the patients understand themselves better.

Emotions

Emotion is usually considered to be a feeling about or reaction to certain important events or thoughts. An emotion can be either pleasant or unpleasant. An individual also may have a mixture of both pleasant and unpleasant emotions. People enjoy feeling such pleasant emotions as love, happiness, and contentment. They often try to avoid feeling unpleasant emotions, such as loneliness, worry, and grief. However, people are sometimes not fully aware of their own emotions.

Although most people believe they know what an emotion is, psychologists have not yet agreed on a definition that applies to both human beings and other animals. Individuals communicate most of their emotions by means of words, a variety of other sounds, facial expressions, and gestures. For example, anger causes many people to frown, make a fist, and yell. People learn ways of showing some of their emotions from members of their society, though heredity may determine some emotional behaviour. Research has shown that different isolated peoples show emotions by means of similar facial expressions. Even children who are born blind have facial expressions like those of sighted children.

Theories about emotions

Charles Darwin, the British scientist who developed the theory of natural selection, also studied emotion. In his book *The Expression of the Emotions in Man and Animals* (1872), Darwin said that emotional behaviour originally served both as an aid to survival and as a method of communicating intentions. For example, angry people show their teeth because they have inherited behaviour patterns that their prehistoric ancestors needed for fighting. Bared teeth also signal an intention to attack.

During the 1880's, the American psychologist William James and the Danish physiologist Carl G. Lange independently reached another conclusion about emotions. According to their theory, the James-Lange theory of emotions, people feel emotions only if aware of their own internal physical reactions to events, such as increased heart rate or blood pressure. Some psychologists still believe in the James-Lange theory, but there is little evidence to support it.

John B. Watson, an American psychologist who helped found the school of psychology called behaviourism, believed emotions were psychophysical (mental and bodily) reactions to specific events. He observed that babies stimulated by certain events, such as falling, having their arms held tightly, or being stroked, showed three basic emotions. He labelled these emotions fear, anger, and love. Watson's view that there are only three basic emotions has been challenged frequently since he proposed it in 1919.

In 1927, the American physiologist Walter B. Cannon and his associate Philip Bard proposed the Cannon-Bard theory of emotions. Cannon and Bard thought emotions arose only when the hypothalamus, a part of the brain, was stimulated. They believed the hypothalamus was the "seat" of emotions. Several researchers have since shown that stimulation of different parts of the brain, especially the limbic system, triggers emotions. .

Modern theories about emotion. In 1962, the American psychologist Stanley Schachter proposed a two-factor theory of emotion, based on an experiment he conducted with Jerome E. Singer. The two factors that determine different emotions, he claimed, are physical changes in a person's body plus the reason the individual gives for those changes. This theory states that emotions result from people's interpretations of their situations after they have been physiologically stimulated. Later research shows that the physiological stimulation may be less important than originally thought.

The most widely accepted view is that emotions occur as a complex sequence of events. The sequence begins when a person encounters an important event or thought. The person then interprets the meaning of the encounter, and the interpretation determines the feeling that is likely to follow. For example, someone who encounters an escaped lion would probably interpret the event as dangerous. The sense of danger would cause the individual to feel fear. Each feeling is followed by a series of physical changes and impulses to action, which are responses to the event that started the sequence. Thus, the person who met the lion would probably run away, increasing the person's chances of survival.

Several American psychologists have independently developed the theory that there are eight basic emotions. These emotions—which can exist at various levels of intensity—are anger, fear, joy, sadness, acceptance, disgust, surprise, and interest or curiosity. They combine to form all other emotions.

Extrasensory Perception

Extrasensory perception, usually abbreviated to ESP, describes a way of communicating or of being aware of something without using the known senses. An awareness of another person's thoughts without the use of sight, hearing, taste, touch, or smell would be an example of ESP. The study of extrasensory perception is part of the field of psychology called parapsychology. Most scientists believe ESP is something whose existence is yet to be proved.

Extrasensory perception is commonly divided into three kinds of phenomena—(1) telepathy, (2) clairvoyance, and (3) precognition. Telepathy is the sensing of the thoughts or feelings of one person by another in some unknown way. Clairvoyance is an awareness of objects, events, or people without the use of the known senses. Precognition is knowledge of a future event by means of telepathy or clairvoyance. Some parapsychologists also study phenomena related to ESP, such as psychokinesis. Psychokinesis is the mental control of physical objects and includes effects such as influencing the fall of dice by concentration.

Many classic ESP experiments, developed and used mainly between 1930 and 1960, involved card guessing. A pack of 25 special ESP cards (also called Zener cards, after the American psychologist Karl E. Zener) was often used. Each ESP card has one of five different symbols on it, such as a circle or cross. In a simple test of telepathy, a person called the sender would look at or think of a given card and concentrate on its symbol. A second person, called the receiver, was usually in another room and would attempt to name the symbol that the sender was thinking of. In an experiment on clairvoyance, cards would be taken from the pack one at a time, and the receiver would try to name the symbols on the cards. In this case, the person taking the cards would not look at the symbol.

The use of computers and electronic random-number devices has almost entirely replaced the use of cards in ESP experiments. Some such research has produced controversial claims that subjects are able to influence or predict the decay of radioactive substances. This kind of influence or prediction is impossible in terms of modern scientific understanding. Possible misunderstandings. In spite of the lack of widely accepted evidence about ESP, many people believe that it is valid because of personal experiences that seem to be unexplainable otherwise.

But most of these experiences can be explained by psychological processes that most people are not aware of. People often do not know how events around them set off their thoughts. Two people who know each other well may both experience a similar chain of thoughts when exposed to a common stimulus. For example, a husband and wife may be reading together and not paying much attention to music on a radio. Then certain music triggers in each of them the memory of a person they met several years ago but have not encountered since. Just as one of them is about to bring up the person's name, the other one mentions it. These similar thoughts may seem to be an instance of extrasensory perception. But neither person is likely to realize that both of their thoughts were actually set off by the music in the background.

One of the most noted ESP researchers was J. B. Rhine, an American who headed the Parapsychology Laboratory at Duke University in the United States for many years. Rhine conducted a number of card-guessing experiments to test clairvoyance, precognition, and telepathy. Some researchers claim that evidence based on the work of Rhine and other investigators, most of them in England, has established beyond question the existence of ESP.

But other researchers believe that the evidence is questionable. In the early days of ESP research, when fairly crude experiments were used, some people put on rather remarkable telepathic or clairvoyant performances. Today, however, when experiments are more carefully controlled, similar performances are rare. In science, the trend should generally be in the opposite direction. That is, if the phenomena under investigation are real, improved experiments should produce more significant and well-defined results.

Another reason for scepticism is that after more than a hundred years of research, no scientist has been able to produce a repeatable demonstration of ESP that can be performed before a group of neutral scientists. Some parapsychologists have responded to this criticism by arguing that the fault may lie with the experimenter. These parapsychologists suggest that sceptical researchers may have attitudes that prevent them from producing or witnessing ESP.

Continued belief in ESP is likely to endure regardless of the weakness of the evidence. Many people strongly believe that some elements of human existence are not subject to physical laws or methods. ESP, if it could be proved to exist, would help to explain these elements.

ESP might also give insights into the possibility of life after death. Rhine, for example, investigated the potential link of ESP to life after death. The Society for Psychical Research, founded in England in the late 1800's, made similar investigations. Interest in ESP and other parapsychological phenomena will probably continue as long as people hope to survive after death or to bypass limits imposed by science.

Extrovert Personality

Extrovert, when used nontechnically, means a sociable person who makes friends easily. In psychiatry, the word has a somewhat different meaning. The Swiss psychiatrist Carl G. Jung defined extroversion as turning the interests and energies of the mind toward events, people, and things in the world about us. As a result, extroverts are more interested in what is going on around them than in their own thoughts and feelings.

In normal people, extroversion is counterbalanced by introversion, and a wholesome balance is maintained between the two tendencies. But in an extrovert, the tendency toward extroversion is greater than the tendency toward introversion.

Habit

Habit is something a person learns to do over and over again without thinking about how to do it. Many everyday actions are habits. Imagine how difficult it would be to tie your shoelaces if you had to think of every action needed to complete the bow. A habit is different from an instinct. An instinct is behaviour that is inborn, instead of learned.

How we learn habits

Most habits begin as actions that a person is aware of. The more the person performs an action, the easier it becomes. Strong habits become automatic, and require little or no thought.

Psychologists generally agree that a stimulus (something that starts an action) must be present each time the habit is carried out. For example, a red traffic light is a stimulus to an experienced driver. It triggers the response of pressing the brake pedal. To learn this habit, each new driver must practise under actual traffic conditions, learning to press the brake pedal when the light is red.

Many psychologists believe that people will learn a habit only if it benefits them. Psychologists call this satisfaction a reward or a reinforcement. If the habit satisfies people, they tend to keep it. When a habit offers no reward or becomes unpleasant, they may break it. For example, some people get pleasure from smoking. Because of the pleasure (reward), smoking becomes a habit. If the habit becomes unpleasant, a person may stop smoking.

Psychologists who support the reward idea of habit formation disagree with an older idea. The older idea said that "paths" were made in the nervous system when an act was repeated. However, psychologists have taught rats habits and then cut their nervous systems at many points. Despite the cuts, the rats continued to perform the habits. This result suggests that the learning of habits does not depend on specific nerve connections and does not occur only in particular parts of the brain.

Kinds of habits

Some habits are simple and require only movements of the muscles. When approaching a door, a person grasps the doorknob. This action is called a simple motor act. The movement seems quite natural, but the person once had to learn this habit. A doorknob is a strange thing to a child when first encountered. The child may play with the doorknob many times before learning to open the door by turning the knob.

Some habits are more than simple motor acts. They are thoughts and attitudes we have about things and people. Psychologists call them habits of adjustment. Some of these habits are "good" and others are "bad", depending on how they affect other people. We learn "good" habits to act as others expect us to act. Neat appearance and pleasant manners are considered good habits. A person may learn "bad" habits, thinking something can be gained from them. But such habits may be annoying to others.

Instinct

Instinct is behaviour that is inherited rather than learned. We might say that a person who often fights has an aggressive instinct. But the person may not have been born with a desire to fight—and, with a different home or school background might never have developed that trait. Scientists use the terms instinct and instinctive behaviour only for activity that involves neither experience nor learning. To be truly instinctive, a behaviour trait must be typical of almost all members of one or both sexes of a species of animal.

The mating behaviour of a fish called the three-spined stickleback includes many examples of instinct. The male stickleback chooses a mating area and drives other fish from it. He then collects plants and forms them into a small mound. He wriggles through the completed mound, creating a tunnel. This tunnel, which is slightly shorter than the fish, becomes his nest. Meanwhile, his normally dull-coloured body has changed colour. His belly becomes bright red and his back bluish-white. He then starts to court females. Whenever a female, her abdomen swollen with eggs, enters his mating area, he swims toward her and performs a zigzagging "dance." He continues this dance until a female follows him to his nest, where she lays her eggs. She then swims away, and the male fertilizes the eggs. He stays near the nest to protect the eggs and, later, the young.

The stickleback does not learn his complicated mating ceremony. Yet all male sticklebacks perform basically the same actions. They are born with the pattern built into their nervous system. In some cases, individual animals of the same species vary the details of an instinctive behaviour pattern. Individual goldfinches may use different proportions of various materials to build their nests. They may also carry the materials in different ways. But most instinctive behaviour is relatively rigid. Members of any species do not usually differ greatly in carrying out the built-in pattern.

Instinctive Behaviour Works

The releasing stimulus. Most instinctive behaviour is released (brought about) by a stimulus, something that makes the animal act as it does. For example, scientists have learned that a male stickleback begins to court a female when he sees her swollen abdomen. In laboratory experiments, male sticklebacks also court cardboard models—but only if the models have swollen abdomens.

The female stickleback is attracted by the male's bright red belly. Females also follow crude models with red bellies more often than they follow exact copies of males without red bellies. The swollen abdomen of the female and bright red belly of the male are both examples of releasing stimuli. A reflex, such as blinking at a bright light, is also a type of unlearned behaviour released by a stimulus. But reflex actions are less complicated than instinctive behaviour.

Hormone changes. In many cases, a releasing stimulus acts on one or more glands in an animal's body. For example, seasonal changes in the amount of daylight affect the glands of some kinds of birds. The glands secrete fluids called hormones. A change in the amount of hormones secreted stimulates the birds to migrate. If a gland does not secrete a certain hormone properly, an animal may not be able to carry out the instinctive behaviour associated with that hormone. Some glands produce hormones only at a certain stage in an animal's life. The sex glands, for instance, do not function completely in young animals.

Instinct and learning: All animals perform both instinctive actions and learned actions. Instinct almost completely determines the behaviour of insects, spiders, and crustaceans (such animals as crabs and lobsters). These animals can learn only a little, and so their survival depends on built-in behaviour patterns. Higher animals, including fish, amphibians, reptiles, birds, and mammals, can learn more. They also modify their instinctive behaviour by learning. Young chicks, for example, crouch motionless when any moving object appears above them—even if it is only a falling leaf. Older birds have learned that leaves will not harm them, and so they do not react as they once did. But older birds do crouch motionless at the approach of a hawk.

The higher the animal, the more it can learn and the less it depends on instinct. Fish behave more by instinct than do birds, and birds perform more instinctive actions than do mammals. Among human beings, infants smile and suck instinctively. But as human beings grow older, most of their acts are learned.

Imprinting: One type of behaviour pattern is called imprinting. It occurs when an animal learns to recognize a stimulus that will later release instinctive behaviour. For example, a gosling follows the first moving object it sees after hatching. The young goose "recognizes" the moving object as its parent. It later "recognizes" similar objects as members of its own species. The gosling's behaviour works out well if the first moving object is an adult female goose. But young geese hatched in an incubator may see human beings first—and become imprinted on them. That is, the goslings act toward human beings as they should act toward other geese. After they mature, they even court human beings. In many cases, animals that become imprinted toward animals of another species never learn to recognize members of their own species.

Combining instinct and learning: Survival for animals higher than insects depends on a combination of instinct, learning, and body changes. For an animal to develop normally, it must come in contact with the normal releasing stimuli for members of its species. Scientists have reared monkeys separately from all other monkeys. Such monkeys do not display normal social or sexual behaviour if, after reaching adulthood, they are placed with other monkeys. Normal adult monkey behaviour results from the experiences of growing up as a member of a group of monkeys. These experiences enable a monkey to perfect its instinctive behaviour through learning.

Intelligence

People differ in the speed with which they learn things and how well and how long they remember ideas. They also differ in their ability to understand ideas and to use their knowledge in solving problems. For example, some people can solve mathematical problems rapidly. Others quickly understand how machines work. Still others can easily learn new words or a foreign language. All these abilities—and many more—are factors in what is called intelligence.

There is no universally accepted definition of the word intelligence. But a person is considered intelligent to the degree that he or she has the abilities mentioned above. Although such abilities are somewhat related, a person may be high in some and low in others. A person who can memorize names and dates may have trouble with long division. Another who has creative talent in art or music or has inventive ability may lack other abilities associated with intelligence. Although creativity and intelligence are known to be related, some people of above-average intelligence do poorly when faced with problems that are new to them.

Intelligence is sometimes regarded as a combination of qualities that lead to success in school. But some abilities, such as mechanical skill, are not used much in school. As a result, tests designed to measure intelligence include few questions that deal with mechanical skill. In addition, IQ (intelligence quotient) tests do not emphasize originality. Thus, they provide an incomplete picture of the many factors involved in intelligence.

A person's intelligence depends on heredity and environment. Every person is born with a certain mental capacity that influences how intelligent he or she will be as an adult. The development of this capacity is influenced by the person's background. Youngsters who are severely undernourished in infancy may be unable to develop their natural abilities. Similarly, children who are beaten or ridiculed by their parents may become so upset that their intellectual talents remain underdeveloped. Many children who face discrimination because of their race or nationality or a physical handicap also fail to develop their capacities to the fullest extent possible.

Scientists have long disagreed about the relative importance of heredity and environment in determining intelligence. In the 1960's, investigators found that children who had completed special preschool programmes experienced IQ score gains of as much as 15 points. Other studies have shown that children have suffered in intellectual development if they have been severely neglected or have received too little mental stimulation. Therefore, some psychologists emphasize the importance of the environment in determining IQ.

Other psychologists, however, attach greater weight to heredity. They note that identical twins, who have exactly the same genes, have nearly identical IQ's. On the other hand, fraternal twins, who are about as genetically similar as ordinary brothers and sisters, are not as similar in IQ as identical twins. In addition, identical twins who are adopted into different families as infants still have similar IQ's as adults. As a result, most psychologists conclude that both heredity and environment are important in determining intelligence, but that each limits the other. That is, they believe a person's genetic potential for intelligence can only be reached in a favourable environment. But they also believe that environment, no matter how favourable, cannot create a potential that is not present genetically.

Intelligence quotient

Intelligence quotient, or IQ, is a number used to indicate a person's intelligence. A person's IQ is based on a comparison of his or her score on an intelligence test with the scores of others on the same test.

Testing intelligence.

Educators and psychologists use an intelligence test to determine a person's mental age (MA)—the level of understanding and performance that the person has reached. Such a test consists of a series of mental tasks arranged in order of difficulty. Most intelligence tests include tasks involving memory, reasoning, definitions, numerical ability, and recalling facts.

Psychologists have worked out the age at which most people can correctly answer each question of an intelligence test. Suppose that a 10-year-old is asked to define certain words, to work out relationships of words and ideas, to solve simple arithmetic problems, and to remember certain facts. The child does as many of these tasks as possible. A child who completes the tasks expected of a 9-year-old but cannot complete those of a 10-year-old has a mental age of 9 years.

Calculating IQ

A person's intelligence cannot be determined by mental age alone. A 6-year-old with an MA of 8 years is more intelligent than a 10-year-old who also has an MA of 8 years. The original IQ test divided the MA by the age in years and then multiplied the result by 100 to avoid fractions. Thus, a 4-year-old with an MA of 6 had an IQ of (6 divided by 4) X 100, or 150. A 10-year-old with an MA of 8 had an IQ of (8 divided by 10) X 100, or 80. In most IQ tests, 100 indicates an average score for a person's age level.

Since 1960, all IQ tests have determined IQ by assigning a value of 100 to the average score of those tested. Then the testers assign values above and below 100 to the other scores, depending on how much above or below average the score is. Intelligence develops at a slower rate during adulthood, and so testers use this method to assign IQ scores to adults.

Uses of IQ tests.

Teachers in some countries use IQ scores to help judge whether children are progressing as well as their ability permits. If a child scores high on IQ tests but does poorly in class, the teacher may try to determine what circumstances keep the child from learning. If a child scores low on IQ tests and is doing poorly in class, the teacher may try to separate learning tasks into smaller or more familiar units. With such help, the child may progress more rapidly. IQ tests can also provide a means of grouping individuals with similar abilities. Classroom instruction can then be adapted to each group of students. Some school authorities use IQ scores to help determine whether to allow a student to be in special courses or programmes.

Problems of intelligence testing

In designing an intelligence test, psychologists try to use questions on subjects to which every person to be tested has been equally exposed. But this cannot be done perfectly. As a result, every intelligence test measures experience to some degree. For example, a child who has always spoken only English is likely to score higher on a test given in English than a child who spoke only Spanish until learning English in school. Similarly, a child whose family reads and travels widely may score higher than a child who lacks these experiences.

A home and school life that encourages learning may result in higher IQ test scores as a child grows older. On the other hand, deprived youngsters who go to an inferior school may score lower and lower through the years. Their falling scores could reflect the lack of many experiences that other children have had. Children may also score low because of malnutrition in their early years. IQ thus depends on both heredity and environment.

Many people have tried to create culture-fair or culture-free tests. Such tests include only ideas, symbols, or words that are recognized by persons of different backgrounds. Sometimes they are called nonverbal (wordless) tests to contrast them with verbal tests, which use words. Some such tests consist only of pictures and diagrams that people of many cultures can understand.

The IQ score of most persons does not change much from year to year. But scores of some individuals can vary from one test to another. People may score somewhat higher if they take a test feeling well, rested, and confident than if they feel ill or tired. Some educators and psychologists oppose using IQ tests for grouping students. These experts fear that a teacher may treat a child according to the "label" of the youngster's group. Thus, children labelled "slow" may think they are expected to learn slowly—and do so, even though they could progress more rapidly.

Two French psychologists, Alfred Binet and Theodore Simon, developed the first modern intelligence tests in 1905. In later tests, Binet and Simon introduced the idea of measuring mental age. They wanted to separate children who probably would have difficulty with schoolwork from those who probably would succeed. Binet checked the accuracy of the tests against the children's actual classroom performance. He then dropped or revised parts of the tests in which an individual's schoolwork showed his or her abilities to be stronger or weaker than the test scores indicated. These tests have since been widely adopted in many countries.

Introvert Personality

Introvert, when used non-technically, usually means a shy, unsociable person. Psychiatrist Carl Jung defined introversion as a turning of mental interests away from people and events of the outer world to the inner world of one's own thoughts. He believed that in a normal person, introversion is balanced by extroversion . But in an introvert, the tendency toward introversion is greater than toward extroversion. Jung thought that if the tendency toward introversion became extreme, it would dominate a person's unconscious mental life and create a conflict between the two tendencies. This conflict would result in a neurosis, which is a kind of mental illness.

Learning

Learning is an important field of study in psychology. Psychologists define learning as the process by which changes in behaviour result from experience or practice. By behaviour, psychologists mean any response that an organism makes to its environment. Thus, behaviour includes actions, emotions, thoughts, and the responses of muscles and glands. Learning can produce changes in any of these forms of behaviour.

Not all changes in behaviour are the result of learning. Some changes result from maturation (physical growth). Others, including those caused by illness or fatigue, are only temporary and cannot be called learning. We can see learning taking place all the time, but there is no simple explanation of the process. Psychologists have examined four kinds of learning in detail: (1) classical conditioning or respondent learning, (2) instrumental conditioning or operant learning, (3) multiple-response learning, and (4) insight learning.

Classical conditioning is based on stimulus-response relationships. A stimulus is an object or a situation that excites one of our sense organs. A light is a stimulus because it excites the retina of the eye, allowing us to see. Often a stimulus makes a person respond in a certain way, as when a flash of light makes us blink. Psychologists say that in this instance the stimulus elicits (draws forth) the response. In classical conditioning, learning occurs when a new stimulus begins to elicit behaviour similar to that originally produced by an old stimulus. For example, suppose a person tastes some lemon juice, which makes the person salivate. While the person is tasting it, a tone is sounded. Suppose these two stimuli—the lemon juice and the tone—occur together many times. Eventually, the tone by itself will make the person salivate. Classical conditioning has occurred because the new stimulus (the tone) has begun to elicit the response of salivation in much the same way as the lemon juice elicited it.

Any condition that makes learning occur is said to reinforce the learning. When a person learns to salivate to a tone, the reinforcement is the lemon juice that the tone is paired with. Without the lemon juice, the person would not learn to salivate to the tone. The classical conditioning process is particularly important in understanding how we learn emotional behaviour. When we develop a new fear, for example, we learn to fear a stimulus that has been combined with some other frightening stimulus.

Studies of classical conditioning are based on experiments performed in the early 1900's by the Russian physiologist Ivan P. Pavlov. He trained dogs to salivate to such signals as lights, tones, or buzzers by presenting these signals when he gave food to the dog . Pavlov called the learned response a conditioned response because it depended on the conditions of the stimulus. To emphasize the fact that a stimulus produces a response in this kind of learning, classical conditioning is often called respondent learning.

Instrumental conditioning. Often a person learns to perform a response as a result of what happens after the response is made. For example, a child may learn to beg for sweets. There is no one stimulus that elicits the response of begging. The child begs because such behaviour occasionally results in receiving sweets. Every time the child receives sweets, the tendency to beg becomes greater. Sweets, therefore, are the reinforcer. Instrumental conditioning is also called operant conditioning because the learned response operates on the environment to produce some effect.

The American psychologist B. F. Skinner performed important experiments with instrumental conditioning in the 1930's. He trained rats to press levers to get food. In one experiment, a hungry rat was placed in a special box containing a lever attached to some concealed food. At first, the rat ran around restlessly. Eventually, it happened to press the lever, and the food dropped into the box. The food reinforced the response of pressing the lever. After repeating the process many times, the rat learned to press the lever for food.

Skinner's experiments were based on those performed earlier in the 1900's by the American psychologist E. L. Thorndike. In Thorndike's experiments, an animal inside a puzzle box had to pull a string, press a pedal, or make some other response that would open the box and expose some food. Thorndike noted that the animal learned slowly and gradually. He called this type of learning trial-and-error behaviour.

Multiple-response learning. When we learn skills, we first learn a sequence of simple movement-patterns. We combine these movement-patterns to form a more complicated behaviour pattern. In most cases, various stimuli guide the process. For example, operating a typewriter requires putting together many skilled finger movements. These movements are guided by the letters or words that we want to type. At first, a person has to type letter by letter. With practice, the person learns to type word by word or phrase by phrase.

In verbal learning, such as memorizing a poem or learning a new language, we learn sequences of words. We then combine these sequences of responses into a complex organization. Learning that involves many responses requires much practice to smooth out the rough spots. To examine this kind of learning, psychologists have observed animals learning to run through a maze. Starting at the beginning, the animal wanders through the maze until it finds food at the end. The animal periodically comes to a choice-point, where it must turn right or left. Only one choice is correct. Eventually the animal learns the correct sequence of turns. Psychologists have found that the two ends of the maze are learned more easily than the parts near the middle. In the same way, when we learn a list of things, we usually find the beginning and end easier than the middle.

Insight learning: The term insight refers to solving a problem through understanding the relationships of various parts of the problem. Insight often occurs suddenly, such as when a person looks at a certain problem for some time and then suddenly grasps its solution. The psychologist Wolfgang Kohler performed important insight experiments in the early 1900's. He showed that chimpanzees sometimes use insight instead of trial-and-error responses to solve problems. When a banana was placed high out of reach, the animals discovered that they could stack boxes on top of each other to reach it. They also discovered how to put two sticks together to reach an object that was too far away to reach with one stick. The chimpanzees appeared both to see and to use the relationships involved in reaching their goals.

Theories of learning are based on facts obtained from experiments such as those on classical and instrumental conditioning. Psychologists differ in their interpretation of these facts. As a result, there are a number of learning theories. These theories can be divided into three groups. One group of psychologists emphasizes stimulus-response relationships and has performed experiments with classical and instrumental conditioning. They say all learning is the forming of habits. When we learn, we connect a stimulus and a response that did not exist before, thus forming a habit. Habits can range from the simplest ones to complex ones that are involved in learning skills.

These psychologists believe that when we meet a new problem, we use appropriate responses learned from past experience to solve it. If this procedure does not lead to the solution, we use a trial-and-error approach. We use one response after another until we solve the problem. The stimulus-response approach has been used to explain and modify bad habits.

For example, when a person is irrationally afraid of dogs, methods called behaviour modification can be used to replace the fear response to a dog with a more relaxed response. A second group of psychologists stresses cognition (the act of knowing) above the importance of habit. These experts feel that experiments with classical and instrumental conditioning are too limited to explain such complex learning as understanding concepts and ideas. This approach emphasizes the importance of the learner's discovering and perceiving new relationships and achieving insight and understanding.

A third group of psychologists has developed humanistic theories. According to these theories, much human learning results from the need to express creativity. Almost any activity, including athletics, business dealings, and homemaking, can serve as a creative outlet. The psychologists in this group believe that each person must become involved in challenging activities—and must do reasonably well at them—to have a satisfying life. The individual gains a sense of control, growth, and knowledge from such activities.

For learning to occur, people must feel free to make their own decisions. They also must feel worthy, relatively free from anxiety, self-respecting, and respected by others. Under these conditions, their own inner drives will lead them to learn. Some kinds of group therapy try to provide an accepting, supporting environment. Such an environment is intended to increase people's awareness of their own thoughts and of the world around them.

Learning involves changes in the nervous system. Scientists are trying to discover the processes that take place in the brain to produce learning. Such research may lead to a physiological theory of learning.

Efficient learning

Learning occurs more efficiently if a person is ready to learn. This readiness results from a combination of growth and experience. Children cannot learn to read until their eyes and nervous systems are mature enough. They also must have a sufficient background of spoken words and prereading experience with letters and pictures.

Motivation

Psychologists and educators also recognize that learning is best when the learner is motivated to learn. External rewards are often used to increase motivation to learn. Motivation aroused by external rewards is called extrinsic motivation. In other cases, people are motivated simply by the satisfaction of learning. Motivation that results from such satisfaction is called intrinsic motivation. This type of motivation can be even more powerful than extrinsic motivation. Punishment, particularly the threat of punishment, is also used to control learning. Experiments have shown that intrinsic and extrinsic rewards serve as more effective aids to learning than punishment does. This is due largely to two factors:

(1) learners can recognize the direct effects of reward more easily than they can the effects of punishment; and

(2) the by-products of reward are more favourable.

For example, reward leads to liking the rewarded task, but punishment leads to dislike of the punished deed. Psychologists also look at the motivation of learning from the point of view of the learner. They tend to talk about success and failure, rather than reward and punishment. Success consists of reaching a goal that learners set for themselves.

Failure consists of failing to reach an intended goal. An ideal learning situation is one in which learners set progressively more difficult goals for themselves, and keep at the task until they succeed.

Skill learning and verbal learning

Through research, psychologists have discovered some general rules designed to help a person learn. The following rules apply particularly to learning skills. (1) Within a given amount of practice time, you can usually learn a task more easily if you work in short practice sessions spaced widely apart, instead of longer sessions held closer together. (2) You can learn many tasks best by imitating experts. (3) You should perform a new activity yourself, rather than merely watch or listen to someone. (4) You learn better if you know immediately how good your performance was. (5) You should practise difficult parts of a task separately and then try to incorporate them into the task as a whole.

Two additional rules apply mainly to verbal learning. (1) The more meaningful the task, the more easily it is learned. You will find a task easier to learn if you can relate it to other things you have learned. (2) A part of a task is learned faster when it is distinctive. When studying at school or college, for example, underlining a difficult passage in your notes in red makes the passage distinctive and easier to learn.

Transfer of training

Psychologists and educators recognize that new learning can profit from old learning because learning one thing helps in learning something else. This process is called transfer of training. Transfer of training can be either positive or negative. Suppose a person learns two tasks. After learning Task 1, the person might find Task 2 easier or harder. If Task 2 is easier, then the old learning has been a help and positive transfer of training has occurred. If Task 2 is harder, the old learning is a hindrance and negative transfer has occurred.

Whether transfer is positive or negative depends on the relationship between the two tasks. Positive transfer occurs when the two tasks have similar stimuli and both stimuli elicit the same response. For example, if we know the German word gross, it is easier to learn the French word gros because both words mean large. In this case, similar stimuli (gross and gros) elicit the same response (large).

Negative transfer occurs when the two tasks have similar stimuli, which elicit different responses. After you learn the German word Gras (grass), it is harder to learn the French word gras (fat). The words are spelled the same way, but they have different meanings. In this case, similar stimuli (Gras and gras) elicit different responses. Psychologists believe new learning can profit from old learning because of three factors: (1) positive transfer of training, (2) general principles that we learn in one task and apply to another task, and (3) good study habits that we learn in one task which help us learn another task.

Memory

Memory is the ability to remember something that has been learned or experienced. Memory is a vital part of the learning process. If you remembered nothing from the past, you would be unable to learn anything new. All your experiences would be lost as soon as they ended, and each new situation would be totally unfamiliar. Without memory, you would repeatedly have the same experiences for the "first time." You would also lose the richness that memory gives to life—the pleasure of happy remembrances as well as the sorrow of unhappy ones.

Scientists know little about what happens in the brain when it stores memories. However, storing new memories seems to involve both chemical changes in the nerve cells of the brain and changes in their physical structure. Research indicates that these chemical and physical changes occur in a tiny section of the brain called the hippocampus when a person stores new memories. The hippocampus is part of a larger structure called the cerebral cortex, which controls most higher brain functions. Such functions include problem solving and the use of language. Scientists have found that a memory is acquired by means of a series of consolidating events in the brain. However, more research will be necessary to discover precisely how memories are consolidated.

The memory system

Psychologists divide a person's memory system into three stages, each of which has a different time span. These stages are called sensory memory, short-term memory, and long-term memory.

Sensory memory holds information for only an instant. Suppose you look at a picture of a mountain. Information about the mountain passes through your eyes to your sensory memory, which briefly holds a nearly exact image of the picture. However, the image quickly fades, and it disappears in less than a second. For the information to last, you must transfer it rapidly to short-term memory.

Short-term memory can hold a fact as long as you actively think about it. You use short-term memory when you look up a telephone number and repeat it to yourself until you dial it. Unless you continually repeat this information to yourself, it will fade after about 20 seconds. However, some information from short-term memory enters long-term memory, where it may last a long time.

Long-term memory includes a huge amount of information, some of which lasts a lifetime. Information enters long-term memory as a result of either of two factors: (1) repetition or (2) intense emotion. A casual acquaintance, met briefly but on many occasions, will be remembered for a long time. The strong emotions of the first experience of falling in love or of the moments surrounding a car crash help place these events in long-term memory.

Measuring memory

There are three commonly used methods to measure how much a person remembers. These methods are (1) recall, (2) recognition, and (3) relearning. Suppose you give a party and someone asks you a few weeks later who was there. The simplest way to find out how much you remember is to list as many names as you can. This is the method of recall.

In *recognition,* the person asking about your guests would give you a list of names. The list would include names of people who were at the party and of others who were not. You could then indicate which people were there. Most people can recognize more facts than they can recall. As a result, most students perform better on multiple-choice tests than on essay tests.

In *relearning,* you would memorize the guest list after apparently forgetting it. Most people relearn information faster than they learned it the first time. Scientists regard the difference in the time required for the original learning and for the relearning as evidence of how much was remembered.

In general, people forget more and more as time passes. An hour after a party ends, you probably could remember most of the people who were there. Two days later, you might recall only a few of the guests. A month later, you probably would remember even fewer. Scientists have devoted much study to why the passage of time makes people unable to remember things they once knew. The chief explanations for forgetting include interference, retrieval failure, motivated forgetting, and constructive processes.

Interference occurs when the remembering of certain learned material blocks the memory of other learned material. If a friend moves, you may have difficulty recalling his or her new telephone number. The person's old number may keep coming to mind and interfering with your remembering the new one. But after you have thoroughly learned the new number, you may not even be able to recall the old one.

The above example illustrates two types of interference. Previously learned information may hamper a person's ability to remember new material. This hampering process is called proactive interference or proactive inhibition. Likewise, the learning of new facts may interfere with the memory of something previously learned. Such interference is known as *retroactive interference or retroactive inhibition*.

Retrieval failure is the inability to recall information that has been stored in the memory. You probably have had the experience of being unable to think of a name or some other piece of information that was on the tip of your tongue. Later, the information came to you naturally and effortlessly. Such temporary loss of memory, which occurs frequently, is called retrieval failure. Scientists compare it to trying to find a misplaced object in a cluttered room. The information is not gone, but neither can it be recalled immediately.

Motivated forgetting is a loss of memory caused by conscious or unconscious desires. Scientists believe we forget many things because we want to do so. Motivated forgetting is related to a psychological process called repression. Repression involves forcing unpleasant feelings or painful experiences from the conscious mind into the unconscious. For example, people who like to gamble tend to remember most of the times they won—and forget those when they lost.

Constructive processes involve the unconscious invention of false memories. When you try to remember an event that happened months or years ago, you may recall only a few facts. Using those facts, you fill in the gaps with details that seem to make sense but may be untrue. The process of constructing probable happenings to tell a complete story is called *refabrication or confabulation*. Refabricated memories seem real and are almost impossible to distinguish from memories of events that actually occurred.

Improving memory

Memory experts believe that people can, with practice,

increase their ability to remember. One of the most important means of improving memory is the use of mental aids called mnemonic devices. A number of other techniques can be used to help people improve their memory.

Mnemonic devices are memory aids that include rhymes, clues, mental pictures, and other methods. One of the simplest ways is to put the information into a rhyme. Many people remember the number of days in each month by using a verse that begins, "Thirty days hath September. . . ." Another method provides clues by means of an acronym, a word formed from the first letters or syllables of other words. A mental picture can be provided by the key-word method, which is particularly useful in learning foreign words.

Mental pictures can also be used to remember names. When you meet a person for the first time, pick out a physical feature of the individual and relate it to his or her name. For example, suppose you meet a very tall man named Mr. Shackley. You could imagine his bumping his head on the roof of a shack. In the future, this image will help you remember his name when you see or think of him.

To use mnemonic devices, one must first learn them—and often invent them. After mastering a mnemonic device, however, you can use it at any time you wish. Other ways to improve memory. A good way to ensure remembering a piece of information is to study it long after you think you know it perfectly. This process is called *overlearning*. The more thoroughly you learn something, the more lasting the memory will be. Another memory aid involves making the surroundings in which you remember material similar to those in which you learned the material. For this reason, soccer coaches require players to practise under conditions similar to those of an actual game. Students often find it helpful to study in the room where they will be tested.

Uncommon memory conditions

We sometimes hear of someone who has a "photographic

memory," which supposedly works like a camera taking a picture. A person with such a memory would be able to take a quick mental picture of a textbook page or a scene. Later, the person could describe the page or scene perfectly by causing the image to reappear in his or her mind.

No one actually has a photographic memory. However, some people have a similar ability called eidetic imagery. An eidetic image is a picture that remains in a person's mind for a few seconds after a scene has disappeared. People who have eidetic imagery can look at a scene briefly and then give a thorough description of the scene based on a mental image. But the image fades quickly and may be inaccurate. Eidetic imagery is rare. Only 5 to 10 per cent of all children have this ability, and most of them lose it as they grow up.

Amnesia can result from disease, physical injury, or emotional shock. Many cases of amnesia, even severe ones, are temporary, and the amnesic person regains his or her memory. A person who suffers a brain injury may forget events that occurred just before the injury. This inability to remember past events is called retrograde amnesia. The more severe the injury, the greater the memory loss. Boxers who receive a blow to the head might forget a few seconds of their lives. Someone who suffers major brain damage in a car accident might lose months or even years of memories. Some brain-injured people also have anterograde amnesia. This condition involves difficulty remembering events that occur after the injury is sustained. Both these types of amnesia also can be produced by emotional shock

Motivation

Motivation commonly refers to anything that causes people to behave as they do. Most people have a clear sense of what it feels like to be motivated to do something. But scientists have found it difficult to define motivation. When studying motivation, most psychologists and behavioural scientists focus on two specific aspects of motivated behaviour—the arousal of behaviour and the direction of behaviour.

Arousal of behaviour involves whatever brings an organism to action. Arousal means being "stirred up" or "ready for action." It may result from stimuli inside or outside the body. Inside, or internal, stimuli include the sensation of dryness that produces thirst and the stomach contractions that cause hunger pangs. Outside, or external, stimuli include the heat that causes pain when a person touches a hot stove.

An aroused organism's response to stimuli depends on habits and other ways of acting that it has learned. Based on such learning, the organism may act either aimlessly or highly purposefully in a particular situation. Direction of behaviour is determined by several influences. These influences include an organism's habits, skills, and basic capacities.

Motives themselves may also direct behaviour. For example, differing motives may direct the behaviour of two football coaches when their teams face much stronger opponents. One coach's behaviour may be motivated by—that is, directed toward—competition or winning. That coach may concentrate on seeking an upset victory. However, the behaviour of the other coach may be motivated by the players' feelings and may focus on keeping the players from being discouraged by the probable loss.

Physiological conditions can direct behaviour by making organisms sensitive to stimuli from the environment. For example, many types of birds may become sensitive to available mates and also direct their behaviour toward nest building when the birds' hormones reach a certain level.

Kinds of motives

Most behavioural scientists place all motives into one or more of three groups. These groups are (1) homeostatic motives, (2) nonhomeostatic motives, and (3) learned, or social, motives.

Homeostatic motives include hunger, thirst, respiration, and excretion. They work to keep the body in a balanced internal state. The term homeostasis refers to the body's tendency to maintain such a balanced internal state. Many homeostatic motives are set in motion either by bodily deficits or bodily excesses. When the body needs water, for example, changes occur that cause thirst and motivate the person to seek something to drink.

Nonhomeostatic motives include sex, such activity as nest building, and curiosity about the environment. These motives are aroused by occasional forces. In the absence of such forces, nonhomeostatic motives may be inactive. In contrast, the needs for food, water, and air—homeostatic motives—have almost continuous influence.

Learned motives, or social motives, include curiosity, a desire for novelty, and the need for such things as achievement, power, social affiliation, and approval. These motives seem to develop through experience, especially through social experience, such as early experience in the family or with friends during adolescence. Learned motives continue to evolve and influence behaviour throughout life. However, their exact origins are not clear. Some babies have strong needs for social affiliation that may result from conditions during pregnancy and birth as well as, perhaps, other factors.

The three kinds of motives often overlap. For example, desire for new experiences may be homeostatic as well as learned. This is because people differ as to the level of novel stimulation their homeostatic mechanisms seek to maintain. As a result, some people always seem to be looking for something new while others seem too content with the familiar.

Theories of motivation

Some general theories of motivation identify a limited number of central motives, such as sex and death instincts, from which other motives develop. Other theories support a single, main motive in human development, such as a person's need for power or to fully realize his or her potential. In contrast, some psychologists argue that many different motives guide behaviour. These motives include needs for order, understanding, and independence. Other theories of motivation try to identify the physiological mechanisms underlying a wide range of motives. For example, researchers exploring the relations between behaviour and brain function have identified chemical and electrical processes in the brain that influence behaviour in people and animals.

Applications

Motivation plays an important role in informal relationships, but also in highly structured relationships, such as those found in industry and education. In industry, managers use motivation techniques to promote cooperation between employers and employees. Such cooperation enables employees to satisfy certain needs through their jobs, including security, career interests, and respect. If employees expect their jobs to help satisfy these personal needs, they will probably be more motivated to ensure that the company's business objectives are achieved.

In education, teachers sometimes use rewards to motivate students to learn. They may also motivate students to find satisfaction in the learning activity itself by emphasizing the value of being able to work through problems. Such an approach encourages students' mastery of problem-solving techniques and an increased expectancy of success in future tasks.

Perception

Perception is the process by which we receive and interpret information from the world around us. The world around us consists of various kinds and levels of physical energy. Our knowledge of the world comes through our sense organs, which react to these energies. Certain wavelengths of electromagnetic radiation stimulate our eyes. Our ears sense certain kinds of mechanical vibrations in the air. Our noses and tongues are sensitive to certain chemical stimuli. Sense organs in our skin respond to pressure, temperature changes, and various stimuli related to pain. Sense organs in our joints, tendons, and muscles are sensitive to body movement and position.

The sense organs change the various environmental energies into nervous impulses, which go to the brain. Through the psychological process of perception, the patterns of energies become known as objects, events, people, and other aspects of the world. The process of perception does not reveal objects and events of the world. We see light and colour, but there is no light or colour in the electromagnetic waves that stimulate the eyes. In the same way, there is no music or noise in the vibrations that stimulate the ear.

The brain organizes and interprets nervous impulses from the eyes as light and colour, and impulses from the ears as sound. Together, the sense organs and the brain transform physical energy from environmental stimuli into information about the events around us.

Factors affecting perception

Various factors influence what and how we perceive. Our perceptions are influenced by the ways our bodies are structured to receive and process stimuli from the environment. Our perceptions also reflect our emotions, needs, expectations, and learning.

Receptors. Each sensory system, such as vision, hearing, or touch, has its own specialized body parts. These parts are called receptors, and they change energies from the environment into nervous impulses. The human eye, for example, has two major kinds of receptors in the retina (the light-sensitive part of the eye). These receptors are called rods and cones. The rods respond to the intensity of light, but not to different frequencies of light (different colours). The cones do respond to different frequencies of light, and are called colour receptors. The rods allow us to see in dim light, and the cones enable us to see colours and sharp detail in bright light. Thus, the particular ways that receptors are structured and function help determine the perceptual effects related to them.

The brain. Certain physical and functional features of the brain also determine some aspects of perception. The part of the brain that serves vision has different kinds of cells that respond only under certain conditions of stimulation. Some of these cells respond only when a light goes off. Others respond when a light comes on, but they stop responding if the light stays on. Such cells also are arranged in special ways in the brain, and this fact is related to how we perceive. For example, some cells are arranged in columns or in clusters. Such arrangements are related to how we perceive edges and forms. Experiments suggest that some cells in the brain allow us to perceive movement. Thus, the structure of the brain is an important element in perception.

Learning, emotion, and motivation

Much evidence points to the conclusion that early experience, learning, emotion, and motivation are important in defining what and how we perceive. Part of this accumulating evidence comes from experiments that compare how people in different cultures perceive things. The perception of such things as form, colour, pain, and touch may differ from culture to culture, depending on habits and customs, and training of children.

Most people do, and some continue to do so even with many repeated readings. In learning to perceive words and sentences, we learn not to perceive each letter and word separately. Instead, we become able to scan the overall pattern and "fill in" the remainder. A poor reader is more likely than a good reader to see the duplicate word in each phrase.

Some illusions are related to learning and past experience. An illusion is not a false perception, as many people believe, but one that is inconsistent with another perception. Since perception does not literally reveal the environment, no sensory system is closer to some absolute truth than any other.

Emotions and motivation can have an important effect on perception. Sometimes a severe emotional disturbance can prevent perception completely, as when emotional shock causes individuals to lose their hearing temporarily. We are more likely to perceive those aspects of our environment that are related to our motives. For example, motivation can affect the perceived characteristics of objects. To hungry people, food may appear larger or more colourful than usual.

Types of perception

Perception has three levels of complexity:

(1) detection,

(2) recognition, and

(3) discrimination.

Detection refers to whether people can sense that they are being stimulated by some form of energy. For example, a light may be so dim they can barely detect its presence. Recognition means being able to identify as well as detect a particular pattern of stimulation. Discrimination means being able to perceive one pattern of stimulation as different from another. For example, a person may hear slight differences between two similar musical tones.

The field of study that deals with levels of perception is called psychophysics. Experimental psychologists investigate the relationships between the physical properties of stimulus patterns and the perceived effects of the stimuli. For example, they may study the relationship between sound frequency and the perceived pitch of sound.

Principles of perception

There are a number of general principles that help us understand the process of perception. One of the most important is the principle of closure. It tells us that we have the general tendency to perceive things as complete and unified. We tend to "fill in" parts that are missing, or parts that conform to an overall impression. The principle of constancy states that despite changes that occur in stimulation, we have a strong tendency to perceive objects as constant in size, shape, colour, and other qualities. For example, an orange will be perceived with its characteristic colour under different kinds of light.

Personality

Personality is a term that has many general meanings. Sometimes the word refers to the ability to get along well socially. For example, we speak of experiences or relationships which are said to give a person "more personality." The term also may refer to the most striking impression that an individual makes on other people. We may say, "She has a shy personality." To a psychologist, personality is an area of study that deals with complex human behaviour, including emotions, actions, and cognitive (thought) processes. Psychologists study the patterns of behaviour that make individuals different from one another.

The nature of personality

Personality types. For hundreds of years, people have tried to group the vast differences among human beings into simple units. Some of the resulting groupings divide people into personality types based on certain characteristics. The ancient Greek doctor Hippocrates divided individuals into such types as *sanguine* (cheerful) and *melancholic* (depressed). He attributed their behavioural differences to a predominance of one of the body fluids. For example, Hippocrates believed that a person was cheerful if blood (sanguis) was the dominant influence on his or her behaviour.

Some of the more recent theories about personality types have tried to associate body build and temperament. Classifications based on body measurements were developed by two psychiatrists, Ernst Kretschmer of Germany and

William Sheldon of the United States. The Swiss psychologist Carl Jung, who studied psychological characteristics, classified people as *introverts* or *extroverts*. The simplicity of personality-type theories is appealing, but it also limits their value. An individual's behaviour is so complex, diverse, and variable that the person cannot be sorted usefully into a simple category.

Personality traits

Related to personality-type theories is the search for broad traits or dispositions to describe enduring differences among people. One of the early workers in this field was the British psychologist William McDougall. Personality traits are regarded as dimensions that range from high to low. For example, anxiety is a trait that varies from the greatest anxiety to the least anxiety. Most people have some degree of anxiety along the scale between the two extremes. Psychologists have studied such personal attributes as aggressiveness, dependency, and extroversion-introversion.

Studies of personality traits help reveal the relationships between an individual's different personal attributes. For example, a group of children may be tested for intelligence and may also be given questionnaires about their attitudes. In addition, they may be asked to rate their own characteristics, and may be rated by their teachers. The results are then correlated statistically to discover the relationships among all this information.

Ratings and self-reports

Research on personality traits tends to rely heavily on broad ratings of personality. In self-ratings, a person indicates the degree to which he or she thinks he or she possesses certain personality characteristics. Ratings may also be obtained from teachers, or others who know the person or who have watched the person in special situations.

These judgments may be affected by many types of bias. A person may give the responses that he or she thinks are expected and socially desirable, even if they are not true. Moreover, the answers may reflect preconceptions and stereotypes (fixed ways of thinking), rather than an accurate description of behaviour. Tests that ask a person to rate such attributes as friendliness or adjustment provide broad self-characterizations rather than detailed descriptions of behaviour.

Consequently, the findings of such tests may partly reveal the concepts and stereotypes that people apply to themselves and to others. These findings may not necessarily reflect the people's actual behaviour outside the test. Some techniques are designed to reduce the role of personal meanings and concepts. Other approaches deliberately seek to clarify the individual's concepts about himself or herself. These personal concepts are especially important in theories that stress the role of the self and one's image of oneself. For example, in his theory of self-realization, the American psychologist Carl R. Rogers focuses on phenomenology—a person's private experiences and perceptions.

Projective tests

Some investigators have tried to avoid the problems of relying on a person's ratings or reports about himself or herself by creating indirect clinical techniques in the form of projective tests. These methods require the person to respond to a situation in which there are no clear guidelines and no right or wrong answers. The person may be asked how inkblots appear to him or her on the *Rorschach Test*. Or the person may be instructed to create a story about the characters in a series of pictures in the *Thematic Apperception Test*. Projective techniques rely on a trained clinician to interpret the person's attributes indirectly from test behaviour. The value of this approach for revealing aspects of personality is controversial and is still being studied.

Freud's psychoanalytic theory

According to the Austrian physician Sigmund Freud, the personality has three parts: (1) the id, which represents instinctive impulses of sex and aggression; (2) the ego, which represents the demands of the real world; and (3) the super-ego, or conscience, which represents standards of behaviour incorporated into the personality during childhood.

According to Freud, mental life is characterized by internal conflicts that are largely unconscious. Impulses from the id seek immediate gratification, but they conflict with the ego and the superego. When unacceptable impulses threaten to emerge, a person experiences anxiety. To reduce this anxiety, the person may use various personality defences. The person may, for example, displace (transfer) his or her emotions to less threatening objects. A child who is afraid to express aggression toward his or her father may become angry at his or her pet dog instead.

Freud's ideas have had great influence on the study of personality, but they are highly controversial. Many of his ideas had to be modified severely by psychologists to take greater account of social and environmental variables.

Personality and environment

Trait theories and psychoanalytic theories both assume that broad internal personality dispositions determine behaviour in many situations. However, research on the consistency of various personality traits indicates that what people do, think, and feel may depend greatly on the specific conditions in which their behaviour occurs. People may be honest in one situation and dishonest in another. They may be passive in some situations but aggressive in other situations or with different people.

Many contemporary approaches to the study of personality therefore emphasize the role of specific social experiences and environmental events in the development and modification of behaviour. Psychologists are gradually moving away from broad theorizing about the nature of personality. Instead, they are studying the conditions that determine complex behaviour.

Personality development

Some psychologists have examined the effects of early experiences on later personality development. Other investigators have studied the stability of particular patterns of personality over long periods of time. Their findings suggest that such tendencies as striving to achieve may persist to some degree from childhood into adulthood. However, research has also shown that personality continues to change as a result of new experiences and modifications in the environment.

Throughout their development, people learn about themselves and their world by observing other people and events. They also learn by trying new kinds of behaviour directly. The rewards and punishments they receive after trying various patterns of behaviour affect their future behaviour in similar situations. People also learn by observing the results of the behaviour of such social models as their parents. Suppose children repeatedly see adults succeed in antisocial or criminal acts.

As children develop, they copy some of the behaviour of many models, including their friends as well as their parents. They combine aspects of their behaviour into new patterns. Through direct and observational learning and cognitive growth, they also acquire standards and values that help them regulate and evaluate their own behaviour. Gradually, people develop an enormous set of potential behaviours. The particular behaviour patterns they show in specific situations depend on motivational factors.

People's cognitive and social learning experiences vary as a result of the particular social and cultural conditions to which they are exposed in the home, at school, and in other environments. Personality traits may predict many important aspects of behaviour. But the setting in which behaviour occurs often provides the best predictions about what people will do. Thus, although extensive differences among people are found in most human actions, considerable uniformity and regularity can occur when environmental conditions are very powerful.

Strong success experiences in a new situation, for example, may override the effects of past failure experiences and of personality traits in determining future reactions to that new situation. Similarly, prolonged or intense environmental changes, such as lengthy hospitalization or imprisonment, may lead to major personality changes. A person who has severe difficulties in personal relationships is said to be suffering from a personality disorder.

Emotional reactions: During the course of development, we acquire intense emotional reactions to many stimuli. Events that once were neutral may become either pleasurable or painful as the result of conditioning. Some reactions may involve strong anxiety and can have crippling effects. For example, children who have frightening experiences with dogs may become afraid of all dogs. This fear may generalize (spread) even more widely to other animals and to such objects as fur coats, or hair. Such fears are especially hard to unlearn because these people tend to avoid all contact with situations that provoke fear. Consequently, these people prevent themselves from having experiences that might eliminate their fear—petting harmless dogs, for example. Emotional upsets of this kind may also be acquired by observing the fear reactions of other people.

Research on cognitive and social learning processes is leading to new forms of psychotherapy to help people who have psychological problems. Some of these problems are the result of learning deficits. For example, some people lack fundamental academic and vocational skills, such as reading proficiency. Individuals who have inadequate relations with others need to learn essential interpersonal skills. Some people have these basic skills, but they suffer because of emotional fears and inhibitions.

Psychotherapy aimed at changing personality tends to stress insight into the history through which the problems developed. Learning methods try to change the disturbing behaviour itself by carefully planned relearning and conditioning techniques. Still other forms of personality change may be achieved by creating special environments for learning more adaptive personality patterns.

Importance of testing in Psychology and education

Testing, in education and psychology, is an attempt to measure a person's knowledge, intelligence, or other characteristics in a systematic way. There are many types of tests. Teachers give tests to discover the learning abilities of their students. They also give tests to see how well students have learned a particular subject. Some tests help people choose a vocation, and other tests help them understand their own personality.

Standardized tests

Most printed tests taken by students and others are standardized. A test has been standardized after it has been used, revised, and used again until it shows consistent results and average levels of performance have been established. Firms that prepare standardized tests include information with them on how to give and score each test. The results of one person's performance may be compared with those of many others who have taken the same test. Most teachers also use nonstandardized tests that they make up themselves. The quality of a test is judged by three major standards: (1) validity, (2) reliability, and (3) practicality.

Validity reflects how well a test measures what it is intended to measure. For example, a test of reading comprehension could lose validity if it allows too little time for taking the test. It might actually measure reading speed rather than comprehension.

Reliability refers to the consistency of results achieved by the test. To establish reliability, a test may be given to the same group several times. If very similar results are obtained each time, the test may be considered highly reliable.

Practicality involves the cost and convenience of the test. If a test requires too much expense or effort, it may be impractical. It also may be impractical if the results are too difficult to interpret.

Kinds of tests

Most tests are designed to measure one of several characteristics:

(1) learning ability,

(2) learning achievement,

(3) aptitude and interest, or

(4) personality.

Tests of learning ability attempt to predict how well an individual will perform in a situation requiring intellectual ability. These tests are sometimes called intelligence tests, mental ability tests, academic aptitude tests, or scholastic aptitude tests.

A learning ability test consists of a standard set of tasks or questions. It enables a student to demonstrate the skills learned throughout the individual's life, both in and out of school. Tests of learning ability do not measure how "bright" a person is. Educators use the terms intelligence and mental ability simply to describe a person's ability to solve certain kinds of problems typically involved in schoolwork. These terms do not reflect a person's ability in all areas.

Achievement tests try to measure how much an individual has learned about a particular subject, rather than the general ability for learning. Schools use achievement tests more than any other kind of test. Throughout primary school, secondary school, and college, most teachers rely on such tests when rating a student's progress. Special achievement tests are used to licence people in such professions as law, medicine, and accounting.

Many teachers prepare achievement tests that closely follow their own method of instruction. They also use standardized achievement tests. Some schools ask students to take standardized achievement tests, as well as scholastic ability tests, for admission or placement. There are two types of achievement tests—*norm-referenced* and *criterion-referenced.* In norm-referenced tests, each person's performance is compared with those of others who took the test. A student who answers some questions incorrectly would still rank highly if most other students answered a larger number of questions incorrectly. But in criterion-referenced tests, each person's performance is compared with a predetermined standard or criterion. For example, a teacher might decide that 90 per cent of the questions on a test must be answered correctly for a student to earn a passing grade.

Aptitude and interest tests reveal an individual's talents or preferences for certain activities. A person who likes to tinker with machinery would probably score highly on a test of mechanical aptitude. Such a person has an aptitude for mechanical work—and at least a fairly good chance of succeeding at it.

Interest tests are also known as interest inventories. In them, a person indicates his or her preferences among large groups of activities, ideas, and circumstances. One of these tests might ask, "Would you rather fix a broken clock, keep a set of accounts, or paint a picture?" Most individuals prefer certain types of activities over others. The pattern of answers reveals the strength of a person's interest in various fields.

Personality tests attempt to measure an individual's personal traits scientifically. Some standardized personality tests consist of lists of personal questions requiring yes or no answers. The answers can be analysed for various characteristics. For example, a person might score high in social introversion, which would indicate a strong preference for being alone. Such a person might find scientific research more satisfying as a career than teaching science in a classroom.

Another type of personality test, the *projective test*, requires individuals to tell what certain images mean to them. In a Rorschach test, for example, a person describes what he or she sees in a number of standardized inkblots. A trained counsellor can often recognize behavioural tendencies in these descriptions. Psychologists use personality tests as clues for further study of an individual. They do not regard them as conclusive evidence about the individual's personality. Most personality tests are less reliable and less valid than the other kinds of tests discussed here. Some people criticize their use as an invasion of privacy.

Knowing how to take tests does not increase anyone's learning ability or achievement. But it does help a person avoid losing points unnecessarily. Experts in testing offer the following suggestions:

1. Get all the experience you can in taking tests. The ability to take tests improves with practice.
2. Cramming before a test is better than no study at all. But a careful review spread over several days is better than cramming.
3. Be sure you understand the directions at the beginning of a test. Otherwise, you may get a lower score than you deserve because you failed to follow certain instructions.
4. Answer the questions that are easy for you, and then go back to the hard ones.
5. If there is no penalty for guessing, answer every question.

If there is a penalty, you may still gain points by guessing some answers. On a multiple-choice question, for example, you may know enough about the subject to eliminate some answers. If so, your chance of guessing the correct answer improves considerably.

Interpreting test scores

There are several points to keep in mind about test scores.

First, a test reflects only a sample of a person's skill or knowledge, not everything about an individual. A test score can tell only how well the person performed on one particular test on one particular day.

Second, a score on a standardized test compares one person's performance with the performance of others. Such a comparison may provide useful information if all the people taking the test are alike in some important way. Most standardized tests give scores for persons of the same age or in the same class.

Third, every test score is an estimate rather than a precise measurement. To remind people of this, some scores are reported as bands rather than as a single number. The bands show the range in which a person's actual ability probably lies.

Testing often has far-reaching effects, and so it receives much attention from educators and social scientists. Criticism has been directed both at the limitations of tests and at their influence.

Some educators believe multiple-choice tests penalize a student who has an expert knowledge of a subject. Such a student may see flaws in the answer generally accepted as correct. Other critics say that standardized tests discriminate against disadvantaged and minority groups. These students may be unfamiliar with words, terms, and concepts used in the tests. To give these students an equal chance, educators have tried to prepare culture-fair or culture-free tests. Such tests might consist of pictures, symbols, and nonsense syllables that are equally unfamiliar to everyone taking the test. This type of test reduces the influence of cultural background on performance. Tests that use no words at all are called nonverbal tests.

The general effect of testing on education has also caused concern. Standardized tests sometimes lag behind educational thought and practice. If tests do not measure the content of new syllabuses, they may fail to encourage educational progress. Many educators believe there is at least some truth in criticisms of tests. But they also know that testing is necessary in teaching. Tests can determine whether one method of teaching works better than another. Tests can also tell a teacher what help a student needs most. No better way has been found to determine how much students have learned, what they seem able to learn, and how quickly they might learn it.

3

Meaning and Definition of Sports Psychology

Several studies have revealed the importance and acceptance of sport psychology. However, the crucial question about the real nature of sport psychology is difficult to answer precisely. Although many definitions have been suggested, there is no comprehensive and internationally accepted definition of sport psychology until now. There is, therefore, a need for a clear description and definition for this area of growing importance.

Although some cultures and languages use distinct terms for different types of physical activity, in this statement the term sport is used as an umbrella term including all kinds of exercise, sport and physically active pursuits. Sport psychology is concerned with the psychological foundations, processes and consequences of the psychological regulation of sport-related activities of one or several persons acting as the subject(s) of the activity. The focus may be on behaviour or on different psychological dimensions of human behaviour, i.e. affective, cognitive, motivational or sensori-motor dimensions.

The physical activity can take place in competitive, educational, recreational, preventative and rehabilitation settings and includes health-related exercise. Subjects are all persons involved in the different sport and exercise settings, e.g. athletes, coaches, officials, teachers, physiotherapists, parents, spectators etc.

How is sport psychology constituted?

Sport psychology as a scientific discipline, as well as a professional field, is loosely associated with, and draws upon, the three areas of (1) sport practice, (2) psychology and (3) other sport sciences. These areas are considered equally valid. All of them have a bearing on the topics, the theoretical foundations, the methodological approaches, and the scientific and ethical standards of sport psychology. The interrelations between these areas are briefly described as follows:

Sport practice: Sport psychology is faced with issues that arise from exercise and sport practice. It tries to better understand these demands and attempts to give assistance in satisfying them.

Psychology: Sport psychology is an applied subdiscipline of psychology. It partly draws upon knowledge adopted from different branches of psychology and contributes to the further understanding of psychology in general.

Other sport sciences: Sport psychology is one discipline of the sport sciences. The more sport psychology generates specific knowledge by empirical work in the field of sport and physical activity, the more the findings and methods of other sport sciences have to be accounted for. Some questions may only be answered using interdisciplinary approaches.

Sport psychology as a scientific discipline and professional area furthers the understanding of sport. It analyzes, assesses and directs activity in all aspects of sport by means of psychological processes. Thus sport psychology has a responsibility for well-being, the attainment and maintenance of health, and the improvement of performance.

Sport psychology may support the individual or the group with the aim that the actions of the subject master the requirements of the task, fit with situational demands and constraints, and are appropriate to the subject's abilities and needs.

Sport psychology gives the body of knowledge that contributes both to the personal growth and development of the subject and to the formation of the conditions under which exercise and sport are performed.

We use the term 'sport psychologist' in a broad sense including all qualified persons working in the field, independent of their academic education. Different countries may have restrictions on the use of the term 'psychologist'. Sport psychologists have three interrelated tasks:

Research:

Research is needed to understand the psychological regulation of activity in the setting of sport. The following types of research are conducted: Theoretical or empirical, basic and applied, laboratory and field studies. All contribute to the construction of a specific body of knowledge.

Education:

Sport psychology is an important subject in the education of almost every person involved in sport. Three different groups of people may be given knowledge and competence in sport psychology:

a) on an academic level, students in psychology, the sport sciences and physical education;

b) on a professional level, psychologists moving into the field of sports, coaches, training supervisors, officials and administrators; and finally

c) sport participants, e.g. top level athletes, health-related exercise participants, participants in adventure sports, or rehabilitation patients.

Application

Knowledge and competence in sport psychology may be applied to two main functions, namely (1) diagnosis and assessment (e.g. talent detection, testing of cognitive or sensori-motor skills, or evaluation of the needs of participants), and (2) intervention (e.g. guidance in cooperation with – other responsible persons in the field, counselling, or consulting in special problem situations).

Mental Toughness in Sports Psychology

There are certain moments during competition that appear to carry great psychological significance, when the momentum starts to shift in one direction or another. These situations require athletes to remain completely focused and calm in the face of difficult circumstances. Tennis players talk of the 'big' points during a tight match, such as a fleeting chance to break serve; for an athlete, it could be the final triple-jump in the competition after seriously under-performing; for a footballer, it could be how you react to a perceived bad refereeing decision or to going behind in a match your team are expected to win. Think about times when things have not gone quite to plan and how you reacted.

Most top athletes and coaches believe that psychological factors play as crucial a role as physical attributes and learned skills in the make-up of champions. When physical skills are evenly matched - as they tend to be in competitive sport - the competitor with greater control over his or her mind will usually emerge as the victor. Mental strength is not going to compensate for lack of skill, but in close contests it can make the difference between winning and losing.

A key question for sport and exercise psychologists is whether champions have simply inherited the dominant psychological traits necessary for success or whether mental toughness can be acquired through training and experience. Recent research has attempted to explore the concept of mental toughness in sport more thoroughly, and it appears that, while some people are naturally more tough-minded than others, people can be 'toughened-up' with the correct approach to training.

Mental Toughness

It is probably easiest to define in terms of how it affects behaviour and performance. A mentally tough athlete is likely to:

— achieve relatively consistent performances regardless of situational factors;

— retain a confident, positive, optimistic outlook, even when things are not going well, and not 'choke' under pressure;

— deal with distractions without letting them interfere with optimal focus;

— tolerate pain and discomfort;

— remain persistent when the 'going gets tough';

— have the resilience to bounce back from disappointments.

The influence of personality

These characteristics are obviously related to success in most life situations. But it seems that some of us may be tougher than others because of personality traits and learned ways of coping. Personality research has always stirred up controversy - usually because researchers have not been able to agree on the correct approach to studying it. Some have taken what is known as the 'trait' approach, which views personality as stable and enduring, based on individual characteristics. However, others see personality as shaped by environmental influences, while 'interactionists' view individual traits and the environment as codeterminants of behaviour.

In recent times, this latter position has tended to predominate, based on the view that personality structure involves both a stable core of attitudes, values and beliefs about self, that remains relatively unchanged after early childhood, and more changeable, dynamic behaviours that are influenced by our environment. Research on the relationship between stress and illness has revealed that some people have characteristics that act as buffers against stressors, making them less likely to succumb to ill health in difficult times.

A researcher Suzanne Kobasa showed in one study that a personality characteristic known as 'hardiness' was a key factor in whether or not highly-stressed executives succumbed to illness. The hardy executives, who avoided illness, tended to perceive stressors as 'challenges' rather than threats, so maintaining a sense of control over events Kobasa suggested that hardiness incorporates three key elements:

— *Control*—the perceived ability of the individual to exert influence rather than experience helplessness;

— *Commitment*—ie a refusal to give up easily;

— *Challenge*—involving a person's ability to grow and develop rather than remain static, and to view change rather than stability as the norm.

Until recently, few studies had attempted to transfer the concept of hardiness to sport and exercise settings, but it seems very similar to the idea of mental toughness. The relationship between hardiness and performance in basketball showed that seven out of eight season-long performance indicators were significantly correlated with a total hardiness score.

More recently, a team of researchers at Hull University have taken the idea of hardiness a step further by proposing a model of mental toughness in sport.

— A key development has been the development of a questionnaire to assess mental toughness that can be used to assess its influence in experimental studies.

The Hull researchers carried out two studies to show how mental toughness was related to performance and cognitive appraisal. In the first study, 23 volunteers performed 30-minute static cycling trials at three different intensities of 30, 50 and 70% of their maximum oxygen uptake, rating the physical demands of the trials at five-minute intervals.

Participants were classified as having either high or low mental toughness based on their responses to the above-mentioned questionnaire and, as predicted, those with higher levels of mental toughness reported significantly lower perceived exertion at 70% of maximum. No significant differences were noted at lower levels of exertion which, as the researchers acknowledged, is consistent with the cliché that 'when the going gets tough, the tough get going'.

The observed differences at higher levels of exertion could reflect a tendency of the more tough-minded to somehow act on the incoming stimuli before it reaches the level of perception, to reduce the perception of strain. Mentally tough exercisers might perceive themselves as having greater control during such conditions, or interpret the higher intensity as a challenge rather than a threat. The key question for the researchers was how participants would respond to feedback that could alter their confidence. As predicted, mentally tough participants performed better on the planning task, delivering relatively consistent performances whether their feedback had been negative or positive. However, those with lower levels of mental toughness performed significantly worse after negative feedback, confirming the greater resilience of those with high levels of mental toughness.

'4Cs' model of mental toughness

Building on the work of Kobasa, the Hull team proposed that confidence was a key element of mental toughness. This has given rise to the '4Cs' model of mental toughness. Research on mental toughness in sport and exercise has focused largely on individual differences, in which mental toughness is viewed as a relatively stable characteristic. However, classic previous research on animals has suggested that 'toughening up' can be achieved through exposure to stressful conditions. Weiss and colleagues observed a toughening phenomenon after exposing animals to cold-water.

— Specifically, the usual decrement in performance following aversive stimulation was not observed after the

14-day period. The intermittent exposure to aversive stimuli had apparently led to the animals becoming more tolerant of - and resilient to - such stimuli.

Although this finding does not necessarily transfer to human subjects, there are distinct parallels with various techniques commonly used as interventions in sport and exercise environments. For example, a technique known as 'stress inoculation training' gradually exposes the individual to more threatening situations while self-control is acquired as a means to combat learned helplessness. The stress response is gradually diminished as exposure renders the situation less threatening and the individual experiences a growing sense of control. Of particular importance here is the idea that exposure to stress in controlled situations is much more powerful than stress reduction or removal, which will not help an individual cope with future exposure to the same stressor. One researcher has proposed four major influences on toughening, as follows:

— *Early life experiences:* Both human and animal studies have shown links between exposure to stressors in early life and reduced fear or emotionality when exposed to threats in adulthood;

— *Passive toughening:* Intermittent exposure seems to protect against depletion of 'stress hormones' and is linked with their quicker returns to baseline levels. In other words, people become less sensitive and more tolerant of stress;

— *Active toughening:* Physical fitness gained through aerobic conditioning is thought to be an important means of self-toughening. This could be related to the application of control;

— *Ageing:*This has the opposite effects to the other three, tending to make people more sensitive to and less tolerant of stress.

Clearly, active and passive toughening are the most relevant manipulations for athletes and can be applied in a number of practical ways. Stress inoculation training is an obvious application, but this is probably best approached with the aid of a sport psychologist. Rod Laver, the Australian tennis legend, has described how he used practice sessions to simulate 'tough' match conditions

Laver felt that fatigue placed great strain on the concentration which was crucial to success in long matches. To simulate these conditions, Laver forced himself to concentrate and work even harder during the latter stages of training sessions, when he was tired, so that he became used to the mental strain of such conditions. He has cited this as one of the key factors in his long-lasting success. Simulation training is a great way to prepare mentally for the challenges of competition, and this can include mental as well as physical stressors.

For example, a tennis player could increase the mental pressures in a practice match by starting each service game 0-15 down, and thus getting used to 'rebounding' after losing the first point. Alternatively a player with an over-reliance on his first serve could be restricted to one serve only and be forced to become extremely focused and accurate with what is, in effect, a second serve. To enhance the stress still further, players could practise by playing tiebreakers, or play practice matches in front of an audience. The coach might use bad line calls, or spectator noise as a way of exposing players intermittently to distractions and giving them practice at dealing with them.

Tennis is a game with plenty of breaks between play that allow time for dwelling on past events or self-doubting. Using imagery and positive self-talk during dead time in order to remain calm and in control can be an effective strategy. Mentally tough competitors are likely to use strategies that reinforce their self-belief at times of crisis. And these strategies can be rehearsed in practice situations. With a little invention, simulation training can be used for most athletes, and the opportunity to deal with mental stressors in controlled situations can be an invaluable way to toughen up in preparation for the very real challenges of competition.

Performance profiling

Where sport psychology is concerned, it is often assumed that performers either have what it takes or are - and forever will be - somewhat lacking in mental skills. We have spent a considerable amount of time in occupation trying to convince both coaches and athletes that mental skills can be learned in much the same way as physical ones can - through systematic training. Think about how often you have heard players attributing their success or failure to confidence, motivation or concentration. Then think about how much time athletes who attribute their failures to mental factors spend on mental training and trying to address areas that could be improved. We can assure you that there is little correlation between recognition of the problem and application of the appropriate remedy.

People who are not familiar with psychological skills training often don't realise the range of options available to help improve performance. Furthermore, the psychological techniques that can lead to performance enhancement are often simple to learn and easy to incorporate into a regular training regime. The real skill of a psychologist or coach is in matching each athlete's requirements to the appropriate techniques. If a 5,000m runner appeared to lack speed towards the end of a race, an effective coach would observe this and design a training programme to tackle the specific problem.

The solution would not be to simply run more laps in a training session, but would involve work on speed-related drills. Similarly, if psychological factors require attention, the intervention must be tailored to specific needs. But whereas speed - or lack of it - can be directly observed, psychological factors are often hidden. A key problem for coaches seeking to address such issues is how to work out what the problem is when they cannot observe what is going on in their performers' minds. A direct question does not always yield useful results since athletes can be reluctant - at least initially - to discuss such things.

One approach that is becoming increasingly popular with sport psychologists and coaches in sport is performance profiling. This has many benefits and is useful for assessing physical and technical prowess as well as psychological factors. Evaluating strengths and weaknesses is a valuable process that can help in the planning of training régimes and the identification of long-term goals as a focus for self-improvement.

For many years the typical psychological evaluation resembled a medical consultation , with the psychologist making his or her assessment and deciding on techniques for a change and the athlete playing a relatively passive role. However, Butler and Hardy identified an inherent weakness in this process since studies had shown that people's intrinsic motivation can be weakened by the application of external controls.

To put it simply, for athletes to remain motivated to adhere to psychological skills training programmes, they need to be more involved in the decision-making processes. With performance profiling the athlete is self-determining and his or her perspective becomes a central rather than peripheral focus. In devising this technique, Butler also provided a mechanism by which athletes could explore aspects of their performance that they may have taken for granted and coaches and psychologists could gain further insight into their athletes' cognitive processes.

The research evidence on performance profiling is certainly supportive. Graham Jones of Loughborough University reported successfully employing the technique with an élite-level racket sport player. This performer had experienced temperamental problems when faced with pressure situations, but the profile identified an intervention appropriate for her specific needs and she showed significant improvements in her ability to cope with pressure following a six-month cognitive-behavioural programme. According to Jones, performance profiling has three major purposes:

— To aid in identifying an appropriate intervention;

— To maximise the performer's motivation and adherence to the programme;

— To monitor any changes over time.

Over the past few years, performance profiling has become a routine aspect of the improvement programmes used by many psychologists and coaches. Most people would agree that the coach-athlete relationship is much stronger when vision, goals and targets are shared and agreed and, conversely, that difficulties can arise when the opposite is true. A boxing coach might place a high priority on punching power and believe his boxer needs to raise his game in this respect because he rates his performance in this respect as 6.

The boxer, on the other hand, might perceive his power as adequate because he rates the construct as less important than the speed of his punch. He may believe that working on his power might compromise his speed and thus may be resistant to any recommendations geared to boosting this. The point about involving both parties in the profiling process is that such differences are highlighted and can then be dealt with effectively through dialogue.

Butler and Hardy explain that, in such circumstances, the coach and athlete might work on developing power through technical modifications in order to preserve the punching speed that the boxer rates as more important. Thus, where conflict might have arisen, the profile helps to focus training in a more productive fashion. Another useful variation on the standard performance profile is for the athlete to compare his or her current status in relation to the agreed constructs with a previous best standard rather than an ideal. If the performer has regressed as a result of an injury, this may provide a more realistic and motivating target in the short term.

According to Butler and Hardy, performance profiling can help coaches and psychologists develop a better understanding of their athletes by:

— Highlighting perceived strengths and weaknesses;
— Clarifying the athlete's and coach's vision of the key determinants of élite performance, and highlighting any differences;
— Establishing areas where the athlete might resist change (as demonstrated by the perceived low importance of one or more constructs);
— Providing a means of monitoring progress;
— Highlighting discrepancies between the athlete's and coach's assessment of performance.

The performance profile appears to be a tool that is particularly useful for aiding the design of specific mental, physical and technical training programmes. The central involvement of the athlete in the process is a key strength that may boost motivation and promote adherence to any intervention strategies devised. It may also facilitate the coach-athlete relationship by promoting dialogue and addressing any perceived discrepancies. Additionally, the profile can be used as a monitoring device to assess the effectiveness of any interventions and highlight areas of good and poor progress.

Sports Coaching

Sports coaching has for too long been based on the dominance of a reductionist approach - the insistence on analysing everything down to its basic components - and lines of authority between coaches in the know and those supposedly without knowledge. This approach goes hand in hand with the denial of the innate, the instinctual and the intuitive, and it has held back sports coaching in UK and elsewhere by 25 years. The beliefs and assumptions that coaches grow up with are the very ones that undermine learning, performance and enjoyment. They can be illustrated by the following statements:

— A person cannot learn a new skill without being told and/or shown by an expert.

— If you try to learn something without expert help, you will develop bad habits.

— Errors and bad habits can only be recognised and corrected by an expert.

— There is a right technique for most activities, one that has to be taught.

— Intellectual understanding is a pre-requisite of learning good technique.

— Coaches must be experts in the particular sport or activity that they coach.

Coach Education Programmes

We believe that the fundamental psycho-physical basis of coaching as practised in sport is flawed and needs to be challenged. We have no doubt that most coaches do the very best they can with the training they have: it is the governing bodies of individual sports and their coach education programmes that need radical review.

The role and influence of the US, National Coaching Foundation, for example, has been disappointing because of its lack of understanding of the bigger picture. Change is made more difficult because academics, analysts and reductionists still dominate our broader educational culture.

More recently, some 30 years ago, the Californian tennis coach Tim Gallwey resurrected the ancient philosopher to help with tennis. Tim wrote a book, The Inner Game of Tennis, that became a best seller not just among recreational players but people from other sports. Many coaches were more sceptical, though, perhaps because the book's message seemed to threaten their livelihood. You start to play the Inner Game when you realise that the opponent within your own head is more daunting than the one on the other side of the net. The outer game is played with a racket and a ball against another player; the Inner Game is played against anxiety, self-criticism, tension, frustration, a lack of self-belief, fear and anger. Your potential is your performance minus your internal obstacles.

The Inner Game process aims to eliminate these internal obstacles to performance, learning and enjoyment and thereby liberate your potential. All sports people are familiar with such internal obstacles and keen to overcome them, but far fewer share Gallwey's confidence that, as these obstacles recede, a natural, technically proficient player somehow emerges from within, without expert input. How does this happen? The best illustrations of this process come, in my experience, from skiing, because skiers of all standards are beset by fears. There is fear of falling, fear of getting hurt, fear of looking foolish, fear of loosing control, even fear of getting left behind or lost; and these fears generate huge amounts of muscular tension and inappropriate defensive body postures. Remove the fear and the posture becomes natural - in other words, it self-corrects.

The increased quantity and quality of feedback and the absence of fear delivers the technically correct position for that person. There is no one correct position for everyone because we all differ in terms of size, weight distribution, strength and flexibility. There is an optimum personal style for each of us, which we only find through self-awareness. Any observer, however expert, sees only the surface, the symptom, and can offer only general advice. The problem is, though, that a learner will often interpret a generality as a specific and strive to apply the advice rigidly, overriding his or her own self-awareness, leading to a counterproductive increase in tension. Let's consider one more example from skiing. A skier's legs are his suspension, and flexible knees with sufficient free movement up or down would seem advisable.

The most frequent technical instruction ski instructors give is 'bend zee knees', in response to which skiers tend to adopt a fixed bent position, which gives rise to stiff suspension and poor ski grip. The instruction was technically correct, but the effect of giving it was counterproductive. This paradox is often unrecognised by conventional sports coaches, who repeat their commands ever more fervently. The most effective way to achieve the desired soft suspension effect is to ask awareness-raising coaching questions, such as: how much do your knees bend; when do they bend most in a turn; what happens when they are most bent, etc?

Learning or performing better through awareness and discovery is massively different from being told what to do. What you are told enters the mind, but it is the body, not the mind, that plays tennis or skis. Awareness results in body-learning and, as we all know from riding a bicycle, the body forgets far less easily than the mind. Tactics are largely intellectual, but technique is physical.

Changes in coaching should keep pace with evolution in psychological understanding, but coach education is slow to respond. Old coaching was based upon longstanding behavioural and cognitive principles, which were discovered to be incomplete and were enhanced by humanistic principles as far back as the sixties. Tim Gallwey grew up in that era, and the Inner Game parallels humanistic principles of which awareness was the key. But Tim and others were already looking ahead to the next evolution of psychology that was waiting in the wings; known as 'transpersonal psychology', this embraces the will, choice and personal responsibility and takes an even more holistic view of people and their development. It is fast finding its way into business practice. Psychological evolution must lead coaching methodology. People from every sport pay lip service to the idea that 'it is all in the mind', but for some coaches technical knowledge remains the be-all and the end-all.

A team of researchers from the University of Western Australia have examined the dubious benefits of thought suppression in a sporting context in two studies using videotaped clips of Australian Rules Football. In the first study, involving 102 under-graduates, participants watched a video with short sequences focusing on players, coaches and umpires, and were then asked to complete a brief questionnaire to assess their awareness of target images. Before this task, they were divided into three groups, as follows:

— General - asked simply to view the video and answer a questionnaire describing what they had seen;

— Suppression of intention to harm - additionally asked not to pay attention to players attempting to harm others;

— Suppression of umpires - asked not to pay attention to umpires.

The researchers also manipulated 'cognitive load' (played distracting background noises to simulate increased stress levels) to test the theory that stressful conditions would aggravate the difficulties of thought suppression. As predicted, analysis of the results revealed that subjects asked to suppress their attention to umpires actually paid more attention to them than those whose thoughts were allowed to roam freely. However, this effect was not apparent in the group asked to suppress awareness of intention to harm, and was not aggravated by distracting external stimuli.

The researchers offer two possible explanations for this discrepancy: first, there were significantly fewer 'intention to harm' images than those featuring umpires; secondly, intention to harm may have been too subjective a focus to be interpreted meaningfully by the students.

Overtraining and Depression

Overtraining syndrome is a very common pitfall for athletes and sports people, affecting more than 60% of distance runners during their athletic careers, more than half of professional players during a five-month competitive season and 33% of basketball players participating in a six-week training camp, according to published research. Yet there is no agreed definition, no objective diagnostic test for the condition, while the underlying mechanism remains unknown. And despite elaborate annual periodisation programmes designed to prevent OTS, even the most experienced coaches admit that they cannot predict which team members will experience performance decrements - the only universal sign of the syndrome.

However, in a comprehensive review of this mystifying syndrome - known variously as staleness, chronic fatigue, overstrain and burnout - a pair of US sports scientists point the way to a greater understanding of the syndrome and even towards a cure. The basic theses outlined by Laurence Armstrong and Jaci VanHeest is that OTS and clinical depression share 'remarkably similar' signs and symptoms, brain structures, neurotransmitters, endocrine pathways and immune responses. This suggests that the two syndromes have similar causes and raised the possibility that medications prescribed for depression - i.e. antidepressants - may effectively treat OTS.

OTS is defined in the review as 'a set of persistent physical and psychological symptoms that occur subsequent to prolonged application of heavy training loads. The critical OTS diagnostic factor is a chronic decrease in performance, not simply the existence of [signs and symptoms]...complete recovery from OTS requires from several weeks to several months'. Up to 90 signs and symptoms of OTS have been identified, of which the most common are:

— Decreased physical performance

— General fatigue, malaise and loss of vigour

— Insomnia

— Change in appetite

— Irritability, restlessness, excitability, anxiety

— Loss of body weight

— Loss of motivation

— Lack of mental concentration

— Feelings of depression.

All except the first of these are also recognised signs and symptoms of major depression.

'Two noteworthy reviews provide a theoretical connection between OTS and depression.' Explain the researchers. 'Both independently hypothesised that highly motivated athletes, consumed with the will to perform well and win, become frustrated by poor performance that may be caused by inadequate recovery during over-reaching and overtraining. Part of this disappointment stems from the athletes' realisation that they are not living up to pre-established aspirations or goals, despite having invested much in their training programme.

'Frustration next leads to increased practice time each day and increased training intensity, which results in less regeneration, increased fatigue and worsening of performance. This progressive cycle of decline also results in deterioration of an athlete's mental well-being. Depression then may manifest itself as altered mood states, sleep disturbances and a loss of zeal for training and competition.' Armstrong and VanHeest cite a fascinating anonymised case report on an elite marathon runner who was laid low with an endless series of illnesses and injuries, accompanied by a decline in performance lasting for more than a decade.

The US researchers strongly recommend controlled research studies to evaluate the effects of various antidepressant medications on variants of OTS. They recognise, though, that the picture is complicated by the existence of two different types of OTS, one primarily involving the sympathetic nervous system and the other the parasympathetic, and also that interactions of different neurotransmitter systems, including noradrenaline and serotonin, are probably involved. They offer the following advice to coaches in relation to OTS:

— Maintain accurate records of performance during training and competition and be prepared to adjust training intensity/volume when performance declines;

— Encourage and reinforce optimal nutrition, hydration and sleep;

— Be aware that multiple life stressors - including, work, home and family pressures - may add to the stress of physical training;

— Treat OTS with rest - but try to find ways to make it appealing to athletes. 'Active recreation' may aid recovery and help deter monotony;

— Encourage athletes to communicate with you about their physical, mental and emotional concerns;

— Consider questionnaires or interviews - after consulting a psychologist - to determine changes in mood states.

Famously, a German researcher called Hans Lenk (1) disproved the notion that only cohesive groups could win by showing data collected from the 'riotous' German Rowing 8 squad that were successful in the 1968 Mexico Olympic Games. Anecdotally, Olympic Rowing provides another famous example of how low cohesion and success can mix, as GB gold medallists Holmes and Redgrave were supposedly not the best of pals! In subsequent Games though, Redgrave and Pinsett were winning Gold and were highly cohesive.

But if the relationship between cohesion and success not cut and dried, this raises more questions:

— If winning is possible without cohesion, how important is cohesion to the winning formula?

— Are there specific aspects of cohesion that are crucial for team success and others that are less important?

Psychology researchers need to be able to analyse and measure team cohesion with validity. In science, the term validity refers to how well your measuring tool actually assesses what you are aiming to measure. In physical terms a ruler is obviously a highly valid measure of length; but in the realms of psychology, which variations in individual perceptions are involved, validity is not so easy to establish. Research led by Albert Carron concluded that much of the early research on cohesion was limited by the less-than-rigorous Sport Cohesiveness Questionnaire in uses at this time. He and his colleagues set about developing a sounder tool, known as the Group Environment Questionnaire (GEQ). These researchers aimed to base this new tool on a sound concept of what cohesion actually involved for sports teams.

The Psychology of Sports Injuries

Contrary to what one might expect, it is not necessarily the most aggressive, risk-seeking athlete who is most likely to be injured in practice or competition. Rather, stressors such as family arguments, disagreements with teachers, or difficult relationships with friends, coupled with an inability to adequately cope with these stressors, may predict the incidence of sports injuries.

Coaches and parents of athletes who stress winning at all costs and who fail to provide adequate psychosocial support can increase the likelihood that athletes will be injured. These problems can be minimized when coaches, parents, athletic trainers, and athletes have open communications with one another.

Athletes and their parents should meet with coaches and athletic trainers at the start of the season so that the risk of injury can be made clear to all and actions that can reduce those risks can be outlined.

During the season, coaches and athletic trainers must be involved in both the psychological and physical development of the athletes. They should teach the athletes to distinguish between discomfort and the pain of injury. Athletes who have a high degree of self concept and good psychological coping skills are likely to recover more quickly from injury than their less confident and capable teammates.

Coaches and athletic trainers can contribute to the athlete's self-confidence by providing counseling and other types of social support. It is essential that injured athletes are treated as important members of the team to prevent any sense of isolation that may otherwise develop.

Stroke Technique in Biomechanics

Biomechanics is the sport science interested in how forces create and modify human motion. Since biomechanics is the science of technique, a primary application of biomechanics for tennis coaches is in the analysis of stroke technique.

Professional Skill of Qualitative Analysis

When a tennis coach observes a player during practice and decides on feedback or certain changes in technique they are performing the professional skill of qualitative analysis. Good qualitative analysis is much more than observing errors and making corrections. Qualitative analysis of tennis strokes can be pictured in a four-task model (Figure 1).

In the preparation task the coach gathers relevant knowledge about the strokes, players, and situation to be analyzed. In observation the coach systematically uses all their senses to gather relevant information about performance. In the evaluation/diagnosis task the coach has two main goals: identify both strengths and weaknesses and then prioritize the weaknesses based on their importance to performance.

In the intervention task the coach selects the most appropriate strategy to help the player improve. During on-court qualitative analysis the coach can immediately return to observation to monitor progress and continue analysis.

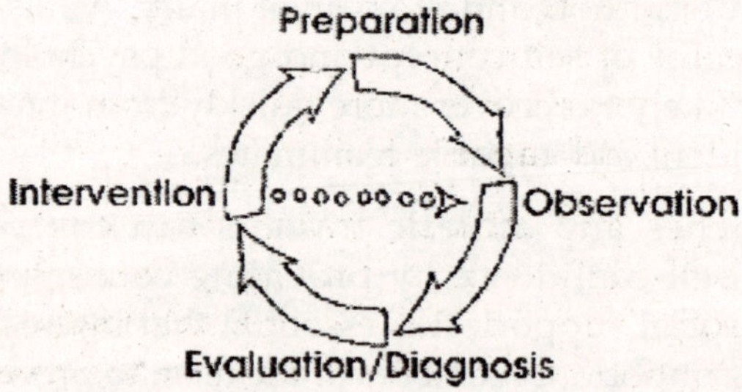

Figure 1. The four-task model of qualitative analysis proposed by Knudson and Morrison (1997).

This larger vision of qualitative analysis helps tennis coaches improve player performance much faster than traditional methods. Noting both strengths and weaknesses helps the coach get a more complete picture of a player's abilities. The diagnosis of performance focuses the coach and player's attention on the most important technique factors, limiting unproductive information overload or attention on irrelevant technique factors. The good coach is skilled at many kinds of intervention (not just verbal feedback) to help players improve.

There is another critical point in the professional qualitative analysis of tennis strokes. A tennis coach/ professional should use an interdisciplinary approach to all the four tasks of qualitative analysis. An interdisciplinary approach is the integration of professional experience and all the sport sciences, not just biomechanics. For example, a coach noting that a young player's strokes have consistently slow racket speeds through impact might decide maturation and conditioning are more important than biomechanical changes in technique.

Nine Principles of Biomechanics

One strategy to apply biomechanics to the qualitative analysis of tennis strokes is through the use of a few generic biomechanical principles. These principles use coach-friendly labels rather than the specific mechanical terminology. Interested coaches can read more about using principles of biomechanics in qualitative analysis in several sources. Following are the principles of biomechanics

— *Balance*: the degree of control over stability/instability

— *Coordination continuum*: organization between simultaneous and sequential actiond

— *Force-motion*: forces are required to change the state of motion

— *Force-time*: the timing/pattern of force application

— *Inertia*: the linear and angular resistance to motion

— *Optimal projection*: impact or release conditions that optimize performance

— *Range of motion*: body motion used in a movement

— *Segmental interaction*: the transfer of energy across body segments and joints

— *Spin*: projectile rotation to stabilize flight and adjust trajectory

The principles of coordination and segmental interaction are becoming even more relevant to tennis coaches because of recent changes in groundstroke technique. For most of the 20th century tennis was played with heavy rackets with small heads. Forehand technique involved a square stance, a weight shift followed by shoulder centered, full-arm stroke. With the lighter, larger and more powerful rackets available today many players are using more open stance and sequentially coordinated forehand techniques.

Sequential coordination (progressive motion from larger to smaller joints tends to transfer energy through the interaction of segments) is the most effective technique for fast movement of small resistances. Recent biomechanical research on tennis groundstrokes has shown evidence of sequential coordination and stretch-shortening cycle muscle actions. Today, groundstrokes are coordinated much like the serve, with well-timed sequential actions of body segments. For example, in an open stance forehand as the speed of trunk rotation peaks this stretches the chest muscles, storing elastic energy. As trunk rotation slows before impact some of this energy is recovered as the chest muscles accelerate the upper arm.

Coaching good sequential coordination is not easy, but obvious pauses or a lack of a stretch on distal muscles as proximal segments reach peak speed are symptoms or poor coordination that coaches should work to eliminate. The principle of optimal projection in tennis suggests that there are optimal angles that strokes are hit given the typical conditions (height, speed, court location). This means that certain stroke paths are more desirable than others to place the ball at typical, strategic targets. For example, virtually all serves are hit with an initially horizontal or upward trajectory. The upward swing of the racket in the serve creates topspin on virtually all serves.

Coaches can apply the principle of optimal projection by evaluating players for signs of "pulling down" on the serve. Beginners often tend to "hit down" on the serve, so coaches need to provide beginners with practice, cues, and the feeling of "hitting up" on the serve. Even advanced players in a hurry to the net or trying to get more weight into their serves can begin to hit their serves at too shallow an angle. Brody has reported typical "windows" or angles of successful shots for most tennis strokes.

Optimal projection is also related to the biomechanical principle of spin. Spin applies to all strokes because virtually all tennis shots are stroked to accommodate the spin on the ball or to impart spin that matches a strategic objective. Research has shown that "flat" strokes are a misnomer since all shots have some spin. In general, the research shows that for typical groundstrokes the racket paths at impact for flat, topspin, and topspin lobs are about 20, 35, and 50 degrees above the horizontal.

Skilled players tend to swing the racket upward near 20 degrees on most strokes, increasing the slope of the racket motion before impact in topspin strokes. Tennis coaches should know that greater topspin on a stroke comes at a cost of lower ball speed. A player using a more steep racket path through impact risks less pace, poorer depth of placement, and greater miss-hits for their heavy topspin. The good tennis coach is able to observe racket motion, ball flight, and impact sounds to evaluate if a player is using appropriate spin on their shots.

Backspin strokes are usually hit with a smaller downward trajectory (15 to 25 degrees) than topspin strokes because the spin of the ball after the bounce does not have to be reversed. A major benefit of spin that must be qualitatively assessed by the coach is the curve in the balls flight. The spinning ball creates a fluid force called lift, tending to curve the trajectory of the ball in the direction of the spin. Coaches need to weigh the strategic advantages of the trajectory and bounce of a player's spin strokes in matchplay.

Focus and Flow

Focus and Flow are at the heart of Sports Psychology:

— Focus is complete attention to the execution of a skill

— Flow is the state of being completely engrossed in the execution of a performance to the exclusion of everything else

When you are in a state of flow, focussing intensely on the execution of skills, you will give your best performances. You enter a state of almost Zen-like meditation in which mood, distraction and different stressors simply have no place in your consciousness. You are free to execute skills just as you have trained to execute them. This is an immensely satisfying state to achieve. The qualities of flow are:

— All your attention is focused either

— on the skills or routine being performed

— or on the input from your senses relevant to the sport

— You are fully focused of the activities being performed, and are:

— not aware of your own awareness, consciousness of self or ego

— not evaluating the quality of execution of skills during performance

— not concerned with distractions such as results, judges, audiences or other peoples expectations

— not making any conscious decisions in your mind or reasoning with words - you are trusting your body to follow its training

— You are in complete control of actions and reactions

— You feel almost in an altered state of consciousness: achieving flow is exhilarating, and gives a powerful feeling of competence.

Achieving Flow

Flow is easiest to achieve when:

— You perceive that your skills are good enough to match the perceived difficulty of the contest.

— The competition is not so easy that you become bored and do not concentrate.

— You have distraction under control

— You are paying full attention to the performance, with no analysis of errors or technique

— You are relaxed and alert

— You are thinking positively, and have eliminated all negative thoughts

— It is allowed to develop, and not forced

— You have practised and trained attention

The Zen Approach

Perhaps the most systematic approach to achieving focus and flow so far is that used in oriental martial arts, such as Karate or Kendo. These adopt a Zen approach to concentration where the fighter is in a state of almost pure flow. In these sports the competitor seeks to lose all distractions of ego, analysis and from surroundings, immersing him or herself completely within the activity. The following things in particular are avoided:

- — Wanting to win
- — Show off
- — Wanting to frighten or terrify the opponent
- — The desire to be reactive and not take the initiative
- — Trying so hard to achieve the correct state of mind that you distract yourself.

Western Sports psychology is now advocating an almost identical set of strategies through a skills based approach. If, however, you appreciate a mystical approach, you may appreciate the Zen approach to focus. Different sports, and different parts or positions in sports, require attention to be focussed on different skills and different cues.

Where success relies on a physical skill being executed, then focus on that skill. In other cases, you may have to make a tactical appreciation before execution of the skill. The appropriate attention should be paid to this. Alternatively where an opponent is involved, study and learn the cues that give away his or her intentions. For example, foot movements, glances in a particular direction or tensing of shoulder muscles can give away the fact that someone is about to throw a punch. Similarly the opponent may give cues as to defensive tactics to be used which may be picked up.

The focus requirements and cues to look for will differ from sport to sport and position to position. You can analyse them effectively by studying video footage of performance. This can be slowed down so that all cues can be examined. You can also pick up information on cues from books or videos on your sport. By understanding the cues to look for, you can separate out the things to which attention should be directed from the clutter of irrelevant stimuli that occur in a competition environment.

Training to Improve Focus

You can improve focus by practice and training, much like any other skill. You can practise it at its simplest almost as a form of meditation - firstly study an object for some time: get completely involved with it, in its shape, colour, texture, smell, etc. Then practise switching the focus to a different object, being completely involved in this, and nothing else.

Similarly you can practise focus on sounds, listening to them and then switching focus to other sounds. This concentrated attention helps you to feel what sporting focus feels like. The rapid switching to another thing practises your ability to switch focus. In normal training, visualise the performance of a skill using imagery, then focus on its execution as you actually perform it. Practise doing the skill without any analysis. Experience the feeling of flow. Associate this feeling of flow with a trigger word in your mind. One thing to watch out for as you get better at a sport is loss of focus. This can happen for two main reasons:

— as your reactions become automatic they hold your attention less, and

— as you get better, you may find that you are not as challenged by other competitors.

You may find that these focus problems have their root in goal setting: if you are setting outcome goals such as 'coming first', then this will not be challenging if you win easily. This can be prevented by setting performance goals that are sufficiently difficult to maintain motivation, a sense of being stretched and concentration on improving skills even when competition is weak.

Mood Control

Bad moods damage your motivation to succeed in training or competition. They make you more prone to negative thinking, and cause distraction, often as you trigger bad moods in other people. Bad moods emerge as bad temper, unhappiness, lethargy and sluggishness. If you are in a good mood, then even dull training can be enjoyable. Your mood is completely under your control - bad moods are an indulgence you cannot afford. You can improve your mood in the following ways:

— Through positive thinking and suggestion - say to yourself 'I feel good' or 'I am going to move faster' or 'I can feel energy pouring into my limbs'. This really does help.

— By treating each element of a performance individually - when you make a mistake, refocus and concentrate on the next separate element of the performance. Treating a performance in this way ensures that a bad move or a missed shot does not effect following moves or shots.

— By using imagery - imagine a beautiful scene or a time when you were performing very well and feeling good. Alternatively, imagine feeling good directly.

— By reviewing your goals to remotivate yourself.

— By smiling! - Forcing a smile onto your face for more than just a few seconds always seems to lift a bad mood. Try it - it really does work!

Distraction Management

Distraction is damaging to your performance because it interferes with your ability to focus and disrupts flow. It interferes with the attention that you need to apply to maintain good technique. This causes stress and consumes mental energy that is better applied elsewhere.

Sources of Distraction

Distraction can come from a number of sources, both internal and external, such as:

— the presence of loved ones you want to impress

— family or relationship problems

— media - photographers, interviewers, cameras, heat form lights, etc.

— teammates and other competitors
— coaches who do not know when to keep quiet
— underperformance or unexpected high performance
— frustration at mistakes
— unjust criticism
— poor refereeing decisions
— changes in familiar patterns etc.

You can prepare for and deal with all of these sources of distraction.

Coping with distraction

Coping with distractions and minor irritations is mainly a matter of attitude - you can either dwell on them and blow them up out of all proportion to their significance, or you can accept them and bypass them. If you waste mental energy fretting over a trivial problem, then this is energy that cannot be spent maintaining good technique. Over long events or competitions, this wastage of mental energy can seriously damage your performance.

What is worth remembering is that when you are distracted, lose concentration and make a mistake, you have not lost your skills. All you have lost is your focus. The following points may help you to deal with distractions:

— Remember that although events may be beyond your control, your reactions to events are entirely controlled by you.
— Think positively - recognise petty irritations as such, and let them go
— Know you can perform well despite distraction
— Prepare for and expect more distraction at bigger events

— Expect other competitors to be more nervous at big events - use your ability to resist stress and distraction as a competitive advantage

— Develop a refocussing plan and practice using it when you are distracted

— Learn how to change bad moods to good moods

— Sleep and rest more before big events so that you have more mental energy to devote to distraction, mood and stress control.

Stress, Anxiety and Energy

Too much stress and anxiety can seriously affect your ability to focus on your skills and flow in a performance. This section examines the causes of excess stress and anxiety, explains their symptoms and then explains techniques that you can use to manage them. It is important that you recognise that you are responsible for your own stress levels. Very often they are a product of the way that you think. Learn to monitor your stress levels, and adjust them up if you need more arousal, or down if you are feeling too stressed. Also learn that other people may seek to manipulate your stress levels: if you are feeling stressed and uptight, the last thing you may need is a motivational talk from a coach or manager who may not be able to see your stress.

Stress

A certain level of stress is needed for optimum performance. If you are under too little stress, then you will find it difficult to motivate yourself to give a good performance. Too little stress expresses itself in feelings of boredom and not being stretched. At an optimum level of stress you will get the benefits of alertness and activation that a good level of stress brings.

Excessive levels of stress damage performance and damage your enjoyment of your sport. These excessive levels occur in the following circumstances:

— When you think that what is being asked of you is beyond your perceived abilities

— When too much is asked of you in too short a space of time

— When unnecessary obstacles are put in the way of achieving goals

The negative effects of stress are:

— That it gets in the way of judgement and fine motor control

— It causes competition to be seen as a threat, not a challenge

— It damages the positive frame of mind you need for high quality competition by:

  — promoting negative thinking

  — damaging self-confidence

  — narrowing attention

  — and disrupting flow

  — It consumes mental energy in, for example, worry. This is energy that you could devote to keeping technique good.

Very often stress can be caused by negative thinking as well as being a result of negative thinking: If you interpret a situation saying 'I'm in trouble', then you are much less likely to do well than if you think positively, seeing a new situation as an opportunity to exhibit your skills at a higher level.

Stress and Adrenaline

When you are in a competitive environment or are in an

environment in which you are being evaluated, adrenaline may enter your bloodstream. This has the following positive and negative effects on your body:

Positive Effects:

— Adrenaline causes physiological arousal

— It causes alertness

— It prepares the body for explosive activity

— Negative Effects:

— It inhibits judgement

— It interferes with fine motor control, and makes executing complex skills difficult.

You will experience the preparatory flow of adrenaline into your body typically as 'Butterflies in your stomach'. In sports such as shooting where fine motor control is important, adrenaline may be a negative factor. However in sports like sprinting or power lifting, where explosive activity is required, adrenaline may be useful in generating optimum performance.

You may currently view high levels of adrenaline in your body negatively as stress. You may need to review this, perhaps welcoming adrenaline as an aid to your performance. Similarly you might like to consider using 'Psych Up' routines to raise your adrenaline levels if you are not sufficiently aroused.

Anxiety

Anxiety is different from stress. Anxiety comes from a concern over lack of control over circumstances. In some cases being anxious and worrying over a problem may generate a solution. Normally, however, it will just result in negative thinking. Albert Ellis listed the five main unrealistic desires or beliefs that cause anxiety:

— The desire always to have the love and admiration of all people important to you. This is unrealistic because you have no control over other peoples minds: people can have bad days, can see things in odd ways, can make mistakes, or can be plain disagreeable and awkward.

— The desire to always be thoroughly competent. This is unrealistic because you only achieve competence at a new level by making mistakes. Everybody has bad days and makes mistakes. One of the benefits of training with better athletes is that you can see them making mistakes and having bad days too.

— The belief that external factors cause all misfortune. Often negative events can be caused by your own negative attitudes. Similarly your own negative attitudes can cause you to view neutral events negatively. Another athlete might find something positive in something you view as a problem.

— The desire that events should always turn out the way that you want them to and people should always do what you want. Other people have their own agendas and do what they want to do.

— The belief that everything that has happened in the past will inevitably condition and control what has happened in the future. Very often things can be improved or changed if you try hard enough, or look at things in a different way.

Mental Energy

You need mental energy to be able to concentrate your attention and maintain good mental attitudes. If you are concentrating effectively then you can conserve physical energy by maintaining good technique when your muscles are tired, can maintain focus and good execution of skills, and can push and drive your body through pain and fatigue barriers.

You can waste mental energy on worry, stress, fretting over distractions, and negative thinking. Over a long competition these not only damage enjoyment, but also drain energy so that performance suffers. It is therefore important to avoid these by good use of sports psychology, and by resting effectively between events and by ensuring that you sleep properly.

Optimum Stress Levels

The level of stress under which you operate is important: if you are not under enough stress, then you may find that your performance suffers because you are bored and unmotivated. If you are under too much stress, then you will find that your results suffer as you find it difficult to focus on technique and fail to flow with the performance.

Where stress is low, you may find that your performance is low because you become bored, lack concentration and lack motivation. If this state persists for a long time, then you may find the sport tedious, and give it up. Where stress is too high, your performance can suffer from all the symptoms of stress. Your flow can be disrupted, you can be distracted, and competition can become threatening and unpleasant.

In the middle, at a moderate level of stress, there is a zone of best performance. If you can keep yourself within this zone, then you will be sufficiently aroused to give a high quality performance, while not being over-stressed and unhappy. This zone of optimum performance is in a different place and is a different shape for different people. Some people may operate most effectively at a level of stress that would leave other people either bored or in pieces. It is possible that someone who functions superbly in a low level competition might experience difficulties in high level competition. Alternatively someone who performs only moderately at low level of competition might give exceptional performances under extreme pressure.

Not only will the zones of optimum performance be in different places for different athletes, they will also be different heights and different widths. This is why you must take responsibility for controlling your own levels of stress, particularly in a team situation: if the team generally needs motivation, but you are in an optimum zone, then paying attention to a motivating team talk may move you to a state of being over-stressed. Similarly if some team members need to be relaxed, then relaxation techniques applied to an entire team may move you to a state of bored demotivation. You may also find that fine and complex skills are less tolerant to stress than simple skills - your zone of optimum performance may be narrower for very difficult skills than for the basic skills of the sport.

An effective way of finding the stress level at which you operate best is to keep a training and performance log. In this record the quality of every training session or performance, along with the level of stress that you felt during that performance. If you have stress monitoring equipment, and can score your performance, then this gives you hard, objective figures to use in your training log. If you do not have the ability to do this, then record your subjective views of the stress levels you felt and the quality of the session.

The following is a list of the major symptoms of stress that you might feel:

Physical Symptoms - mainly in response to increased levels of adrenaline:

— Increase in heart rate

— Increase in Sweating, and a cooler skin as this combines with a reduction in the blood flow to your skin.

— 'Butterflies' in your stomach

— Rapid Breathing

— Tense Muscles

— Dry Mouth

— A desire to urinate

— Mental Symptoms

— Worry

— Confusion, inability to concentrate or difficulty making decisions

— Feeling ill or odd

— Feeling out of control or overwhelmed

— Behavioural Symptoms

— Talking rapidly

— Nervous mannerisms: nail biting, foot tapping, increased blinking, twitching, pacing

— Scowling

— Yawning

These symptoms of stress should not be taken in isolation - they could be caused by other factors. However if you find yourself exhibiting or recognising a number of them, then it would be worth investigating stress management techniques.

Increasing Stress Levels

Where you are not feeling motivated towards an event, either because you are bored by it, because there is no serious competition or because you are tired, you may need to psych yourself up. This will raise your level of arousal so that you can perform effectively. The following techniques can be used to psych up:

— Warm up faster and harder

— Use imagery - for example, a swimmer might imagine himself being chased by a shark!

— Use suggestion - 'I can feel energy flowing into me'

— Focus on the importance of the event

— or Focus on personal goals, such as running a race in a particular time, rather than unchallenging outcome goals such as winning (when competition is not intense).

Stress Reduction Techniques

This section shows you effective methods of reducing stress to a level where you can perform most effectively. The techniques that you select depend on the cause of the stress and the situation in which the stress occurs. In choosing methods to combat stress, it is worth asking yourself where the stress comes from: if outside factors such as relationship difficulties are causing stress, then a positive thinking or imagery based technique may be effective. If the stress is based on the feeling of adrenaline in the body, then it may be effective purely to relax the body and slow the flow of adrenaline.

As with all sports psychology skills, the effectiveness of the stress reduction technique depends on practice. Stress Reduction Techniques Explained:

— Environmental Methods

* Reduce the Importance of the Event
* Reduce Uncertainties
* Listen to Music or Relaxation Tapes

— Physical Techniques: these are most effective where stress is driven by excessive levels of adrenaline.

* Progressive Muscular Relaxation
* Breathing Control
* Biofeedback

— Mental Techniques: most effective where psychological factors are driving stress.

* Imagery Relaxation

* Thought Awareness, Rational Thinking and Positive Thinking
* Remembering past good workouts, performances and achievements
* Self-Hypnosis and Auto-Suggestion

Burnout

Burnout is a very real threat to people in challenging and stressful jobs, as it can quickly cause the end of otherwise promising careers. Because of this, it is something that is deeply feared by many successful people.

This simple tool gives you the opportunity to identify what you want to get out of your job, and then to compare this with the reality of your situation. This allows you to identify possible areas of mismatch, as these mismatches are possible pressure points that may develop into burnout. Knowing these pressure points helps you to manage the situation to avoid burnout.

To start using this tool, list the things that give real meaning to what you do.

Write down what attracted you to your current job or profession in the first place. List the things about it that you find fulfilling now. Write down the value of the profession to humanity and what excites you about it. Think about what you want to achieve within it, and what you think is important to doing the job well.

This will give you a long list of things that are good about what you do. From this list, identify the five things that give the greatest meaning to what you do. These should be the things about the job that most inspire you. Write these down in order with the most important item at the top of the list. This list shows you the important things that you should protect as far as possible.

Next, write down the things that frustrate you most about your work. This may involve things like inadequacy of resource, lack of recognition or bureaucracy. As well as this, list the factors that are causing you difficulty and which are likely to cause stress in the future.

Now work through the list of things that give you meaning item-by-item. For each item, look at the list of frustrations and see if any of these threaten the item. While many of the frustrations on your list may be significant, these ones are particularly important as potential burnout pressure points.

Think these through carefully, and plan in advance how you will handle build-ups of stress in these areas. Our article on avoiding burnout can help you to do this.

The Burnout Self-Test

This tool is a useful self-check for burnout. By using it on a regular basis, you can keep a check on yourself to see whether you are at risk of burnout, and therefore whether you need to take action to avoid it. The tool is a simple self-test that you can run through to check whether you are at risk of burnout.

Avoiding Burnout

So far, we have looked at identifying your personal burnout pressure points and have shown how you can check yourself for burnout. If you need more help in identifying the most important sources of stress in your life, then use the Schedule of Recent Experience to get a view of the long term stress you are experiencing, and keep a Stress Diary to see what is causing stress in your day-to-day life.

Consider whether you are being too accommodating. Should you let people know that you have too much work to do? Should you be politely turning down new work that people pass you? If this is the case, then improved assertiveness skills may help you to do this in a positive way.

Remember that you will have to say "no" at some stage, otherwise your commitments will get bigger and bigger. You must learn to say no to commitments that you should not take on, otherwise you will be in severe danger of becoming intensely stressed and exhausted.

Finally, be aware that it is just not possible to do some jobs. Sometimes organizations commit themselves to projects that they do not have the capabilities, resources or skills to complete. These quickly become "projects from Hell". Beware of these projects - they can be traps from which it is difficult to escape, even if you are at severe risk of burning out.

Political and people problems

Where politics seems to be a problem, you need to check that you are allocating enough time to managing your stakeholders and that you are correctly managing your support network. It is very easy when under stress to stop communicating with people, and this can lead to political problems that compound with other issues to create a toxic cocktail of stress.

Alternatively, a major cause of burnout can happen when too many people lean too heavily upon you. While it is important to provide support to the people around you, some people will suck up as much support as you can give and demand still more. This can be both tiresome and intensely disappointing, as you never seem to be able to meet their needs.

While distancing yourself from people is a symptom of burnout, it is also a defense against it. You need to find the fine balance between being reasonably open and available to the people you live and work with, while at the same time distancing yourself from people who drain you of emotional energy. A way of doing this may be to involve other people in providing support.

Another area where you need to find a balance is with the different (and often conflicting) demands of different groups of people and organizations. An obvious conflict is between work and family: Both really want as much of your time and energy as possible. You need to find a way of reconciling both, while still leaving time for yourself. However, this is also true of almost all of the people or organizations you deal with. All have their own goals and values, and all have their own ideas of how you should behave. In many cases, these goals will conflict with those of other organizations and in many cases they will conflict with yours. As the only person who is an expert in your own life, you need to find what seems like a reasonable balance and then defend this assertively.

Avoiding Exhaustion

Exhaustion is a major factor in burnout. Going on a good, long vacation is one of the best ways of avoiding burnout. Choose a vacation that does not expose you to the stresses you experience at home or which distracts you from them. Leave your laptop and mobile phone behind. Forget about work completely until your return. Rest, and enjoy life. Similarly, make sure you get enough sleep and rest, and that you frequently use relaxation techniques to calm down and relax.

The other major cause of burnout is disillusionment with your job, particularly when you get a great deal of the meaning in your life from the work you do. The emphasis here is on protecting the parts of your job that give you meaning and satisfaction. If you have trouble in justifying this to yourself, then think about the people you serve: if you burn out, then they will not get the benefit of the energy and enthusiasm you can provide: You owe it to them to enjoy your job!

How to Recover From Burnout

It may be too late to talk about avoiding burnout, as you may have already reached a stage where you are thoroughly disillusioned with your job and where you no longer get anything of emotional value from it. You may feel let down or betrayed by your organization, and may just be going through the motions of doing your job just for the money it brings in.

While you can deal with exhaustion by taking a good break, rest may not cure this sense of disillusionment. The passion and commitment that you previously brought to your job may now have completely burned out. Without this, it is unlikely that your career will progress much further. People deal with this situation in a number of different ways. Some are effective, while others are not so good:

Doing Nothing: One of the worst ways of reacting to burnout is to accept it and do nothing about it. By remaining in place, you risk becoming bitter and angry as opportunities pass you by. Your organization may come to regard you as "dead wood" and if things do not change, you may be doomed to a gradual or sudden decline. You need to change the situation in some way.

Changing Career: If you have lost all interest in the values that led you into your profession in the first place, then career change may be the only option open to you.

The first downside of this, however, is that you lose the benefit of the precious experience that you have gained within the profession. In entering a new profession, you will undoubtedly be competing equally with people much younger than you. These people may be willing to accept much lower salaries.

A second downside is that you risk a strong sense of failure in the way you handled your first profession, whereas burnout will only have been a temporary setback if you succeed in turning the situation around.

Changing Jobs: Job change within the same profession is less of an issue than full-scale career change, in that many of your skills and much of your experience will be transportable. It provides you with the opportunity to rededicate yourself to your original goals. It also provides a fresh start in a new environment, without the constant reminders that come with staying in the same job.

Changing jobs is an appropriate response where you are disillusioned with your organization more than you are with your career. What you risk, however, is ending up in the same situation again: In changing your job, you must make sure that you understand the causes of your burnout and ensure that history does not repeat itself. Looking at this positively, you should now know the signs of impending burnout and should now know how to avoid it!

Using Burnout as a Trigger for Personal Growth:

An important first step in managing burnout is to deal with the sense of failure that you may experience following it. The way to do this is to take a long, rational, dispassionate look at the circumstances leading up to it. A good way of doing this is by talking to someone who you trust and who is experienced in similar situations in similar organizations (you may find a personal coach helpful here). Avoid people within your own organization, as these people will be tainted with its assumptions and thinking habits. These may contribute to the problem. Take the time to talk the situation through in detail, looking at the circumstances before your involvement, your workload, your actions and the actions of other people, and the situations that evolved.

If you are the sort of person who has been committed enough to your work to burn out, it is more than likely that you will have already done everything in your power to resolve the situation. In reflecting, you will probably find that you made some mistakes, but you will most likely see that these are excusable under the circumstances. You will almost certainly see that a great deal of blame should be attributed externally to the situation, to people around you, or to the people who set up the situation in the first place.

Lessons that people typically learn through this process are that they are not superhuman, that hard work does not cure all ills, and that major achievements need the commitment and support of other people: In many circumstances, the intense commitment of only one person simply is not enough. They also learn to look at situations with skepticism as they go into them, and to trust their own judgment in spotting and communicating problems early on.

Inform these processes with the increased wisdom and self-understanding you will have gained by understanding why you burned out. Ensure that you give due weight to the relaxation, quality of life issues and social activities that will help to protect you against burnout in the future. Make sure that your goals are set in a balanced manner so that they do not conflict with one-another, and that they are not so challenging that they become a source of excessive stress in their own right.

Mental Skills Training for Sports

The interface between biomechanical, physiological, and peripheral and central nervous system operation to coordination of movement are mediated by different facets of psychological involvement. To enhance the psychological component of physical movement, mental skills training has been recognised as an effective method. Primarily, mental skills training has developed from the necessity of the athlete to learn more about their individual mental life to allow a degree of control in coordinating effective movement through various psychological states of performance.

There are many different methods used to develop mental skills in task performance, but most can be separated into two basic approaches, cognitive and somatic, even though there is much overlap between the two. Underlying both systems is the aim and motivation of the individual to attain self-mastery, that is, a desire to control their individual psychological world.

The ability of the individual to control mental and emotional elements assists task performance as well as creating a psychological foundation for confidence and well-being. When the individual feels as though they possess a degree of self-mastery in relation to psycho-somatic function, this serves to motivate continued efforts in attempting to increase performance. However, when the ability of the individual to control their psychological state is diminished, especially during times of injury or incapacitation, there is a risk of a decrease in self-confidence, well-being and future performance. Thus, as its first premise, mental skills training relies on a methodology of self-mastery, generated through self-knowledge, to enhance the psychological state of the individual.

Like any form of training, methods to develop self-knowledge require time, and distinct and definite goals. Furthermore, time set aside for mental skills practice, and the belief in the methods employed, require a certain level of motivation, even more so, than physical based training that has quantifiable results from the beginning and can be assessed and measured with regularity. Mental skills training takes a certain degree of patience and trust in their application because results may not come immediately, and are often qualitative and difficult to separate from significant increases in physiological performance. Sustaining individual motivation with patience and persistence is important from the beginning.

The initial difficulties associated with implementing a mental skills training package can be alleviated by ascertaining the motivational characteristics behind the aim of increasing performance. Weinberg identified two distinct motivations underlying the desire for an athlete to improve performance, these were, extrinsic rewards and intrinsic motivation. Extrinsic rewards are those motivations that are essentially external to the athlete. These include the more material aspects of competition, such as prizes, trophies, money and security, and also the more immaterial, egocentric aspects of competitive events, such as recognition and respect from peers. Intrinsic motivations are mainly concerned with the desire for self-development, and to challenge and improve oneself.

Weinberg, Martens and Rushall emphasize that athletes should be encouraged to improve performance from intrinsic rather than extrinsic motivation to help with attaining specific goals. This is because extrinsic rewards tend to govern the concept of self, and event performance, that is, the athlete's self-confidence and overall satisfaction with training and performance are influenced and defined by external factors out of the control of the individual.

For example, if an individual obtains a good result, even though they may have performed below personal expectations, they may find satisfaction in his or her performance. If the individual obtains a poor result, despite having performed above personal expectations, they may be very self-critical and produce within themselves a depressed state that may affect future performance. In either case, if performance is evaluated by external factors, such as what other people may think of them, or what material gains may be made from competition, an egocentric, almost narcissistic psychology may be developed. Furthermore, this may decrease the objectivity the individual requires to learn from failures, and face personal challenges that may be inhibiting further development.

Motivation derived from external rewards appears to underlie the phenomenon of learned helplessness in sport, or the continued failures of the athlete despite no obvious, external cause being identified. This is because those individuals whose definition of self lies with external elements tend to attribute failures to others, or outside events, and only successes to themselves. If the athlete only ever learns from past successes, as a sign of the appropriate path to follow to increase performance, there will be a limited scope in development. In general, there are far more failures in fine tuning performance than there are successes, and learning from failure becomes a success if taken from the perspective of intrinsic motivation in self-mastery.

Intrinsic motivation derives from a desire to achieve for achievement's sake. Instead of defining oneself from the perspective of external agents, the individual measures themselves by themselves, success attributable only inasmuch as how they performed previously, regardless of the external reward. Intrinsic motivation allows the athlete a more objective perspective of themselves, decreasing an egocentric position that would normally be associated with external motivation, and freeing the individual to see performance as a means of self-development. Understanding this, the individual places awareness upon the importance of persistence in training, vital to the adherence of psychological and physiological based training.

Moreover, the athlete is not limiting themselves by external events, that is, only setting goals to merely "beat" their opponent for some material or ego-oriented gain, but opens the door for much higher aims in performance. This is because goals set as a construction of external events, i.e., whether one "wins" or "loses", has been shown to be a source of great stress and anxiety due to the inherent uncontrollability of external events. Furthermore, one's goals will be focused mostly on those things believed to be controllable in the external environment, instead of focusing internally on the way one perceives external events.

Under intrinsic motivation, a greater scope for self-development and self-improvement exists in comparison to external rewards because intrinsic motivation assists in changing perception of external events, rather than external events precipitating a change in perception. Therefore, before mental skills training can begin an assessment of underlying motivation is important because of the qualitative nature of results and gradual progression of training.

Methods of Mental Skills Training

Most mental skills training techniques can be grouped into two basic categories, cognitive and somatic methods. Cognitive methods include mental rehearsal, mental imagery and visualization, visuo-motor behavior rehearsal, and cognitive-behavior therapy. Somatic methods include biofeedback, progressive muscle relaxation and meditation. Although cognitive and somatic methods develop the psychological apparatus of the individual from different perspectives there is much overlap because of the nature of psycho-somatic function. Therefore, elements of each tend to permeate elements of all, but an explanation of a variety of approaches is useful to characterize the different aspects of human nature that contemporary psychology has undertaken to enhance the mental development of the athlete.

Cognitive Methods

Mental Rehearsal: Most of the methods used to increase performance of a given task involve the individual mentally rehearsing the motor skill or strategy intended for training or for the event. Cohn has reviewed much theoretical and practical research citing mental rehearsal as an effective tool for performance. The theoretical support for mental rehearsal comes from a variety of sources.

Schema Theory

This theory developed by Schmidt describes movement as being primarily controlled by central structures with minimal input from sensory information that stores pre-programmed commands in the form of generalized motor patterns that are retrieved and executed upon demand. However, these commands, once executed, especially during quick movement, requires an almost absence of sensory information, otherwise, disruption of the motor pattern becomes inevitable and execution malformed. This is because conscious intervention is too slow to accommodate changes in motor coordination, and thus, unconscious execution is desirable.

By mentally rehearsing the specific motor pattern the psychological "script" becomes more explicit in its expression, and tendencies to intervene at critical moments can be alleviated when the requisite cues have been made aware to the individual. Without awareness of the script, or motor pattern, to allow execution from start to finish without intervention, motor skills may not be effective.

Stages of Motor Learning

Much like Schema Theory, Fitts, and Fitts and Posner describe the stages of motor learning as (a) the cognitive phase, i.e., consciously learning a new skill, (b) the associative phase, i.e., making minor adjustments to the newly learned skill in striving for perfection, and (c) the autonomous phase, i.e., the newly learned skill is capable of being executed unconsciously. However, even if the cognitive and associative phases are properly performed the autonomous phase may not be sufficiently reinforced within neural structures to allow proper unconscious activation. Practiced mental rehearsal can help to reinforce the appropriate neural coordination to allow the specific motor patterns to be retrieved and used. If not, conscious processes may still have to intervene and slow down, or even destroy the coordination process.

The Set Hypothesis

This hypothesis proposes that before a successful motor skill can be executed a specific internal state is necessary for optimal conditions of activation, especially after prolonged periods of specific motor skill inactivation, such as the nature of golf and bowls. That is, adjustments in the level of arousal and attention need to be modified depending upon the particular demands of the task, and this must be repeated each time. By rehearsing this aspect of skill performance the individual will be able to practice eliciting those psychological states conducive for performance. If not, then before the skill has a chance to be executed the risk of failure is high because the requisite psychological background conditions are not sufficient for optimal activation.

Cohn describes some of the practical implications of mental rehearsal from the theories extrapolated above. Depending upon the nature of the task and the skill level of the individual, the advantages of mental rehearsal are two-fold.

First, mental rehearsal can be used to reinforce unconscious processes executing specific motor skills to increase skill efficiency. This is because conscious control of quick and/or complicated movements are too slow in their intervening power, and thus, contribute to disrupting, or destroying the intended movement.

Secondly, initiation of a specific skill requires specific psychological conditions for optimal performance, such as specific arousal and attention processes. Therefore, the motor skill component and the pre-skill, or pre-performance lead-up, need to be rehearsed for efficient execution.

Cohn provides evidence of pre-performance routines used to facilitate sports performance in open- and closed-chain skills that include golf, tennis service, basketball free-throw, soccer, volleyball service, bowling, gymnastics, wrestling, skiing and skating, and diving. Lobmeyer and Wasserman investigated the effect of a pre-performance training routine upon a free-throw shooting task. Subjects showed a 7% increase in free-throws during practice when using their pre-throw routine versus not using it.

Wrisberg and Anshel found that mental imagery in conjunction with arousal control was an effective pre-shot strategy to enhance the free-throw shooting performance of young athletes. Moore evaluated the effects of an overt-covert routine training program on adherence to, and performance of, a pre-service routine in tennis. Overt, or behavioral based strategies such as practice swings, setting and aligning feet and hands, etc., and covert, or cognitive based strategies such as picking a target, visualizing the ball in flight, etc., were used. The study showed that tennis players' adherence to a pre-service routine increased following the intervention program, but there were only slight increases in serving accuracy. The players reported in follow-up interviews that the intervention had a positive effect on second-serve aggressiveness and target selection.

A similar study investigated the effects of self-recording (a technique of self-monitoring) on adherence to a tennis service routine. The results indicated that self-monitoring had improved adherence to service routines, with only slight but consistent improvements in serving accuracy. Moore and Lloyd concluded that small increases in performance with advanced athletes is still meaningful because of a "ceiling effect" that leaves only a small margin of improvement. Furthermore, a study using bowlers demonstrated that a positive self-monitoring technique enhanced performance for low-skilled bowlers.

Cohn et al. showed that cognitive behavioral intervention improved adherence to pre-shot routines in golf, and follow-up measures revealed that performance improved in actual competitions. In follow-up interviews, golfers reported that the intervention helped to improve concentration as well as deciding which club to select and the type of shot to be hit, and that it improved confidence and decreased controlling tendencies.

Heishman tested the set hypothesis versus the schema theory as alternate explanations for when to introduce a service routine in volleyball. The study attempted to determine whether learning the serve in conjunction with a routine (as schema theory suggests) was more beneficial than acquiring the serve first and the routine later in learning (as the set hypothesis suggests). The results showed that both groups made significant gains in service accuracy scores compared to controls, but the stage in which the routine was taught did not influence the accuracy or form scores.

A retention test revealed that the set hypothesis group did not decline in accuracy whereas the schema theory group did. Heishman concluded that pre-service routines were effective for improving serving accuracy and form. Furthermore, the routine should be taught after the basic skill has been learned (supporting the set hypothesis), if the main objective is to enhance skill retention. Another advantage of mental rehearsal is the absence of major physical exertion that the individual would have to perform under traditional physical training regimes. This can alleviate the risk of over training that is a constant source of anxiety amongst many amateur and professional athletes.

Fundamental Methods in Mental Skills Training

Therefore, mental rehearsal has been demonstrated to be an effective tool to increase performance. Though there are many varying techniques in mental skills training, some fundamental methods are described below.

Mental Imagery and Visualization

The brain regions responsible for motor execution (specifically the prefrontal cortex and its connections to the basal ganglia maintained in working memory) appear to be also responsible for imagery processes under conscious thought without the intended movement being evoked. That is, those neural operations involved in executing motor coordination also play a role in mentally representing those actions in conscious thought, through imagery, without generating the actual movement. However, imagining the event happening is not enough to elicit the correct imagery process, and like motor skills, if the mental imagery technique is performed inadequately, without sufficient attention on appropriate execution, subsequent gains in motor performance will be substandard.

There are many requirements in achieving the desired effect of mental imagery, but the first is the approach to teaching and learning the specific techniques. The visuo-spatial and temporal components form the "procedural" knowledge required for effective mental imagery, while conceptual (ideas of movement) and symbolical (language representations) elements form the "declarative" knowledge of mental imagery. Procedural knowledge is the knowledge of "knowing how" to do mental imagery based on performance results, i.e., the success achieved in mentally forming the correct image in the mind.

Declarative knowledge is different because it is the knowledge of "knowing that", or the concept or idea behind the mental imagery method in order to gain an understanding of the mental imagery process, and intervening conceptually, or symbolically to assist understanding. This sort of distinction has a similar foundation in "implicit" and "explicit" knowledge in cognitive psychology, in that, these terms signify whether the individual knows what they are doing (explicit) compared to the individual knowing how they are doing it (implicit). These two forms of knowledge are critical if the individual is to learn the techniques needed to perform mental imagery properly. This is because imagining the skill, and actually performing the skill, needs to be as closely executed as possible for effective transfer and reinforcement to neural structures.

Thus, mental imagery competency requires a degree of attention and psychological effort to elicit the desired effect. Once declarative knowledge has been absorbed and understood and conscious attention to detail during mental imagery forms a reinforcing feedback loop that enhances neural structures, then procedural knowledge can begin. There are many guidelines to enhance the imagery process, and most, if not all, fit within the spectrum of techniques in mental imagery training. Some of these guidelines include:

The individual practices mental imagery with the aim of recruiting as much sensory information of the actual skill as possible. That is, not only are visual and temporal data used, but also acoustic (hearing), olfaction (smell), gustation (taste), and kinesthesia (body awareness). By drawing in as much of the sensory information as possible concerning the conditions of skill performance the more realistic simulation of the mental imagery process can be created.

The ability to mentally control the image in a dynamic mode is important. For example, visualization of the image dynamically in first person and third person, or the individual attempts to "see" the performance of the motor skill through their eyes (first person), as well as the eyes of another person observing them (third person). Creating third person and first person visualization allows a multiply perspectives to the continually changing environment to make the process more objective that would be difficult in first person imagery. However, ultimately, the individual must master first person perspective in order to simulate actual events.

In 'Mental Rehearsal', specifically The Set Hypothesis, creating the appropriate psychological background pre-performance is essential in effective initiation of the required motor skill. Therefore, not only should the individual draw in as much sensory information as possible, and the necessary conscious control of the image, but also evocation of the emotional content specific to the skill intended. That is, retrieving the desired arousal and attentional processes involved before the initiation of the skill sequence.

These aspects of the mental imagery process need to be constantly practiced in order to elicit results. Even though individual differences exist in mental imagery ability, generally, better imagery control correlates to better performance in the motor skill. Another approach is to combine the techniques of mental imagery with physical practice of the intended skill labeled visuo-motor behavior rehearsal.

Visuo-Motor Behavior Rehearsal

Visuo-motor behavior rehearsal (VMBR) is an extension of mental imagery, in that, it combines the psychological aspect of generating the mental image with feedback from the performance of the physical skill. This method has been used successfully, especially with closed motor skills, in a number of sports including Karate, basketball, racquet ball, tennis, and cross-country running, golf, track and field, gymnastics, and diving. VMBR involves three phases, first, an initial relaxation phase to retrieve a psychological state conducive for mental imagery, second, visualizing performance through various imagery techniques, and finally, performing the actual skill under realistic conditions.

By repeating this process with the intended skill during training it is hoped that real-time feedback ensues between mentally coordinating the visualization and imagery component with actual performance, thereby, minor changes in either the skill, and/or the imagery process, can be maintained in parallel. The rationale behind VMBR is keeping mental imagery and skill performance closely associated in training, which should correspond to an increase in performance because the individual can fine-tune both processes simultaneously.

Before VMBR can begin, the mental imagery techniques are required to be learnt and understood within the context of performance, otherwise, VMBR can be detrimental to the motor skill activity. This is because insufficient attention during motor performance may result if the individual is concentrating to heavily on the method of mental imagery due to unfamiliarity with procedure. VMBR can be used as an effective extension of mental imagery training. An alternative method is cognitive-behavior therapy that attempts to change skill performance, and behavior towards performance, through altering the way one cognizes the event or events.

Cognitive-Behavior Therapy

Cognitive-behavior therapy (CBT) has been used successfully in a wide range of applications, from developing social skills, dealing with psychiatric disorders, to the treatment of depression. Primarily, CBT focuses on methods that strengthen positive behavior and weaken negative behavior towards a desired goal. Over time, and with maintenance of treatment, it attempts to condition the individual to cognize in specific ways to create desired psychological states as a foundation for psycho-somatic events. This approach has found favor amongst sport psychologists and educators because athletes' attitudes to the way they approach training and competition, and the cues they use to adapt to given situations, influence sporting performance.

CBT is a method to alter perceptions and conceptions about given situations that create a psychological atmosphere conducive for other mental skills techniques to be used effectively, such as mental imagery and VMBR. Many factors appear to influence the success of CBT in any intervention strategy, such as, the interpersonal relationship between trainer and trainee, quality and quantity of feedback, athlete motor skill level (closed/open) and gender, recreational versus elite athletes, and state and trait anxieties.

However, Gordon has reviewed CBT in relation to sports performance and has concluded that, although there are many ways with which to use CBT in an individual and team sport's environment, guidelines can be followed as a fundamental design procedure in any CBT strategy. The central problem of CBT as self-regulation. That is, attempting to alter habits, whether psychological or physical, in order to change attitudes toward a given situation, or motor coordination to a given task, depends on the individual's ability to regulate their own behavior. A five stage process of self-regulation to change behavior towards a given task is offered as a guideline.

The first stage in self-regulating is problem identification. Athletes can become so task focused and rigid in their training routines that the perception of significantly improving performance above and beyond their current level may be non-existent. This may be especially applicable for elite athletes who think that they have already "peaked" and that further improvements are unlikely. Therefore, the main concern at this stage is to assist the athlete in evaluating their training and behavior for possible ways to enhance performance. It does not analyze the specific task for improvement, but attempts to identify ways the athlete can strategically alter their psychological approach to the given task, thereby, opening up new and possible paths to increase performance.

The second stage in self-regulating is commitment. If the athlete does not want, or does not see the need for changing behavior, then any CBT method will not work. Commitment to schedules and training sessions, taking responsibility for their behavior, and a desire to succeed, are based upon the motivational perspectives involved, as for example if the athlete possesses characteristic extrinsic or intrinsic motivations. Without commitment, and the motivational factors that compose commitment, no CBT strategy can be effective.

The third stage in self-regulating is execution. This concerns the actual method of regulating behavior in order to change it. Generally, observation of one's behavior (self-monitoring) and evaluating one's behavior in relation to the set goal (self-evaluating) is coupled with communicating feedback to oneself (self-consequating). For example, after self-monitoring and evaluating a specific behavior that has been identified as positive in light of the expected goal, then affirmation and reinforcement of that behavior can be given in the form of positive self-consequating, such as saying to oneself "keep up the good work, that's it!" Behavior identified as negative in light of the expected goal can be negated by negative self-consequating, such as "it's not working, leave this and try something else to help reach that goal."

The emphasis behind the self-monitoring to self-evaluating to self-consequating and back to self-monitoring schema, is a negative feedback loop. That is, anything self-monitored that negatively affects reaching the specific behavioral goal (over self critical, easily frustrated, etc.) is negated by positive self-consequating techniques. These techniques may include mental rehearsal, mental imagery and visualization, VMBR, and relaxation to help the athlete de-emphasize negative states and allow positive states to permeate their psychological landscape that is more conducive for performance. Of course, employment of these techniques will depend upon the various factors that affect CBT interventions as stated above, specifically because every CBT strategy needs to be individualized.

The fourth stage in self-regulation is environmental management. This stage can affect all others if not properly done. This is because the athlete's environment, the social and physical support networks associated with attaining the desired goal, such as friends, family, colleagues, coaches, management services and facilities, are the foundations for psychological and physiological security. Without this, anxiety levels concerning the support framework in place for the athlete may adversely affect attempts at self-regulation. Therefore, when the first three stages have been identified and mapped out, environmental management is necessary to allow concentration on the important aspects of CBT.

The fifth stage in self-regulation is *generalization*. In order to change behavioral habits in the long term, and maintain a consistent CBT strategy throughout the lifestyle of the athlete, the specific CBT method can be generalized or translated into all aspects of life, such as work and study. Altering behavior is a time consuming effort that, in order to be successful, should be promoted into as many aspects of the athlete's life as possible. If not, deviation from the original goal of the CBT strategy may occur because of constant distracters, such as irrelevant thoughts and stresses, from other areas of life. Thus, by combating these issues with similar or different CBT plans, the constant, and consistent improvement of the individual as a whole is more likely.

The overall goal of CBT is to strategically plan and execute a definite approach that the athlete can follow according to relevant cues indicated by the mutual agreement of the therapist and athlete. CBT attempts to change the way the athlete approaches the given task in order to lay the foundation for specific performance enhancement techniques to occur, like mental rehearsal, mental imagery and VMBR. Thus, CBT concentrates more on the general aspirations and psychological profile of the athlete, rather than specific task affective actions.

Another way of attempting to improve performance is through somatic methods. Somatic methods employ a number of self-awareness approaches that directly support the modalities of CBT but are primarily concerned in gaining control of various bodily functions.

Somatic Methods—Biofeedback, Progressive Muscle Relaxation, and Meditation

To increase the level of self-awareness, that contributes to enhanced self-monitoring and self-regulation, employment of somatic methods to improve performance begins with concentrating on physical sensation to heighten attention of the perception of movement or non-movement. Often, to start the athlete focusing on thoughts and emotions can be difficult because of the subjectivity of experiential content, whereas awareness of bodily sensation can give a more objective sense of self. One approach in the somatic method is biofeedback, that is, employing various devices that amplify specific body functions for psychosomatic feedback.

Biofeedback has been demonstrated to increase running economy in long distance runners by presenting the athletes, when treadmill training over a six week period, their heart rate (heart rate monitor) and ventilation (VO2 spirometer) data. Treadmill running with additional electromyogram (EMG) data, used as a feedback treatment, demonstrated significant increases in running efficiency. The three above mentioned biofeedback devices have also been used in various ways to increase performance in basketball free throw scores, mental skills training, arousal regulation, and especially anxiety reduction in athletes.

Though biofeedback appears to be an effective method of increasing performance, either directly through the applied task, as in running and free throwing, or indirectly through anxiety and arousal regulation, the biofeedback devices can be impractical and sometimes difficult to ascribe causes of results if two or more modalities are used. Another somatic modality similar to biofeedback is progressive muscle relaxation (PMR). Unlike biofeedback, PMR attempts to use the athlete's awareness of muscle contraction/relaxation sensations to derive degrees of self-awareness. This method has been successfully used in decreasing anxiety for optimal psychological states of performance and pain tolerance.

PMR is performed by instructing the athlete to contract then relax specific muscles in a definite order. Normally, this starts with the facial muscles because of their role in gesture and expression of psychological states, and then progresses to larger muscles that have a lesser role in postural awareness. Depending on the sport and individual this sequence may change. For example, a weight-lifter may need to relax specific muscles not associated with the lifting movement to allow an energy efficient execution during performance. Conversely, an archer may need to focus on relaxing facial and upper extremity muscles to assist in concentration when pulling and releasing the arrow.

However, PMR is often combined with biofeedback methods to enhance self-awareness during training that can be transferred to the competitive environment where biofeedback equipment is impractical. The somatic method of meditation, though it combines frequently with biofeedback and PMR, is another way of increasing awareness of self in sport performance. Meditation derives from yogic science but has been transferred to sport because of its holistic emphasis in integrating psychophysical function.

Meditation is defined as mental exercise and by focusing on particular aspects of physical sensation the individual can begin to be aware of the correlations between physiological functions and psychological activity. For example, when certain muscles tense before a specific task, and are detrimental to that task, meditation can be a way to identify what is happening within self and intervene before undertaking the activity, thereby, averting a possible poor performance.

There are many methods to develop meditation and the appropriate intervention strategies to improve performance, but the fundamental principle is beginning with an awareness of the physical self as a tangible expression of the psychological self. Eventually, meditation can be a practical extension to biofeedback because there is no use of equipment, and as an extension to PMR because there is no specific muscular activity. The meditative state requires awareness of internal physical and psychological cues, and thus, may be useful as a mental skills technique during competitive situations.

Visualization in Sport

Visualization is also referred to as guided imagery, or the process of creating a scene in the athlete's mind of what she wants to happen. An athlete will create images, like pictures or movies, that recreate her best performances, or she will envision a desired outcome. While imagining these scenarios, the athlete actually imagines every detail and the way it feels to perform just the way she wants.

Both physical and psychological reactions in certain situations can be improved with such visualization. Such repeated imagery can build both experience and confidence in an athlete's ability to perform certain skills under pressure, and in a variety of possible situations. The most effective visualization techniques result in a very vivid sport experience in which the athlete has complete control over a successful performance.

Guided imagery and visualization can maximize the efficiency and effectiveness of an athlete's training. In a world where sports performance and success is measured in one hundredths of a second, most athletes will use every possible training technique at hand. Visualization is used by many to gain that very slim margin. How to psyche yourself up, calm yourself down and overcome performance anxiety.

Many athletes perform their best during training or practice and find that they choke during competition. If this happens to you take heart because there are some simple steps you can take to overcome such anxiety.

Choking is described as a decrease in performance due to too much perceived stress. The key word here is perceived. Keep in mind that stress lives only in your mind and in the way we interpret a situation. Ultimately, it is not the external situation that causes stress, but the way we think about that event that creates feelings of stress, anxiety and fear. For athletes who choke during competition it is important to understand that you can control the thoughts you have regarding the event. Are your thoughts of doubt, failure and a lack of confidence in your ability? If so, such negative thinking often breeds feelings of anxiety, nervousness, and tension.

Traditional coaches and trainers may try to help the athlete understand why those thoughts and feelings develop and then try to change or modify that process with limited amounts of success. Why such thoughts arise may be of interest, but knowing the answer isn't always necessary to overcome them.

Allow a few minutes to visualize yourself doing everything right. Breathe easy, close your eyes and use mental imagery to visualize yourself performing well. This positive self-talk can change your attitude. While athletes need to be flexible enough to react during the event, you should enter the event with a general strategy of how you want to race. Your strategy can be simple (maintain a steady pace or maintain a steady heart rate) or complex.

Focus on the task at hand rather than the outcome. Stay present in the moment and avoid thinking too far into the event or thinking about the finish. If you find yourself thinking negative thoughts or negative self-talk, stop and focus only on your breathing. Focusing on your breathing rhythm will automatically pull you back into the present. Force a smile. Really. If you are struggling with negative thoughts and can't break out of the cycle, simply force yourself to smile, even if only for a few seconds. This simple action will change your attitude in a split second. Perhaps that is all the time you need to relax back into your performance.

Race like you don't care about the outcome. If you find yourself caught up in negative thoughts and find that you suddenly expect the worst it will be impossible to perform at your peak. If you begin to race like you don't care about the outcome, you may relax and enjoy the event for what it is -

another day in your life. Not the most important thing in your life.

Review the race and recall the things you did well. Focus on actions, thoughts and behaviors that helped you perform. Acknowledge, but quickly dismiss things that hindered your performance. This is the same principle as avoiding an obstacle while driving - look where you want to go, not where you don't. When you focus on the pothole, you invariably hit it. Focusing on the negative aspects of the event will not help you improve in the future.

Rather, you want to focus on the times when you 'got it right.' This is a form of mental rehearsal where you practice skills that will be used in the next event. Design a training program that mimics race-like conditions. Teams and clubs often do such training. If you always train alone, consider joining a group so you can do this type of simulation. Practice is most effective if you can mimic the conditions you will be faced with in competition. Coaches can also help or hinder an athlete's ability to overcome choking during competition. Coaches often inadvertently reinforce a pattern of choking when trying to encourage. Such talk only increases the pressure an athlete feels to perform.

Remember that choking can be dealt with if you are aware of the pattern of negative thoughts that snowball before and during competition. If you find yourself in such a downward spiral, simply acknowledge those thoughts and let them go. Focus on your breathing and play as though you are enjoying it. Chances are you will realize that you are enjoying it despite the occasional less than perfect performance.

Sport Psychology Guidelines for Parents of Young Athletes

A recent news media article depicted the dilemma of parents who are attempting to locate the best school for their 6'3" athletically gifted son who plans to enroll for the fall semester.

These parents, however, were not looking for colleges; instead, they were looking for the best high schools offering college scholarship possibilities for their 13-year-old son. They were afraid that the local high school would not draw enough scouts to view their son, so they were conducting interviews with athletic directors of high schools with track records of college scholarship potential. What parents do not realize is that this process may put undue pressure on a child to live up to parental expectations. Some parents have gone to great lengths, such as moving to another town just for the opportunity to better their child's chances for attaining a college athletic scholarship.

Statistically, the chances for college scholarships are slim. What happens when children don't get the recognition their parents believe they deserve? They may develop feelings of inadequacy and tend to drop out of sport; in fact, by the age of sixteen, eighty percent of children will have dropped out of a sporting activity. Fortunately, most parents are not putting excessive tension on their young athletes. Children will have a greater likelihood of staying in sport and enjoying it more if they don't perceive undue pressure. The following guidelines are suggested in order to help parents and coaches ensure that children experience positive feelings from engaging in sport and to help to create a physically active life that continues through adulthood.

— Focus on your children's effort and performance rather than the outcome of a competition. Teach children that success means achieving their personal goals rather than winning a contest.

— Help your children to set realistic goals that are measurable and attainable. Goals that are too vague or difficult lead to a high ropout rate. Goals that are performance directed rather than outcome directed lead to greater likelihood of success. All goals must be numerically quantifiable.

— Make sure your children know that whether they win or lose, whether they play a lot or a little, you love them unconditionally. Give just as much praise for a loss as you do for a win.

— Show respect for your children's coaching staff. If you're not happy with the coaching style or manner, discuss your concerns with the coach. Don't coach your children from the sidelines.

— Show support for your children's teams by attending games and cheering for all team members. Don't express criticism towards opponents or referees during competition.

— Accept any limitations in your children's physical abilities. Studies suggest that children with less than average skills would rather play on a losing team than a winning one if it means that they can play more often.

— Make sure your children are having fun. Ask your children if they are enjoying their participation in sports and want to continue or try something else.

— Place your children in sports best suited to them rather than forcing your children into sports you prefer or that are most popular.

— Be careful not to relive your sport experiences exclusively through your children. Let them play for themselves, not for you.

— Keep sport in perspective. Remember — the purpose of sport for children is to create an opportunity for fun and growth. All the triumphs and heartaches that are inherent in sport for children can provide learning experiences and lessons that help pave the road to adulthood. These experiences also lead to better sport parenting.

4

Meaning and Definition of Personality

In psychology, personality refers to the emotion, thought, and behavior patterns unique to an individual. The DSM-IV defines personality as:

> "Enduring patterns of perceiving, relating to, and thinking about the enviroment and oneself. Personality traits are prominent aspects of personality that are exhibited in a wide range of important social and personal contexts. ..."

Through the course of western thought, different theories have been put forth to explain the human personality:

Sigmund Freud broke the human personality down to three significant components: the id, the ego, and the superego. Personality is shaped by the interworkings and conflicts of the three. Katherine Briggs and her daughter Isabel Meyers alleged that the writings of Carl Jung delineated personality types. B. F. Skinner, a proponent of behaviorism, suggested that the human personality is developed through external stimuli.

Albert Bandura, a social learning theorist suggested that the forces of memory and feelings worked in conjunction with environmental influences.

Gordon Allport delineates three kinds of traits with varying degrees of intensity: cardinal traits, central traits, and secondary traits.

Raymond Cattell's research propagated a two-tiered personality sturucture with fifteen "primary factors" and five "secondary factors".

Building on the work of Cattell and others, Lewis Goldberg proposed a five dimension personality model, nicknamed the "Big Five":

1. Extroversion
2. Agreeableness
3. Conscientiousness
4. Emotional Stability
5. Intellect

Holland proposed a "RIASEC" model of personality widely used in vocational counseling. The RIASEC is a circumplex model where the six types, which are represented as a hexagon where physically closer types are more related than distal types:

— Realistic - Physical, hands-on, tool-oriented, masculine

— Investigative - Scientific, technical, methodological

— Artistic - writing, painting, singing, etc.

— Social - nurturing, supporting, helping, healing

— Enterprising - organizing, activating, motivating

— Conventional - clerical, detail-oriented

A Typology of Personality Models

Modern personality models may generally be broken into three types: factorial models, typologies, and circumplexes.

— *Factorial models*: Factorial models posit that there are dimensions along which human personality differs. The main purpose of a personality model is thus to define the dimensions of personality. Factor analysis is a primary tool of theorists composing factorial models. Such models arise directly from a classical individual differences approach to the study of human personality. Goldberg's Big Five model may be the best-known example of this type of theory.

— *Typologies*: Typologies or type models arise naturally from some theories that posit types of people. For example, astrological signs represented a well-known, pre-scientific typological model. Typological models posit a relatively small number of modal types and possibly some interaction between the types. The Jungian typology implemented in the MBTI may best represent the typology approach.

— *Circumplexs*: Circumplex models may resemble factorial or type models but further specify a relationship between the different types or factors. Typically, some types or factors are more related than others and can be presented on a polygon. Holand's RIASEC may be the best-known example of this type of theory. Correlations of personality scores should resemble a simplex form where opposing types have low correlation and close types have a high correlation.

Personality Tests

Types of personality tests include the Rorschach test, the Minnesota Multiphasic Personality Inventory, Myers-Briggs Type Indicator, and the Thematic Apperception Test. Critics have pointed to the Forer effect to suggest that some of these appear to be more accurate and discriminating than they really are.

Alter Ego

Alter ego is also a game for the Commodore 64 computer. An alter ego (from Latin, "other I") is another self—a second personality or persona within a person. The term is commonly used in literature analysis and comparison to describe characters who are psychologically identical. For example, in Dr. Jekyll and Mr. Hyde, Mr. Hyde was Dr. Jekyll's evil alter ego (same person, different personalities). The term and concept are also frequently used in popular fiction, like comic books, for the secret identity of a superhero. Superman's alter ego is Clark Kent, Batman's is Bruce Wayne and Spiderman's is Peter Parker.

Dissociative Identity Disorder (DID)

In psychiatry DID is the current name of the condition formerly listed in the Diagnostic and Statistical Manual of Mental Disorders as Multiple Personality Disorder (MPD) and Multiple Personality Syndrome. The International Statistical Classification of Diseases and Related Health Problems continues to list it as Multiple Personality Disorder. This is a controversial diagnosis. The manuals do not agree; the professionals do not agree. People diagnosed with MPD/DID may disagree with the professionals. Skeptics doubt that the supposed disorder exists at all. Also, there are many points of disagreement: Whether MPD/DID is a real disorder, or just a fad. If it is real, is the appearance of multiple personalities real (MPD) or delusional (DID)? Whether it can be cured. Whether it should be cured. Who should primarily define the experience — therapists, or multiples.

In rough terms, believers in DID or MPD argue that children who are stressed or abused (especially sexually abused), split into several independent personalities as a defence mechanism. For example, Marti Em described her childhood abuse as one of disbelief: she couldn't believe she was being abused, so she detached herself from those events and watched it happen to someone else. That someone else developed a personaly over time, and the process repeated itself. Her current treatment is focussed on dealing with the trauma, not the MPD itself. How people with MPD perceive their actions varies, but often only one personality (or "alter") can control the body at any one time. Sometimes alters are co-conscious and share all memories. Sometimes each alter remembers only the times when he/she/it controlled the body, and has amnesia for all other periods.

People diagnosed with DID will exhibit erratic alterations of personality and may "lose time". Skeptics claim that people diagnosed with DID have learned to exhibit the symptoms in return for social reinforcement, either from therapists, from others with DID, or from society at large — or from any combination thereof. Believers in DID as a disease retort that victims really *do* have multiple selves or experience themselves so, really cannot control their behaviors, and should be treated with the same respect and consideration afforded those with other mental disorders.

In addition, some people would argue that it is normal to experience oneself as multiple, and that "multiplicity" is not necessarily a disorder. The debate over DID and MPD has been inextricably mixed with the furor over recovered memories of childhood sexual abuse, the child sex abuse panic of the 1980s, and associated tales of satanic ritual abuse. In the U.S. (and to a much lesser extent in other English-speaking countries, like the U.K. and Australia), it was widely believed that sex and satanic abuse were rampant and that they often caused MPD. More people began to suspect that their psychological problems were caused by childhood abuse and that they had MPD. As the stories told by the clients grew ever more bizarre and unbelievable, as the numbers of people claiming MPD spiked, as public prosecutions of daycare workers began to seem like Salem witch trials, the public at large eventually grew less accepting and more hostile to stories of recovered memories, ritual abuse, and MPD.

However, there are still many mental health workers who would argue that while there was much exaggeration and bad therapy during the 1980s and early 1990s, and a few supposed MPD clients who were merely suggestible, that it is a real disorder, with real victims. This view is common enough that DID and MPD still figure in the diagnostic manuals. At stake is how we are to treat those claiming multiple selves. If DID is *real*, then they are victims. If it is factitious, then the supposed victims have something like histrionic disorder; the adoption of a less-than-ideal strategy for controlling others. Given that the stakes are so high and opinions so fundamentally opposed, it is extremely difficult to present information about DID in a way that all sides will accept. Perhaps the best solution is to give each side a chance to state its case. These sides (there are more than two!) might be said to be:

— Those who argue that we must trust and believe those who claim to have DID/MPD and to have recovered memories of childhood sexual abuse. Let us call them "true believers".

— The skeptics — mental health professionals, scientists, and others who have challenged the true believers. Most would argue that DID is a fad rather than a real disease.

— Mental health professionals, scientists, and others who believe that DID is a valid diagnosis, while distancing themselves from the perceived excesses of the true believers.

— People who believe that it is possible to be multiple *and* psychologically healthy. Arguments that assume DID is a disorder do an injustice to healthy multiples.

True Believers

The basic premise of the true believers is that child abuse or child sexual abuse are trivialized and under-reported. We do not want to believe that real mothers and fathers would abuse their children or allow them to be hurt; we shut our ears to the survivors who dare to speak up. Believers say that we must believe them, even when they say things that we do not want to hear. Otherwise, we are protecting the pedophiles who prey on children, smugly sure that any children who do complain will not be believed. Not only should we believe the children, we should believe the adult survivors who have struggled to recover repressed memories of childhood abuse. Believers trust that hypnosis, dream analysis, body memory analysis, and other such techniques are valid ways to uncover the repressed memories.

Believers may differ in how far they will accept all details of children's accounts and recovered memories. When survivors report satanic ritual abuse and alien abduction, some people say that we must still believe the survivors. Others would say that while not all details may be accurate, it is still likely that something untoward occurred. Believers are particularly incensed by the False Memory Syndrome Foundation, a support and advocacy group for parents accused of child sexual abuse. The FMS supports pedophiles, they say, by encouraging the public not to believe the victims.

The Skeptics

Skeptics would say that humans often lie, exaggerate, and fantasize, and that it is a mistake to demand uncritical belief in stories of child abuse, recovered memories, and multiple personality. To do so is to invite misuse of the blank check given the story-tellers. If we are told we must believe the children, what are we to make of the daycare child abuse trials?

— The McMartin Preschool trial

— The Fell's Acres trial

— The Little Rascals trials

These trials received much publicity and are still controversial. The MacMartin trial ended without a conviction; convictions in the Fell's Acres and Little Rascals cases have been reversed. After the children in these cases were questioned at length, they told stories of underground tunnels, secret rooms, children being thrown to sharks, trips in rocket ships, etc. Believers would say that we must believe "something happened" because children do not lie. If we are told we must believe recovered memories, what of the people who recover memories of alien abductions and satanic ritual abuse? There is no scientifically acceptable evidence for any such events. What of the people who recover memories and later disavow them? Skeptics point to cases like the following:

Dr. Bennett Braun was a respected therapist and a founding member of the International Society for the Study of Multiple Personality and Dissociation. In 1993 he was accused of malpractice by one of his patients, Pat Burgus. Under Braun's treatment at a Chicago area hospital, Burgus discovered that she had 300 personalities and recovered memories of a long career as a satanic priestess presiding over cannibal feasts. Eventually she rejected Braun's diagnosis and sued. In 1997, Braun settled for 10.6 million dollars. He was sued by other patients and lost his medical licence for a time.

Other such material has been collected by the False Memory Syndrome Foundation, founded in 1992. Skeptics state that the child abuse/recovered memories/ritual abuse/ MPD panic bears all the signs of a mass mania, like the Salem Witch Trials or the New Delhi monkeyman hysteria. DID cannot be a real disease or it would be much more widespread. But DID is limited to a specific place (the United States and to a much lesser extent, other Western countries exposed to the U.S. media) and time (roughly, the period from 1976 through 1996). As media coverage spiked, cases climbed. There were 200 reported cases of MPD from 1880 to 1979, and 20,000 from 1980 to 1990. Per Joan Acocella, 40,000 cases were diagnosed from 1985 to 1995. Not only is DID centered in the U.S., it is centered in a few practitioners. Most mental health professionals have never seen a patient with DID; others apparently see nothing but! This does not inspire confidence in the diagnosis.

Skeptics would argue that by lavishing attention and care on persons diagnosed with DID/MPD, we reward them for the supposed disease. The current trend for multiples to conceptualize their alters as "littles" or child-like others is revealing in this regard: multiples, by presenting as "littles", can demand to be treated with the indulgence we afford to real children.

There is now a vast psychological literature on memory and recovered memory, as well as arguments pro and con for the usefulness of the DID diagnosis. Many professionals would admit that uncritical belief and questionable therapeutic practices were rife during the heyday of the recovered memories/ritual abuse/MPD mania. However, they insist that publicity or no publicity, some patients would still have DID and still require treatment. Mainstream opinion now says:

— A pushy therapist can lead patients to recover false memories. Many supposed memory recovery methods, like hypnosis or dream work, are unreliable. Any therapist working with patients who claim to be abuse survivors (or whom they suspect to be abuse survivors) should be scrupulously neutral, careful to avoid suggestion, and wary of uncorroborated claims.

— A therapist should work with "alters" if they come up spontaneously, but should not reward the patient for displaying them.

Mental health professionals and researchers working with dissociative disorders can join an organization called the The International Society for the Study of Dissociation.

Healthy Multiplicity

Some professionals and multiples would say that multiplicity is not inherently dysfunctional. So long as there is co-consciousness and no loss of memory, so long as the various "selves" can communicate and negotiate with each other, multiples can lead happy and productive lives. It is mere prejudice and bigotry to insist that everyone be a singleton (have a single "self"). Some would say that the unity of the self is an illusion (as some religions, like *Buddhism*, do indeed teach) and that everyone is fundamentally multiple. Others take the position that some people are inherently singletons, some inherently multiple, and that people should be allowed to express themselves as they are.

Truddi Chase, author of the widely read When Rabbit Howls, is one believer in healthy multiplicity. Her "selves" rejected integration and live as a cooperative. Another is therapist Dr. David Caul, who treated Biily Milligan. He said of multiplicity therapy "It seems to me that after treatment you want a functional unit, be it a corporation, a partnership, or a one-owner business." There is a fair bit of cross-cultural evidence to suggest that a small but persistent fraction of humans everywhere experience themselves as multiple. Many religions feature shamans, people who say that they are possessed by gods or spirits. Devotees visit the shaman, who may go into trance and speak as the god's voice. Religions may also diagnose some illnesses as spirit possession. Those who recover from possession may go on to become shamans. This could be seen as a transition from dysfunctional to functional multiplicity.

In yet other religions, like *voodoo* and the *orisha* religions of Africa, all devotees aim to be possessed by the gods. Multiplicity is not a dysfunction, but a spiritual goal. While such evidence suggests a common psychological mechanism for multiplicity, it also highlights the influence of the surrounding culture on the perception and subjective experience of multiplicity. For example, people in other cultures who are multiple do not express their other selves as "parts of themselves", but as spirits. There is no evident link between childhood abuse and dissociation, nor between multiplicity and any recovered memories. This constellation of features may characterize the "late 20th century Western" template for multiplicity, known in the psychiatric community as "the post-Wilburian paradigm".

Personality Disorder

Personality disorders form a class of mental disorders that are characterized by longlasting rigid patterns of thought and behaviour. Because of the inflexibility and pervasiveness of these patterns, they can cause serious problems and impairment of functioning for the persons who are afflicted with these disorders. Personality disorders are seen by the American Psychiatric Association as an enduring pattern of inner experience and behaviour that deviates markedly from the expectations of the culture of the individual who exhibits it. These patterns are inflexible and pervasive across many situations. The onset of the pattern can be traced back at least to the beginning of adulthood. To be diagnosed as a personality disorder, a behavioural pattern must cause significant distress or impairment in personal, social, and/or occupational situations.

Personality disorders are represented on Axis II of the diagnostic manual of the American Psychiatric Association, the DSM-IV. Personality disorders are somewhat controversial for various reasons. One point of critique is that their comorbidity rates is high, which suggests that they may not be separate independent disorders. Another objection is that the diagnosis of personality disorders relies heavily on the judgement of a single psychologist or psychiatrist. Individual clinicians can have different opinions about the difference between a personality disorder and a personality style.

The DSM-IV lists ten personality disorders, which are grouped into three clusters:

1. *Cluster A (odd or eccentric disorders)*
   - Paranoid personality disorder
   - Schizoid personality disorder
   - Schizotypal personality disorder
2. *Cluster B (dramatic, emotional, or erratic disorders)*
   - Antisocial personality disorder
   - Borderline personality disorder
   - Histrionic personality disorder
   - Narcissistic personality disorder

3. *Cluster C (anxious or fearful disorders)*
   — Avoidant personality disorder
   — Dependent personality disorder
   — Obsessive-compulsive personality disorder (not the same as obsessive-compulsive disorder)

The DSM-IV also contains a category for behavioral patterns that do not match these ten disorders, but nevertheless have the characteristics of a personality disorder. This category is labelled *Personality Disorder NOS* (Not Otherwise Specified). The previous version of the DSM also contained the *Passive-Aggressive Personality Disorder* and the *Self-Defeating Personality Disorder*. Passive-aggressive personality disorder is a pattern of negative attitudes and passive resistance in interpersonal situations. Self-defeating personality disorder is characterised by behaviour that consequently undermines the person's pleasure and goals. These categories were removed in the current version of the DSM, because it is questionable whether these are separate disorders.

Personality Development

The concept of personality refers to the profile of stable beliefs, moods, and behaviors that differentiate among children (and adults) who live in a particular society. The profiles that differentiate children across cultures of different historical times will not be the same because the most adaptive profiles vary with the values of the society and the historical era. An essay on personality development written 300 years ago by a New England Puritan would have listed piety as a major psychological trait but that would not be regarded as an important personality trait in contemporary America.

Contemporary theorists emphasize personality traits having to do with individualism, internalized conscience, sociability with strangers, the ability to control strong emotion and impulse, and personal achievement. An important reason for the immaturity of our understanding of personality development is the heavy reliance on questionnaires that are filled out by parents of children or the responses of older children to questionnaires. Because there is less use of behavioral observations of children, our theories of personality development are not strong. There are five different hypotheses regarding the early origins of personality.

One assumes that the child's inherited biology, usually called a temperamental bias, is an important basis for the child's later personality. Alexander Thomas and StellaChess suggested there were nine temperamental dimensions along with three synthetic types they called the difficult child, the easy child, and the child who is slow to warm up to unfamiliarity. Longitudinal studies of children suggest that a shy and fearful style of reacting to challenge and novelty predicts, to a modest degree, an adult personality that is passive to challenge and introverted in mood.

A second hypothesis regarding personality development comes from Sigmund Freud's suggestion that variation in the sexual and aggressive aims of the id, which is biological in nature, combined with family experience, leads to the development of the ego and superego. Freud suggested that differences in parental socialization produced variation in anxiety which, in turn, leads to different personalities.

A third set of hypotheses emphasizes direct social experiences with parents. After World War II, Americans and Europeans held the more benevolent idealistic conception of the child that described growth as motivated by affectionate ties to others rather than by the narcissism and hostility implied by Freud's writings. John Bowlby contributed to this new emphasis on the infant's relationships with parents in his books on attachment. Bowlby argued that the nature of the infant's relationship to the caretakers and especially the mother created a profile of emotional reactions toward adults that might last indefinitely.

A fourth source of ideas for personality centers on whether or not it is necessary to posit a self that monitors, integrates, and initiates reaction. This idea traces itself to the Judeo-Christian assumption that it is necessary to award children a will so that they could be held responsible for their actions. A second basis is the discovery that children who had the same objective experiences develop different personality profiles because they construct different conceptions about themselves and others from the same experiences. The notion that each child imposes a personal interpretation to their experiences makes the concept of self critical to the child's personality.

An advantage of awarding importance to a concept of self and personality development is that the process of identification with parents and others gains in significance. All children wish to possess the qualities that their culture regards as good. Some of these qualities are the product of identification with each parent. A final source of hypotheses regarding the origins of personality comes from inferences based on direct observations of a child's behavior. This strategy, which relies on induction, focuses on different characteristics at different ages. Infants differ in irritability, three-year-olds differ in shyness, and six-year-olds differ in seriousness of mood.

A major problem with this approach is that each class of behavior can have different historical antecedents. Children who prefer to play alone rather than with others do so for a variety of reasons. Some might be temperamentally shy and are uneasy with other children while others might prefer solitary activity. The current categories of child psychopathology influenced the behaviors that are chosen by scientists for study. Fearfulness and conduct disorder predominate in clinical referrals to psychiatrists and psychologists. A cluster of behaviors that includes avoidance of unfamiliar events and places, fear of dangerous animals, shyness with strangers, sensitivity to punishment, and extreme guilt is called the internalizing profile.

The cluster that includes disobedience toward parent and teachers, aggression to peers, excessive dominance of other children, and impulsive decisions is called the externalizing profile. These children are most likely to be at risk for later juvenile delinquency. The association between inability of a three-year-old to inhibit socially inappropriate behavior and later antisocial behavior is the most reliable predictive relation between a characteristic scene in the young child and later personality trait.

Influences on Personality Development

The influence comes from a variety of temperament but especially ease of arousal, irritability, fearfulness, sociability, and activity level. The experiential contributions to personality include early attachment relations, parental socialization, identification with parents, class, and ethnic groups, experiences with other children, ordinal position in the family, physical attractiveness, and school success or failure, along with a number of unpredictable experiences like divorce, early parental death, mental illness in the family, and supporting relationships with relatives or teachers. The most important personality profiles in a particular culture stem from the challenges to which the children of that culture must accommodate.

Most children must deal with three classes of external challenges:

1. unfamiliarity, especially unfamiliar people, tasks, and situations;
2. request by legitimate authority or conformity to and acceptance of their standards, and
3. domination by or attack by other children. In addition, all children must learn to control two important families of emotions: anxiety, fear, and guilt, on the one hand, and on the other, anger, jealousy, and resentment.

Wiggins has described sports psychology as studying "the effect of psychological factors on behavior in sports, or the psychological effect that participation in sports or physical activity has on the performer." Over the last two decades psychology has become increasingly involved in athletics and sports, both as an area of scientific study and as an applied field. Applications of psychology to sports and athletics are numerous. They focus both on the individual athlete and on the team. Psychology is increasingly involved with athletes, coaches, and trainers to enhance athletic performance through improved physical and mental training.

Examples of psychological techniques applied to helping athletes acquire motor skills and improve performance range from visual motor behavior research where athletes mentally practice movements, to anxiety reduction techniques like thought stopping and relaxation training. A knowledge of psychology is essential for understanding each individual's motivation and developing that motivation to an optimal level for athletic performance. In addition to facilitating athletic performance psychology is important in rehabilitating athletes from physical injuries and psychological trauma, as well as in providing more routine counseling services. Sports psychologists work not only with the individual athlete but also with the team. How best to meld a group of individual athletes into a cohesive team performing at its best is an ongoing question and challenge for coaches and team leaders.

A knowledge of group dynamics, social perception—how people perceive, think about, and respond to each other, and individual differences in personality are all essential to motivating and leading a collection of athletes into a smoothly functioning team that makes the best use of each individual player's strengths. In addition to the interventions that are part of applied sports psychology, sports psychologists also study topics like fan behavior, including aggression and mob violence, developmental antecedents of interests in sports and athletics, factors influencing the adoption and maintenance of regular exercise programs, comparative sports, sports as art, etc.

Career Opportunities

The diverse field of sports psychology in "The 1990's" provides the researcher and practitioner alike with an extensive array of interesting and challenging career opportunities. Three major career paths await sports psychologists:

— *Educational*: Primarily teaching activities in both traditional (college university) settings and in non-traditional venues such as at workshops, clinics and seminars.

— *Research*: Sports psychologists are engaged in searching for new knowledge in the "field." Application of psychology to physical performance requires multivariate models that incorporate the simultaneous evaluation of several variables. These research efforts seek to predict performance outcomes in the actual competitive environment.

— *Clinical*: A degree in either clinical or counseling psychology allows the practitioner to focus on personality disorders and behavioral problems affecting the quality of life for athletes. These include anxiety, depression, alcohol and drug abuse, eating disorders, concentration or attention problems, motivation, and burn out.

Table 1. Professional Activities of Sports Psychologists

Coach-Education	Leadership and interpersonal skills, communication, management of human resources
Athlete Preparation	Performance enhancement: relaxation, biofeedback, mental imagery
Research/Teaching	Produce evidence of scholarly contributions to the field; conference and journal contributions
Clinical/Counseling	Guidance and psychological support services, private practice

As psychology has become more closely involved in the activities described above there has been interest by professional organizations in providing training and career planning for students interested in sports psychology. The American Psychological Association (APA)division, Exercise and Sports Psychology Division publishes "Graduate Training and Career Possibilities in Exercise and Sports Psychology." The Association for the Advancement of Applied Sports Psychology (AAASP)defines the criteria for certification as a sports psychologist.

The Sports Psychologists in the 1990's finds a large number of accrediting bodies whom seek specialists in this field. These include providing consulting services to the National Collegiate Athletic Association (NCAA), Sports Medicine Committee, Registry of Approved Sports Psychologists, Psychological Advisory Committee (USOC), National Coaching Certification Program (NCCP), National Coaching Certification Programs (NAC), APA(Committee for the Ethical Standards of Sports Psychology), Professional Golf Association (PGA), Major League Baseball, and the National Football League (NFL).

Sports Psychology Minor

This minor focuses on how psychological factors affect behavior on sports and athletics and on how participation in these activities affects the athlete. Students study social perception, motivation, group dynamics, development of motor skills, leadership, aggression, and other topics essential to working with teams and individual athletes for careers in coaching, education, research/ teaching, or counseling.

Self-Concept

The self-concept (self-identity) is the mental notion an animal has about its physical, psychological, and social attributes; as well as its attitudes, beliefs and ideas, The self-concept consists of the self-image and the self-esteem.

A milestone in human reflection about the non-physical inner self came in 1644, when René Descartes wrote Principles of Philosophy. Descartes proposed that doubt was a principal tool of disciplined inquiry, yet he could not doubt that he doubted. He reasoned th at if he doubted, he was thinking, and therefore he must exist. Thus existence depended upon perception. A second milestone in the development of self-concept theory was the writing of Sigmund Freud who gave us new understanding of the importance of internal mental processes. While Freud and many of his followers hesitated to make self-concept a primary psychological unit in their theories, Freud's daughter Anna gave central importance to ego development and self-interpretation.

Self-concept theory has always had a strong influence on the emerging profession of counseling. Prescott Lecky contributed the notion that self-consistency is a primary motivating force in human behavior. Raimy introduced measures of self-concept in counseling interviews and argued that psychotherapy is basically a process of altering the ways that individuals see themselves. By far the most influential and eloquent voice in self-concept theory was that of Carl Rogers who introduced an entire system of helping built around the importance of the self. In Rogers' view, the self is the central ingredient in human personality and personal adjustment. Rogers described the self as a social product, developing out of interpersonal relationships and striving for consistency. He maintained that there is a basic human need for positive regard both from others and from oneself. He also believed that in every person there is a tendency towards self-actualization and development so long as this is permitted and encouraged by an inviting environment.

While most self-concept theorists continued to write and conduct research during the 1970s and 1980s, general interest in self-concept declined. Patterson presents reasons for the decline of interest in self-concept. He offers four likely causes:

1. A cornucopia of contrived games, gimmicks, and techniques that were introduced and controlled by unprepared professionals.

2. A national mood of "back to basics" in education prevailed where concern for the emotional needs of students was viewed as inimical to academic excellence.

3. Poor judgment by counselors and teachers in selecting suitable materials for values clarification programs resulted in public opposition to any attempt to introduce values in school.

4. Strong opposition by those who objected to any consideration of personal development of students because they believed it to be secular humanism and, therefore, an effort to undermine religion.

Fortunately, there is a new awareness on the part of both the public and professionals that self-concept cannot be ignored if we are to successfully address such nagging problems as drug and alcohol abuse, drop-out rates, dysfunctional families, and other concerns. In addition to this growing awareness, new ways are being developed to strengthen self-concepts. For example, research by cognitive theorists are demonstrating that negative self-talk leads to irrational thinking regarding oneself and the world.

Many of the successes and failures that people experience in many areas of life are closely related to the ways that they have learned to view themselves and their relationships with others. It is also becoming clear that self-concept has at least three major qualities of interest to counselors: (1) it is learned, (2) it is organized, and (3) it is dynamic. Each of these qualities, with corollaries, follow.

1. *Self-concept is learned*: As far as we know, no one is born with a self-concept. It gradually emerges in the early months of life and is shaped and reshaped through repeated perceived experiences, particularly with significant others. The fact that self-concept is learned has some important implications:

   — Because self-concept does not appear to be instinctive, but is a social product developed through experience, it possesses relatively boundless potential for development and actualization.

- Because of previous experiences and present perceptions, individuals may perceive themselves in ways different from the ways others see them.
- Individuals perceive different aspects of themselves at different times with varying degrees of clarity. Therefore, inner focusing is a valuable tool for counseling.
- Any experience which is inconsistent with one's self-concept may be perceived as a threat, and the more of these experiences there are, the more rigidly self-concept is organized to maintain and protect itself. When a person is unable to get rid of perceived inconsistencies, emotional problems arise.
- Faulty thinking patterns, such as dichotomous reasoning (dividing everything in terms of opposites or extremes) or overgeneralizing (making sweeping conclusions based on little information) create negative interpretations of oneself.

2. *Self-concept is organized*: Most researchers agree that self-concept has a generally stable quality that is characterized by orderliness and harmony. Each person maintains countless perceptions regarding one's personal existence, and each perception is orchestrated with all the others. It is this generally stable and organized quality of self-concept that gives consistency to the personality. This organized quality of self-concept has corollaries.

- Self-concept requires consistency, stability, and tends to resist change. If self-concept changed readily, the individual would lack a consistent and dependable personality.
- The more central a particular belief is to one's self-concept, the more resistant one is to changing that belief.
- At the heart of self-concept is the self-as-doer, the "I," which is distinct from the self-as-object, the various

"me's." This allows the person to reflect on past events, analyze present perceptions, and shape future experiences.

— Basic perceptions of oneself are quite stable, so change takes time. Rome was not built in a day, and neither is self-concept.

— Perceived success and failure impact on self-concept. Failure in a highly regarded area lowers evaluations in all other areas as well. Success in a prized area raises evaluations in other seemingly unrelated areas.

3. *Self-Concept is dynamic*: To understand the active nature of self-concept, it helps to imagine it as a gyrocompass: a continuously active system that dependably points to the "true north" of a person's perceived existence. This guidance system not only shapes the ways a person views oneself, others, and the world, but it also serves to direct action and enables each person to take a consistent "stance" in life. Rather than viewing self-concept as the cause of behavior, it is better understood as the gyrocompass of human personality, providing consistency in personality and direction for behavior. The dynamic quality of self-concept also carries corollaries.

— The world and the things in it are not just perceived; they are perceived in relation to one's self-concept.

— Self-concept development is a continuous process. In the healthy personality there is constant assimilation of new ideas and expulsion of old ideas throughout life.

— Individuals strive to behave in ways that are in keeping with their self-concepts, no matter how helpful or hurtful to oneself or others.

— Self-concept usually takes precedence over the physical body. Individuals will often sacrifice physical comfort and safety for emotional satisfaction.

— Self-concept continuously guards itself against loss of self-esteem, for it is this loss that produces feelings of anxiety.

— If self-concept must constantly defend itself from assault, growth opportunities are limited.

Self-Esteem

In psychology, self-esteem or self-worth is to a person's self-image at an emotional level; circumventing reason and logic. The term differs from ego in that the ego is a more artificial aspect; one can remain highly egotistical, while underneath have very low self-esteem. The maintenance of a healthy degree of self-esteem is a central task within psychotherapy, where patients often suffer from excess degrees of self-criticism, hampering their ability to function. Popularised in the 1970s as the cause of the ills of society and of individual humans, and written into Californian law as something to oppose, low self-esteem rapidly became a universal explanation for any personal failing and a staple target for personal development movements, sometimes resulting in narcissistic, over-confident individuals with excessive self-esteem.

Much debate about self-esteem centres on the definition of the term. New Age thought can provide self-serving views of the concept; other views can discount the existence or merely the usefulness of the idea. Some see low self-esteem as a major predisposing factor for crime; others point out that high self-esteem equates with the risk-taking behaviour of criminals.

Will

Will in philosophy refers to the quality that produces conscious and intended actions. It is an important idea in the philosophy of NietzscheSelf-concept.

Athlets and Personality Type

Is there a relationship between personality type and sport preference? How do people choose the sport they participate in? Would it be a matter of personality preference? Are certain personality types more attracted to certain sports, like in careers? Why some people prefer individual sports over team sports? What do basketball players have in common? In order to answer questions related to athletes' personality type, over five hundred athletes were tested and evaluated by this author. To examine the relationship between personality types, sport preferences and performance, team and individual athletes' personality profiles were designed.

Results indicated that teams exhibit a predictable personality profile and that by understanding the psyche of the athlete, performance and team productivity can be enhanced. Interpersonal communication amongst players and coaching staff can improve, players can take advantage of their personal preferences and strengths and work on developing other areas identified in the assessment process. Optimal communication and performance can be achieved by identifying the athletes preferred learning and personality styles. Personality types are attracted to and succeed in certain sports just like they do in certain occupations. The more athletes and coaches understand about their personalities and the team profile, the more productive they can be.

Benefits of understanding the personality profile of athletes are as follows:

1. Helps assess the fit between persons and sports and even positions on a team
2. Helps athletes and coaches value their strengths and become more aware of those areas in which development may be warranted
3. Helps coaches and athletes in a strained relationship analyze the source of the conflict and build a strategy to reduce it

4. Can lead to motivated and committed behavior
5. Useful for the athlete and sports professional in career and life planning, self-management (such as stress/time management) and interpersonal skills areas
6. Many applications in team building and management training

The Myers-Briggs Type Indicator is organized by using eight different personality preferences. The preferences are arranged by four functions and four attitudes. The four functions are composed of two kinds of perception, sensing (S) and intuition (N), and two kinds of judgment, thinking (T) and feeling (F). The four attitudes are composed of extraversion (E), introversion (I), judgment (J), and perception (P). The roles of the functions are as follows:

— Sensing (S) seeks the fullest possible experience of what is immediate and real.

— Intuition (I) seeks the furthest reaches of the possible and imaginative.

— Thinking (T) seeks rational order and plan according to impersonal logic.

— Feeling (F) seeks rational order according to harmony among subjective values.

The roles of the attitudes are as follows:

— Extroversion (E) draws energy from objects and people in society and the environment.

— Introversion (I) draws energy from an inner world of concepts and ideas.

— Judgment (J) seeks to make decisions, closure, plan operations, or organize activities.

— Perception (P) outer behavior is spontaneous, curious, and adaptive, open to new events and changes.

The MBTI can be applied to many different settings, such as, education, counseling, career guidance, athletics and teamwork, and communications.

— In education settings, the MBTI can help to analyze curricula, methods, media, and materials in light of the needs of different types.

— In counseling, it can help couples and families learn the value of both their differences and similarities.

— Using the MBTI in career guidance can help guide individuals in their choice of school majors, professions, occupations, and work settings.

— For athletics and teamwork, it can help select teams, and help team members grow in their own development as each learns from the skills of the other.

— In a communications setting, the MBTI can help to increase understanding by "talking the language" of different types in the group.

The investigation of athletes personality type and its relationship with individual and team performance is innovative; results of the work conducted with NBA players, Olympic athletes and high school athletes have been very positive. Coaches and parents can now better understand the behavior of athletes and teams. Athletes can better understand their preferences and utilize that information to maximize their performance in sport and in their second careers.

Self Confidence

Self-confidence is arguably one of the most important things you can have. Self-confidence reflects your assessment of your own self-worth. It will play a large part in determining your happiness through life.

Sport can be both enormously effective in improving self-worth, and highly destructive in damaging it. Where sport is used creatively, with emphasis on enjoyment, effective goal setting and monitoring of achievement of goals, it can build self-confidence as targets are reached and improvement in performance is noted.

Where children are compelled to participate in a sport for which they have no aptitude, this can be immensely destructive to self-confidence as failure and lack of self-worth are consistently reinforced. Coaches should ask themselves whether they are prepared to take moral responsibility for inflicting this damage, even if numbers are needed to make up a team.

Self-confidence allows you to take risks, as you have enough confidence in your own abilities to be sure that if things do go wrong, you can put things right.

Levels of Confidence

The way in which you are self-confident is important: if you are underconfident, then you will not take risks that need to be taken. If you are over-confident, then you can end up not trying hard enough and losing.

Confidence should be based on observed reality. It should be based on the achievement of performance goals: you should be confident that you will perform up to your current abilities. Good self-confidence comes from a realistic expectation of success based on well practised physical skills, a good knowledge of the sport, respect for your own competence, adequate preparation, and good physical condition. The success attained should be measured in terms of achievement of personal performance goals, not achievement goals such as winning.

Where you are underconfident, you will commonly suffer from fear of failure (which will prevent you from taking risks effectively), self-doubt, lack of concentration, and negative thinking. Often you may find yourself blaming yourself for faults that lie elsewhere.These will damage your flow and disrupt your enjoyment of sport. Here you should use suggestion, visualisation, and effective goal-setting to improve your self-confidence and self-image.

Overconfidence is dangerous - it can lead you into situations which you do not have the ability to get out of. It can set you up for serious failure that can devastate the self-confidence you should have. Overconfidence is confidence that is not based on ability: it may be a result of misleading or pushy parents or coaches trying to help you without understanding your abilities, may be caused by vanity or ego, or may be caused by positive thinking or imagery which is not backed up by ability.

Goal setting

Goal setting is probably the most effective way of building self-confidence. By setting measurable goals, achieving them, setting new goals, achieving them, and so on you prove your ability to yourself. You are able to prove to yourself that you are able to perform and achieve effectively. You can see and recognise and enjoy your achievement, and feel real self-worth in that achievement. Importantly, by knowing what you are able to achieve, you are not setting yourself up for surprise failure - you almost always have a reasonably accurate assessment of what your abilities really are, which is unclouded by ego or vanity.

Imagery

Imagery is useful in building self-confidence, but only if properly applied.

Imagery should be used to imagine achievement of a goal that is being worked towards in order to help you to believe that that goal is attainable.

It should only be used, however, where you are rationally aware that you have the raw ability to achieve a goal if you stretch yourself, but if psychological factors such as lack of emotional self-confidence are interfering with your ability to achieve. For many years psychologists have advocated use of imagery, positive thinking, and suggestion without stressing that it should be based on a rational assessment of abilities. This can easily lead to over-confidence and serious failure.

Unhealthy Expectations

Most athletes maintain high expectations especially if they have had past success in their sport. Expectations are harmful to your performance. When an athlete doesn't meet these expectations, frustration, anger, or feelings of failure emerge. The best option is to replace expectations with confidence. With expectations, you presume many things such as how well you should perform, how many errors you can make, and how smart you should ride. It's do or die. A player's expectation is doomed at the first sign of an error or a loss.

Some people equate expectations with confidence. They are not the same. Confidence is the belief you can perform a task or ride well, but it doesn't mean you absolutely must ride well. Confidence helps you perform better. But expectations are judgments about your performance or how well you are performing in a competition compared to how you think you should perform. As a rider, don't set yourself up for frustration with high expectations. Instead, be confident that you can win, but don't expect it.

A better option is to replace expectations with set goals in which you strive for. Goals are changeable and not as absolute as expectations. You strive for your goals, but that doesn't mean you have to achieve them. Expectations are absolute beliefs about one's talent, which when not achieved can make riders unravel. Goals are more flexible and help the rider to focus on the process of performing. For example, you can set goals related to your jumps, faults, knockdowns, etc. for each show. This way you can focus on the process of good riding instead of making judgments about how you are performing.

Nothing is more important than the feeling of confidence before the start of the game. What is confidence? Confidence is the belief in your ability and it can include two areas: (1) a general belief in your ability to perform well and win the game; and (2) a task-specific belief in your ability to pass, run, tackle, and execute. How do football players develop confidence? Confidence comes from many sources and it varies from person to person. Most players get confidence from one or more of the following: (1) past success, (2) experience, (3) performing well in the immediate past, (4) other persons, (5) practice, and (6) having a good support team.

Here are some ideas to help you feel confident at the start of the race:

Believe in your skills: This is really the definition of confidence. If you believe in your football skills and physical talents, then it is said you have confidence. If you back yourself more than anyone on the field, then you have confidence. This comes from your belief in football skills, such as passing, running, tackling, blocking, etc.

Reinforce why you will succeed: Many athletes don't give themselves enough credit for the successes and other skills that contribute to good play. Athletes sometimes overlooked their own mini successes. Other players disqualify positives in their career. What is your list for the reasons to succeed? It can be comprised of your ability, your team, past success, good coaches, practice, fitness, and many other areas that contribute to confidence.

Battle the doubt: Part of staying confident is battling your own internal doubt. No one is perfect and in times of adversity it's tough not to have any doubts about winning. The first place to start it to identify any doubts you have had in the past and that are themes in your career such as "My team is not good enough to win." The next step is to counter the doubt with statements that turns the situation around into an advantage such as: "I have the confidence that my team can is better than any team we play."

You have to see it before you can achieve it: It's so easy for kids to have big dreams about the future, but as adults that same ability gets beaten down by others. Keeping the dream alive means seeing and feeling success close in hand. To win at your sport, you have to see yourself win over and over again. With the vision, comes confidence that it is all possible.

Use the past to feel confident today: Most football players would say that past success and experience in playing is the number one source for confidence today. You can tap into your success in the past to help you feel confident today by replaying successful games, practices, conversations, and kudos from others. In today's game, you might recall a successful play you had on a similar field or similar conditions.

Patience in a form of confidence: A patient player is a confident player. The challenge in football is to stay patience when thing are not going your way today. It's easy to give in to internal doubt and criticism when you are not on top in your sport. But the better choice is to stay patient with results and wait for good things to happen.

Avoid Putting Other Racers on The Pedestal

Do you pay more attention to other ranked racers in the field that have had success? Do you compare yourself to other riders when you get to the track for qualifying? If you answered yes, then you are a candidate for psyching yourself out of the race. Psych-outs are usually self-induced based on your perceptions of an event or other riders. It happens in all sports—rookies or younger athletes worry too much about the competition instead of what they need to do to race their best. Just the reputation of a rider can make you feel intimidated—if you let it!

Intimidation in part is a confidence breakdown. Meaning you are not confident enough in your own talents to believe that you can race against "legends" in your sport. "How can I beat him—he's a State Champion?" you say to yourself standing in the gate. You have to take the approach that everyone has the same chance of winning and you have earned the right to compete at the event. Do not put others "on a pedestal" before the race even starts or look at riders as superstars. They put one shoe on at a time just like you.

Making comparisons does not help either. Most of the time when you make a comparison to another rider, you compare yourself to drivers who you think are better than you. You then try to find out what makes them better and what you might me missing—a further knock to your own confidence. This is a bad approach to getting ready for any event. It is all about working your pre-race routine and getting your car ready to do your best. The pre-race routine is very helpful for you to stay focused on the race and your race plan. This is when you should be visualizing the sections of the race and anticipating what you might have to do in given situations such as when passing others during a turn. Your routine should also include the usual preparations you take before the start of the race from going over your strategy to getting suited up to getting strapped in the car.

Belief, Self Talk and Performance Enhancement

One of the more frequently faced challenges experienced by athletes is that of how to improve their performance. They express frustration that they often possess identical, if not superior, physical attributes to their competition, yet they're consistently being out performed by that competition. In many of these cases the factor that separates their performance from the competitions has been found to be rooted in their belief as to their ability to outperform the competition.

In other words they are operating with a limiting belief as to their athletic ability and level of performance they are capable of achieving. Yet it is well documented that a individual's core beliefs in any given area of their life will ultimately determine the reality they draw into their life-positive, negative or stagnant. So how does one go about changing a limiting belief to a positive one — one that will result in improving your performance?

It has been established by psychologists and neuroscientists that every person in the world carries on an ongoing dialog, or self-talk, of between 150 and 300 words a minute. This works out to between 45,000 and 51,000 thoughts a day. Most of out self-talk is harmless thoughts that serve our daily activities like, "I need to stop at the cleaners." The danger is when inner dialogue takes on a negative connotation such as, "I'll never be as good an athlete as he is," "I don't have the mental toughness to compete at this level," or "I'll never be that fast." The ongoing negative reinforcement created by habitual negative self-talk results in the creation of a limiting belief(s) that goes on to become self-fulfilling prophecy.

Beliefs — positive or negative — are literally etched into our brain in comfortable grooves or neural pathways. Incoming data from our senses travel on these neural pathways on the way to interpretation in the brain. Therefore, if you desire to change an unresourceful/limiting belief into an empowering belief, you must rewire the negative neural track created in the brain.

This can be accomplished in precisely the same way the tracks were created: by using self-talk or, more specifically affirmations. An affirmation is a statement of fact or belief — positive or negative — that will lead toward the end result you expect. Anything that follows the phrase "I am," such as "I am a peak performance athlete" or "I am quick and agile," is an affirmation. The simplicity of affirmations often causes them to be overlooked. Nonetheless, affirmations are regularly used by professional athletes and successful business people.

The process for changing a limiting belief to a resourceful belief using affirmations is a simple one. First, identify the areas of your life which are not working to your satisfaction. Next, write out the affirmations that represent things the way you desire them to be, they will be the vehicle for creating new resourceful/positive pathways.

Basic to formulating a new self-suggestion is that your affirmation is short and to the point — simple enough that a five year old child will understand it — and is always stated in the positive. Further, your affirmation should be stated in the present tense — as if it has already happened, for example, "I am a strong athlete."

Now you are ready to begin your daily (minimum) reprogramming process:

— Sit upright in a comfortable chair.

— Close your eyes and take a couple of minutes to progressively relax.

— Release your body's tight sharp focus on the physical world by taking yourself to an even deeper level of relaxation.

— Speak your affirmation aloud from five to twenty times (depending on the time you have and the number of beliefs you are reprogramming).

By speaking your affirmation aloud you are down-stepping your thoughts to the brains electrical network to speech, and you are involving more of your brain by including two more of your senses: auditory and kinesthetic. It is important that you trust this process and give your affirmation(s) time to achieve their desired outcome. Worry or self-doubt as to whether your affirmations are working only conveys to your subconscious worry and the belief that your desire may not come to pass or the affirmation may not succeed. Be patient, success is on the way.

The Power of Pre-event Thought

What thoughts go through your mind before an important race? This question may be crucial to your results in the pool. It seems that the more science discovers about the human mind, the more important the power of thought becomes, especially in swimming. Believe it or not, every thought you think, and every word you say in the 5-10 minutes before a race can have a major effect upon your results.

Humans think around 60,000 thoughts a day, and the quality of these thoughts is becoming increasingly important in a sport where a hundredth of a second is an eternity. We already know many of the problems which are associated with a negative attitude, such as fear, intimidation, lack of belief, intimidation ... and so on.

If you still struggle to believe the importance of the mind in swimming, think of this; all of your swimming experience (that is, every lap you have ever swum in your lifetime) is recorded in the archives of your memory bank, and this lies in your subconscious mind. The subconscious happens to be the control-center of all movement, and works just like a computer, and is being constantly programmed by the thoughts, words and statements you choose.

Your results in the pool (the printout) are determined by the quality of the thoughts (the data) which are programmed into your mind. What this all means is this: think negative thoughts before a race, and you will generally get a negative result. Likewise, program your mind positively, and get rid of the mental roadblocks which have been holding you back, and you will get a vastly improved result. Garbage in, garbage out, as they say. The question is: are you satisfied with the results you are getting, or could they improve (a lot)?

One of the best ways to overcome negative thoughts before a race is to re-focus the mind onto something positive, by using an affirmation. This is an ancient technique, where you simply repeat a few words over and over again for 5-10 minutes before a race. This does two things; it focuses the mind onto the positive, and it prevents negative thoughts being programmed in before the race. An example of an affirmation could be 'power and speed', or 'perfect rhythm', but you can just as easily make up your own affirmations using your own words.

If you make up your own affirmation, just ensure you keep them short, positive, and present-tense. Some swimmers even sing a song as an affirmation, and this can also work well. Practice this technique, and see if it makes a difference.

Influence of Stress on Athletic performance

The influence of stress on athletic performance is a legitimate concern for most coaches and athletes. Whether we realize it or not, our emotions affect every cell in our body. Negative emotional reactions are often caused by stress. One of the ways to deal with this phenomenon is to understand the mental and physical effects. Thus, the following quiz is designed to be an initial step in understanding and combating the harmful effects stress has on athletic performance.

All of the questions are to be answered either True or False

— Under high levels of stress, athletes typically have a broad attention span. T or F

— The clammy feeling we often get when stressed is caused by our body's natural defense against bleeding to death. T or F

— Elite level performers have fewer nervous reactions to stress than do non-elite level performers. T or F

— High levels of stress make it more difficult to think clearly. T or F

— Getting sick to your stomach and throwing up when nervous is your body's way of telling you that you are over-stressed. T or F

— Caffeine exaggerates the physical and mental effects of stress. T or F

— The body's stress response, which is commonly referred to as the fight or flight response, allows us to do superhuman feats. T or F

— The only time stress is good is when there is no stress. T or F

— Sighing as you exhale is more relaxing than not sighing. T or F

— Under stress, athletes often revert back to their most well learned behaviors. T or F

Answer Key

— False. Under high levels of stress athletes tend to have a narrow attention span, often referred to as tunnel vision. Attention may also focus on the athlete's internal thought process which can lead to "choking" under pressure.

— True. One of the physical responses of the body to stress is to divert blood away from the small vessels near the skin. This provides a defense against bleeding to death from wounds, but gives the skin a cold, clammy feeling.

— False. Elite level performers have just as many nervous reactions to stress as any other type of performer. However, elite athletes often interpret these reactions as being more positive and beneficial than do other athletes.

— True. Clear thinking is more difficult in pressure situations. This is why coaches and athletes must constantly practice what they are going to do and how they are going to respond in pressured-packed situations.

— False. So that more blood is available to the large muscles of the body in preparation for strenuous physical activity such as fighting or running away, the digestive system shuts down. During this shut down, the acid in your stomach makes you feel nauseated which sometimes results in throwing up. This is a normal reaction to stress.

— True .Caffeine tends to exaggerate the physical and mental effects of stress. Knowing this, coaches and athletes should avoid caffeine products before entering potentially stressful situations.

— True. Under stress, the body produces adrenalin which provides a powerful, quick burst of energy sometimes resulting in superhuman feats.

— False. There are a number of stresses which are good. For example, being elevated to the starting team brings additional stress which most athletes would enjoy. Another example of positive stress is physical and mental training. All athletes are under stress when, during training, they push themselves to the edge so that their body will adapt to the demand and get stronger.

— True. For some reason letting out an audible sigh as you exhale is very relaxing. There are a number of additional relaxation techniques which involve breathing exercises.

— True. In stressful situations athletes often revert back to behaviors they are familiar and comfortable with. This is one of the reasons why athletes should try to learn and perfect new skills and techniques in the off-season.

Preventing 'Choking' and Downward Performance Cycles

Anxiety is a natural part of performing, whether you're on the basketball court, giving a speech, or taking the college boards. Even seasoned veterans get butterflies before the big game. Where problems begin is if you focus on the wrong things. If your attention gets stuck on a mistake you made in the past, or if you zoom in on someone who doesn't seem to like what you're saying, you may forget a play or the answer to a question that you know perfectly well. In other words, it isn't the butterflies that cause you problems, it's the negative thoughts you attach to them that hurt your performance.

When you get anxious or excited, your heart beats faster, you breathe faster, and your muscles tense. You may perspire, or even feel light headed and shaky. These feelings won't ruin your performance, but if you worry about them enough (and that happens when you lack confidence), your worries will join the physical changes to ruin your performance. Athletes and coaches call this "choking."

Failure like this is usually a vicious cycle. Your physical anxiety triggers negative thoughts, which leads to more physical anxiety. These distractions keep you from organizing your thoughts and suddenly you can't solve simple problems, or keep your eye on the ball. Instead of attending to the task, you concentrate on the negatives, and soon you fall farther and farther behind. It's not pretty, but you can take heart in the fact that everyone reaches this point at times.

To prevent choking, you have to keep this negative feedback loop from getting started in the first place. You can do this by taking a slow deep breath from down in your abdomen when you feel yourself getting up tight, or find yourself thinking negative thoughts. On the exhale you direct your attention to relaxing the muscles in your arms, neck, shoulders and legs. Try it now, inhale deeply from down in your diaphragm. As you exhale silently say to yourself "relax the muscles in my neck, shoulders, arms, and legs." As you say those words to yourself let the muscles relax. Good! Try it again, only this time close your eyes as you exhale and tell your muscles to relax.

Breathing Breaks the Downward Cycle

The process you just went through is called "centering". When you center, you use a deep breath to help you prevent and/ or break the negative feedback loop I talked about earlier. To keep that loop from reoccurring, however, you need to quickly redirect your attention to the task at hand. What you direct you attention toward, immediately after you center is very important.

You want to focus attention on what sport psychologists call "process cues." A process cue is a technical or tactical self-instruction that is directly related to successful performance. When you get anxious on the college boards for example you might say to yourself "Read the whole question." to get over the tendency to read half the question and panic. Or you might say "Which of the four answers is definitely wrong?" This would help you narrow down your choices and improve the likelihood that you will pick the right answer. If you were about to inbound the ball late in the game with the score tied, you might center and then immediately remind yourself to "Wait for your teammate to clear." When shooting a free throw you might center and say ".

By directing attention to process or task relevant cues, you are avoiding or blocking out those sights, sounds, and thoughts which remind you of the importance of the "outcome." You stop attending to the clock which would be telling you that time is running out for example. Paying attention to outcome cues when you are nervous or when confidence is low, only makes it harder to concentrate. Under these conditions, outcome cues generate more anxiety and re-establish that choking cycle.

Often, athletes and students know what they should do to be successful, but they become so anxious they forget to do it. You can help yourself remember to center and to concentrate on process cues if you learn to use those highly charged outcome cues (like the amount of time you have left, the closeness of the score, or the importance of your performance to yourself and/or people in the audience), as signals to center and to refocus on the task.

For practice, think about a situation in the past where you paid attention to the wrong things, became anxious, and performed more poorly than you would have liked. Mentally recreate the situation by thinking yourself back into it. Close your eyes and see it, and feel it just like you did then. As you notice the outcome cue (e.g., time left, or a mistake you made), take a centering breath, relax your muscles, then redirect attention to a process cue and see yourself successfully complete the task.

Pschoanalytic Perspective on Anxiety in Atheltes

The most popular conceptual paradigm in sport psychology is a cognitive-behavioral one. Texts used in undergraduate and graduate courses on sport psychology are slanted heavily toward a behavioral/ experimental model of intervention. The standard sport psychology interventions include relaxation training, deep breathing, visualization, imagery, mental practice, self-talk and goal-setting.

Sport psychology has its roots in academic settings which have traditionally been behavioral in orientation. However, if one works full-time in the field of sport psychology, it becomes clear that cognitive- behavioral techniques will only take you so far. These methods have a hard time with issues such as resistance in the athlete and more subtle effects such as shame, embarrassment and guilt when winning.

Symptoms of anxiety as they relate to unconscious conflicts are psychoanalytic ideas. Both the motivation to compete in sports and conflicts about winning are largely unconscious and cognitive-behavioral interventions have little to contribute in the study of these areas. One of the very few psychoanalytic papers on the psychoanalysis of sports was written by Dan Dervin nearly fifteen years ago. He introduced psychoanalytic thinking to the world of the athlete.

Criteria for diagnosing anxiety during athletic performance is from the DSM IV. Under the heading of general anxiety disorder are the symptoms of muscle soreness, trembling, restlessness, fatigue, shortness of breath, tachycardia, sweating, dizziness nausea and vomiting, being on edge, startle response, blank mind, poor sleep and irritability. The prevalence of anxiety disorders, simple phobias, obsessive compulsive disorders and post traumatic stress disorders are common in the general population and common in athletes as well.

These symptoms are familiar to many athletes. It is not at all uncommon to hear of sleeplessness, vomiting, nervousness and restlessness before games. The intensity of the anxiety that is felt before and during sports is so gripping, immediate and debilitating that one feels compelled to provide fast relief for these anxious athletes. The need to offer a quick solution to panicking athletes is so pervasive that it may account for the compulsive use of behavioral techniques even when they are ill-advised or ineffective. For the psychologist that works with athletes full-time and over a long period of time ones soon realizes that these quick fixes are often not fixes at all and at best last for very brief periods. Some psychoanalytic approaches to performance anxiety in sports are following.

An Object Relations Approach

Shame and embarrassment are constant threats in sports because the game is usually played in front of people. Gabbard has written about performance anxiety and shame from an object-relations perspective. He suggests that shame is a narcissistic disturbance that impacts many who perform in front of an audience. Success or winning in an athlete can induce a feeling of separation from the family, the opponent or the crowd and this can produce considerable anxiety and shame. This shame and anxiety can inhibit performance. Conflicts that winning brings loss and separation derive from childhood when the child is given the message to stay close to the mother and never to leave her. Separation anxiety induced by winning or the threat of winning is exceedingly common.

The Dread Of Success

Some athletes carry a dread of winning because it means that they are superior to others. Superiority, for some, means greed and selfishness. We all see this amply displayed by some professional athletes. The dread of success is especially felt in female athletes, some of whom are raised to think aggression is not nice. For many children raised religiously winning implies selfish striving which is considered sinful. Occasionally a child raised in the lower class who later becomes a star with great fame and wealth has a sense of dread that they are leaving their families behind. This explains why you so often hear professional athletes say their true desire is to buy their mothers a home with the money they make.

Success can bring with it great guilt. The recent near disqualification of a pro golfer at a Tour event may have something to do with the dread of success. He had already won three tournaments this year. It was reported that before the tournament he had lost two close friends to sudden death. During the event he was nearly disqualified twice, once due to almost missing a tee time and once by marking his ball on the 72nd green a failing to replace it properly. If he had signed his scorecard without the score adjustment and the two shot penalty he would have been disqualified. A fan whom he later called his "guardian angel" saved him from disqualification by telling him of the infraction in time. These very unusual mishaps were neither accidents as most would think nor divine intervention but may have had to do with the guilt over winning following the loss of his two friends.

Self Psychology And Sports

Self psychology has emerged in the last few decades as an alternative to classical psychoanalytic instinct theory. Kohut moved the focus of psychoanalytic concern away from sexual and aggressive drives and onto self concepts. A cohesive sense of self esteem which is developed in childhood is thought to enable adults to cope with pressures inherent in sports. Conversely, a disordered self will fragment under extreme pressure.

It is very common to observe athletes with low self image fall into rage or despair at the first sign of difficulty. A fragmented or enfeebled self system can give way to temporary states of psychosis when under extreme pressure during competition.

The experience of being "flooded" with affect as one fights for the lead in a sporting event can be explained with the concept of the self and its collapse. The collapse of ego boundaries when under pressure produces disorganization in thinking and what is referred to as choking. Many athletes unconsciously choose the effect of humiliation and depression over the effect of being flooded. As a result, mistakes and missed shots take on a new meaning in this light. Anything that gets them out of the pressure is a defensive maneuver used to remove the self from under pressure. Many of them say they try to "enjoy" themselves while under pressure to inhibit this overwhelming and psychosis producing emotion.

Instinct Theory And Sports

Sports are clearly about aggression. If you work with athletes you soon begin to realize just how much aggression they are capable of. Boxers emanate power and grace as well thereby combining aggression and sexuality, the two basic drive states. The inhibition of aggression occurs as a result of trauma, training in not to be aggressive or through difficulty during the oedipal phase of psychosexual development. Freud suggested that aggression is typically defended against by turning it into its opposite (passivity), turning it against oneself (self-defeat or depression) or by sublimating it through sports. Conflicts with aggression invariably leads to defeat.

Tiger Woods Horner has researched female inhibition of aggression. Women are often taught that aggression is unfeminine, not lady-like and are faced with the conflict of winning versus being seen as "unfeminine." This conflict has an impact on performance and brings us to a discussion of secondary gain over losing.

Secondary Gain

Secondary gain is a standard psychoanalytic concept and is considered a reason that neurotic symptoms are so difficult to give up. The same unconscious dynamic holds for self-defeat in sports. Loss has the potential to produce enormous secondary gain. One need only recall Greg Norman's humiliating defeat by giving up a six stroke lead in the 1996 Masters which was witnessed by millions of television viewers. In the next few weeks he received thousands of sympathy letters as well as supportive articles in all the major newspapers around the world. This sympathy can be quite reinforcing and gives defeat an unconscious appeal to some individuals.

Relationship Between Anxiety and Performance: A Cognitive-Behavioral Perspective

The ability to cope with pressure and anxiety is an integral part of sports, particularly among elite athletes. Researchers have reported that over 50 of consultations among athletes at an Olympic festival were related to stress or anxiety related problems. A great deal of research has been conducted examining the relationship between anxiety and performance within the field of athletics.

Theoretical Constructs of Anxiety

The main problem that research on the relationship between anxiety and performance has encountered is that researchers have not adequately operationally defined the construct of anxiety. Instead, terms such as stress, anxiety, arousal and activation have been used interchangeably. For the purposes of this paper the following operational definitions will be used for the terms anxiety and stress. Stress is a state that results form the demands that are placed on the individual which require that person to engage in some coping behavior.

Arousal can be considered to be a signal to the individual that he or she has entered a stressful state and is characterized by physiological signs. Anxiety results when the individual doubts his or her ability to cope with the situation that causes him or her stress. Another important point that needs to be clarified is the difference between state and trait anxiety. While state anxiety can be considered to be more situational in nature and is often associated with arousal of the autonomic nervous system, trait anxiety can be thought of as a world view that an individual uses when coping with situations in his or her environment.

Trait anxiety influences performances in that individuals with high trait anxiety will attend more to information related to state anxiety. Research on sport and exercise psychology has indicated that individuals with high trait anxiety who are state anxious attend to threat related information, while individuals with low trait anxiety who are state anxious will attend away from threat related information. Within the context of sports, those individuals who are low trait anxious and experience high state anxiety would find it facilitative to a peak performance; but, those individuals with who are high trait anxious and experience state anxiety will find it debilitative to athletic performance.

One of the earliest models that attempted to explain the relationship between arousal and performance was the inverted-U hypothesis. It stated that as arousal increased performance would increase as well; but, if arousal became too great performance would deteriorate. In other words, as stress began to build an individual still felt confident in their ability to control it and performance would improve. However, once a stressor became so great that the individual started to doubt the ability to cope with, performance began to decline.

Although this model gave some explanation as to why performances deteriorated when individuals felt stress, it did not account for the differences in the performance of athletes who are exposed to the same stressor. Researchers attempted to account for the differences in the performances of individuals through the concept of individualized zones of optimal functioning or IZOFs. According to this theory, each individual has an optimal level of pre-performance anxiety which results in peak performances. However, if the pre-performance anxiety lies outside the area of the IZOF, whether too high or too low, then performance will deteriorate.

IZOFs can be determined by repeatedly measuring anxiety and performance or through athlete's recall of anxiety levels prior to peak performances. Indeed, researchers found that IZOFs are better predictors of performance then the inverted U- hypothesis. Although this is a better model then the inverted-U hypothesis, it still fails to explain the factors that account for the individual differences in performance among athletes.

The differences observed between successful and unsuccessful athletes may be the result of their cognitive interpretation of their anxiety states. According to reversal theory arousal is interpreted differently depending on their present state. In telic states athletes are focused on a goal and thus interpret their arousal as anxiety. However, in paratelic states performers are focused on their behavior and therefore interpret their arousal as excitement. Individuals can flip from one state to another quickly and therefore change their interpretation of the arousal that they experience which in turn affects their performance. This theory attempts to incorporate both physiological and cognitive factors in its explanation of the relationship between performance and anxiety but fails to explain their relationship with performance adequately.

Multidimensional anxiety theory expanded on reversal theory's inclusion of cognitive and physiological factors. In this model, cognitive anxiety (the central tenet of which is concerned with the consequences of failure) has been found to have a negative linear relationship with performance. Self-confidence (a separate cognitive component) has been found to have a positive linear relationship with performance. Finally, somatic anxiety (physiological symptoms) has been found to have an inverted-U shaped relationship with performance. Although this model incorporates many elements of anxiety, it still treats them as separate entities. The next model that arose looked at the interaction between two of these three factors.

The catastrophe model of anxiety and performance looks at the interactive effects of physiological arousal and cognitive anxiety upon performance. Physiological arousal can influence performance as a result of the individual's interpretation of their physiological symptoms. According to the model as cognitive anxiety increases it will be beneficial to performance at low levels of physiological arousal but a detrimental effect at high levels of physiological arousal. Furthermore, when cognitive anxiety is at a low level, changes in physiological arousal have little effect upon performance. However, as cognitive anxiety increases physiological arousal can have either a positive or negative effect on performance depending on how much arousal there is.

Once physiological arousal levels are too high there is a steep drop in performance which can only be reversed by a reduction in physiological arousal. Although the model fails to include a self-confidence variable, its interactive approach seems to be the best explanation for observed behavior. Now that we have a good understanding of the interaction of these variables, the question still remains, how do you operationalize these constructs? Two scales have been developed for this purpose.

The Competitive State Anxiety Inventory - 2 (CSAI - 2) developed Martens, Burton, Vealey, Bump, and Smith (1990) seems to be the most widely used. It consists of three subscales: cognitive anxiety (fear of anxiety and negative expectations), somatic anxiety (perceptions of physiological arousal) and self-confidence. Although self-confidenceis not included in the catastrophe model, it has been found to be a separate entity from cognitive anxiety.

The Sport Anxiety Scale (SAS) was developed by Smith, Smoll, and Ptacek. It measures trait cognitive anxiety, somatic anxiety, and concentration disruption. Although it is not used as often, it is still a reliable instrument that also fits within the catastrophe model of anxiety and performance. Use of either of these scales by researchers would be a step in the right direction towards creating appropriate operational definitions.

Effects of Anxiety in Athletics

A great deal of research has been devoted to the effect of anxiety on sports performance. Researchers have found that competitive state anxiety is higher for amateur athletes in individual sports compared with athletes in team sports. In addition, participants in individual non-contact sports have been found to report lower levels of state anxiety than participants in individual contact sports. Cognitive anxiety has been found to exert a powerful influence on performance. This statement holds true regardless of the individual's skill level. Participants in a collegiate softball tournament were put into one of two conditions: high situation criticality or low.

While somatic anxiety did not differ in the two situations, those athletes in the high criticality condition had significantly higher levels of cognitive-anxiety. Clearly the cognitive interpretation an individual gives to a situation exerts an effect. Researchers have found that athletes that are successful interpret arousal to be facilitative. Research conducted with an elite group of swimmers found that anxiety intensity levels were higher in subjects who interpreted their anxiety as debilitative than those who reported it as being facilitative. This has been found to be true of gymnasts as well as basketball players.

Gould, Petrchlikoff, and Weinberg have reported that the strongest predictor of cognitive anxiety was years of experience such that the more experience an individual had the lower the level of cognitive anxiety. This was supported by research conducted with a group of tennis players. Advanced subjects (individuals who had been participating in the sport for an extended period of time) reported more facilitative interpretations of their anxiety than novices. Similar results have been observed among a group of elite swimmers (Jones, Hanton, & Swain, 1994). Perhaps this is due to previous experience with arousal and how to cope.

The amount of self-confidence that an individual possesses has been found to differ among elite and novice athletes. Research with a group of tennis players indicated that the advanced players had significantly higher levels of self-confidence. This has been found to be true of gymnasts as well as swimmers. The predictors of self-confidence identified by research are perception of preparedness, and external conditions. Other researchers have found that the strongest predictor of self-confidence has been found to be the amount of ability that an individual believed he or she had. This makes sense given an individuals previous experience in a given situation.

Self-confidence has been found to account for a greater proportion of variance in performance than cognitive or somatic anxiety. This suggests that the most powerful quality that elite performers posses is a high level of self-confidence which may act as a protective factor from cognitive anxiety.

Although the research conducted focusing on cognitive anxiety and self-confidence provides some insight into their effect on athletic performance, the interaction of these variables in conjunction with somatic anxiety provides a better understanding of the true effects. Among a group of 91 athletes ranging in age from 14 - 36 years old who participated in soccer, swimming, and track and field, those individuals with higher scores on self-confidence and lower scores on cognitive anxiety and somatic anxiety perceived their overall anxiety levels as more facilitative of athletic performance.

Research conducted comparing athletes competing in team sports (basketball) with those competing in individual sports (track and field) has found that subjects competing in individual sports report significantly lower self-confidence and higher somatic anxiety than team sport athletes. This is supported by research that has been conducted with figure skaters as well. Martin and Hall's research demonstrated that skaters experienced grater cognitive and somatic anxiety prior to an individual competitive event than prior to a team competition. Perhaps this is due to a diffusion of responsibility that occurs in the team framework but not in an individual framework. Important gender differences have also been found by researchers focusing on the relationship between cognitive anxiety, self-confidence, and somatic anxiety.

Females had lower self-confidence and higher somatic anxiety scores than males on the CSAI-2. This research also focused on the location of an athletic event as well, finding that away games resulted in increased somatic anxiety and lower self-confidence. Finally, Thuot et al. found that adolescents, regardless of gender, experienced significantly higher levels of cognitive and somatic anxiety and lower levels of self-confidence as the ability of opponents increased. This is partially supported by research that has focused on the determinants of anxiety as well as gender. Among males, cognitive and somatic anxiety was more strongly affected by their perception of opponent's ability and probability of winning.

Female's cognitive anxiety and self-confidence is determined by readiness to perform and the importance they personally placed on doing well. These gender differences are indicative of the need to develop interventions that are tailored to individual needs and the importance of considering all factors when developing an intervention.

Clearly, anxiety exerts a variety of effects on athletic performance. These effects vary based on sport, gender and level of experience. In order to facilitate peak performances by athletes, sport psychologists must consider the three different facts of anxiety: cognitive anxiety, somatic anxiety, and self-confidence. Given the research that indicates that successful athletes who interpret their anxiety as being facilitative is characterized by high scores on self-confidence and low scores on somatic and cognitive anxiety, sport psychologist should work towards achieving this ideal state among their clients.

Cognitive-Behavioral Treatments in Athletics

A large discrepancy between performance in practice and in competition is indicative that the athlete is having a hard time achieving an appropriate level of arousal or may over aroused.

Advances in the field of anxiety reduction in general have transferred over into athletics. Research in the field has identified the following strategies used by elite performers to control their anxiety: goal setting; though control strategies such as positive thinking and cognitive restructuring; relaxation techniques such as diaphragmatic breathing, imagery, and progressive muscle relaxation; and focusing on the task at hand.

In the past, researchers have examined the effectiveness of cognitive-behavioral interventions with a variety of athletes. The treatment modalities that have been used have had considerable variability in content and in format. Early research in the field was based on work for anxiety reduction in clinical settings. Research conducted with two female collegiate basketball players who received training in relaxation, imagery, and cognitive restructuring had significant improvements in concentration problems and in-game anxiety.

One study used the cognitive-behavioral interventions mentioned above in 7 weekly 2-hour group sessions. The results indicated that in comparison to the no treatment control group, the treatment group showed decreases in anxiety. Another study using a multiple baseline design demonstrated that after a cognitive-behavioral intervention there was a significant decrease in cognitive and somatic anxiety as well as an increase in self-confidence. However, the improvement in self-confidence may have been due to the individualized nature of the treatment provided. This is supported by other research conducted with collegiate basketball players who were treated in either a group or a combination group/ individualized program.

Although there was a decrease in cognitive and somatic anxiety for all athletes, only those subjects who participated in the individualized program had improved scores on self-confidence. This indicates that an individualized treatment program may be most beneficial for athletes who are having difficulties with self-confidence, but that treatment of cognitive and somatic anxiety can take place in a group format.

Some research has suggested that any intervention regardless of content was beneficial in reducing anxiety. Tennis players in one of four interventions (imagery, relaxation, relaxation and imagery, and concentration) showed significant reductions in somatic and cognitive anxiety and an improvement in self-confidence. If the researchers would have included a no-treatment control group, then their results might have shown some differences among the groups; but, cognitive-behavioral interventions are effective for the purposes of performance enhancement.

However, research conducted with field hockey players has concluded that anxiety reduction techniques that are directed at the individual's dominant anxiety type (cognitive or somatic) is more effective. It is therefore necessary to asses athlete's needs before instituting interventions. None the less, the above research demonstrates the effectiveness of cognitive-behavioral interventions.

Relaxation is one method that has been discussed in the literature for reducing both cognitive and somatic anxiety. These two strategies have been used successfully in the treatment of clinical populations. Use of progressive muscle relaxation is recommended for this purpose and may be beneficial for athletes who have difficulty sleeping the night before a big competition. Although both of these interventions are beneficial for the purposes of anxiety reduction previous experience indicates that they initially work best when used in conjunction with imagery focusing on relaxation. As the athlete begins to master these techniques the relaxing imagery can be dropped off.

Imagery and mental rehearsal of tasks is also beneficial for the individual seeking to improve athletic performance. It provides familiarity with the task at hand and also provides positive feedback of their imagined performance. This intervention has been proven to be effective with collegiate athletes in all sports. Results of research indicate that individuals who were in the imagery intervention had significantly greater increases in sport performance and sport competition anxiety than did the delayed-training control group. Little is known about how imagery functions. However, researchers have identified visual imagery ability and motivational arousal imagery as predictors of cognitive state anxiety.

Visual imagery ability was also predictive of somatic state anxiety and motivational mastery imagery was predictive of self-confidence. The researchers also found that imagery ability was significantly related to imagery use such that as ability increased so did use. Butler identified the following components a being important to a successful imagery routine:

— Selection of a skill to be imagined. Visualization should be preceded by relaxation. Visualization should also be as a realistic as possible incorporating the use of all senses and the venue of the athletic competition.

— The technique to be imagined should be brought into focus. An internal perspective (as if they are viewing it through their eyes not the eyes of a camera on them performing the skill) is necessary. In addition, an attempt to feel the movement is effective in enhancing the imagery exercise.

— Practice the skill in "real time," there is no need to speed up or slow the skill down. Inclusion of coaches in the development of an imagery routine is important since it incorporates their technical skill and helps to minimize the perception of psychologists as a threat by coaches.

Butler concludes that imagery is an important component of an athlete's pre-competition regimen if they are to be successful. Cognitive restructuring is an important component of treatment since it allows individuals to have a different interpretation of the activation states they are experiencing and thus reduce cognitive anxiety. It can be beneficial for de-emphasizing the importance of competitions which will allow an athlete's true ability to come through.

According to multidimensional anxiety theory, elite performers will have peak performances as cognitive anxiety decreases and self-confidence increases. This suggests that an appropriate intervention might be to de-emphasize the importance of competitions and try to achieve an intermediate level of somatic anxiety. Goal setting is another important part of cognitive restructuring as well. It is important not to set goals that are too overwhelming for individuals since this in turn may result in increases in state anxiety which in turn may result in impaired performance. Instead, it is recommended that a series of smaller goals be set for individuals that break the task down into its component parts.

Although relaxation, imagery, and cognitive interventions are each beneficial for the purposes of anxiety reduction in athletics, they are far more powerful when used in conjunction with one another. Butler suggests a mnemonic device called ***Pressure*** who have a hard time coping in competitions that incorporates all three phases of intervention. The word can be broken down as follows:

— Prepare - Athletes must psychologically prepare for what they will face during the competition.

— Relax - Diaphragmatic breathing exercises, may be necessary prior to competition in order to prevent over arousal which would result in a deterioration in performance.

— Externalize - This involves the belief that problems are not within yourself. This can be of assistance when athletes feel that there are too many demands that are being put upon them.

— Stay Positive - Acknowledgement of the importance that individuals should have confidence in their abilities.

— Single Minded - Stay focused on the task at hand. This can be used both in training and competition.

— Unite - Particularly useful within the framework of teams sports, this component encourages athletes to consider what roles others will fulfill and the importance of working together as a team throughout the competition.

— Re-evaluate - How important is this event in the real world?

— Extend yourself - Give your best performance every time no matter how important, or unimportant, the competition is.

Use of this mnemonic device is warranted with individuals that have problems with the three components of athletic anxiety: cognitive, somatic, and self-confidence. Even the amount of cognitive effort that is used by an individual to use these strategies as an effect on performance. Gould et al., reported that the differences between medal winners and non-medal winners at an Olympic wrestling competition was the degree to which the individuals used these interventions automatically such that winners were more likely to use the interventions automatically.

Most elite level performers have already found ways of achieving the activation state that is necessary for the sport. One of the things that makes athletics so fascinating is the number of different demands that are placed on an individual throughout a competition. It is therefore unlikely that any one intervention will ever be able to be of benefit for everyone. Thorough assessment of the athlete's needs is therefore recommended.

Violence in Sports

Violence in sports involves intentional aggressive violence. Competitive sports, such as football (soccer), ice hockey, basketball, may involve aggressive tactics, but actual violence in sports falls outside the boundaries of good sportsmanship. Particularly contact sports such as American football, rugby union/league, boxing and wrestling. Violence in sports may include threats, verbal abuse, or physical harm and may be carried out by athletes, coaches, fans, spectators, or the parents of young athletes.

Causes

"Intermittent explosive disorder" may be a cause of violence. Some athletes may be genetically predisposed to violence or (particularly in male athlete cases) have unusually high testosterone levels. Animal behaviour ethology studies may also lend a clue, as athletes may resort to violence to establish territory. For example, a 1920s National Hockey League incident involved Eddie Shore's assertion of territorial dominance over newcomers Sprague Cleghorn and Billy Coutu; in retaliation, Coutu severed Shore's ear.

In some sports, such as American football and ice hockey, traumatic brain injury, whose high incidence has only recently been realized, may also reduce players' emotional control. The National Football League and the National Hockey League now have procedures to facilitate the detection of concussion.

In ice hockey, violence is often a tactic. In particular a team's "enforcer" may protect a star player who is a less skilled fighter by fighting players who harass the star. Recent tule changes in the NHL, however, have reduced the incidence of intimidation tactics, such as attacking a player without provocation.

Although criminal justice authorities have historically avoided pressing charges against athletes, these authorities may also come from cultures where domestic violence was or is also tolerated under the guise of a social contract — an unwritten agreement in an ongoing relationship. By pursuing athletes, officials may be seen as interfering in a social contract. It can be difficult to determine whether athletes invoke a social contract for violence each time they step on to the field, stadium or court. However, in some cultures, authorities have stepped in, such when police occasionally press charges in the National Hockey League.

Some sports psychologists and sports psychiatrists have expressed concerns about the impact on children. Media sometimes broadcast unfiltered scenes of violence, sometimes showing shots over and over while the incident is a hot media topic. Critics worry that children may copy activities or become desensitized to violence.

Types of Violence

Physical violence

Athletes sometimes resort to violence, in hopes of injuring and intimidating opponents. Such incidents may be part of a strategy developed by coaches or players. An example of a pre-arranged strategy is the 99-call used by the British Lions Rugby Union team in their 1974 tour of South Africa, as a pre-arranged all-out attack on the South African team if one of the South African players was deemed to have committed a violent infraction that would go unpunished by the home referees. This was arranged on the (correct) assumption that the home referee could not send off all the Lions if they all retaliated simultaneously to violence.

In boxing, unruly or extremely violent behaviour by one of the contestants often results in the fighter breaking the rules being penalized with points taken off, or, in extreme cases, disqualification. Outlawed tactics in boxing include hitting the opponent on the back of the head, under the belly, during clinching, and to the back. Other tactics that are outlawed, but less seen, are pushing an opponent extremely hard to the floor, or hitting after the bell repeatedly.

Verbal abuse

Athletes, fans, parents, and coaches sometimes take part in verbal abuse, screaming at players, coaches, officials, and fans. In European football, UEFA and has had to warn a number of teams about racist chants from supporters, and on some occasions has fined teams or forced them to play home matches with no supporters allowed in the ground due to racist behaviour of supporters.

Fan violence

In the stands and the streets, fans may resort to violence to express loyalty to a team, anger at a team's performance, or to intimidate opponents. Violence may also be related to nationalism or as an outlet for underlying social tensions. It is often alcohol-related.

Violence by supporters of sports teams dates back to Roman times, when supporters of chariot racing teams were frequently involved in major riots. A notable example of this is the Nika riots of 532. Montreal Canadiens fans rioted in the 1950s, after Maurice Richard received a suspension.

The actions of English football hooligans in the 1980s caused English teams to be banned from European competition for six years after the Heysel Stadium disaster in 1985. Although the level of football-related violence was significantly reduced in England after this event, in the recent Euro 2004 tournament, England were publicly warned that any violence by supporters at matches could result in the team's expulsion from the tournament. Many known hooligans were prevented from travelling to the tournament in Portugal. There was a collective sigh of relief from security experts the USA when England faild to qualify for the 1994 Football World Cup. Alan Rothenberg (chairman of the World Cup organising committee in the United States in 1994) said:

> There were three countries in the world whose presence would have created logistical and security problems, so we're very pleased they won't be coming: Iraq, Iran and England."

After Marvin Hagler knocked out Alan Minter in three rounds to win boxing's world Middleweight title at Wembley Arena in 1980, many of Minter's supporters began to throw beer cans, bottles and other objects to the ring. Both Hagler and Minter, along with their respective handlers, had to be escorted out by Scotland Yard.

In 1990, a match between Red Star Belgrade and Dynamo Zagreb was abandoned after ten minutes with thousands of fans fighting each other and the police. One Zagreb player was seen to kick a policeman, and after an hour long riot, the stadium was set on fire.

In 1993, Monica Seles was stabbed by a Steffi Graf fan during a changeover at a tennis match in Germany.

In 1994, Vancouver Canucks fans rioted in the streets of Vancouver after their team lost in the Stanley Cup finals.

During the 1994 World Cup, Colombia football (soccer) player Andres Escobar accidentally scored an own goal (put the ball in his own net), causing the team to lose 2-1 to the United States. On his return to Colombia, Escobar was confronted outside a bar in Medellín by a gunman who shot the player six times, reportedly shouting 'goal' for each bullet fired.

In July 2000, 13 people were trampled to death in a riot at a World Cup qualifying match in Harare, after South Africa took a 2-0 lead.

Parental Violence

The parents of athletes occasionally become violent. Some taunt or hit coaches, players, and other parents. Others bully their own children, lashing out as punishment or misguided encouragement. In 2000, hockey dad Thomas Junta of Reading, Massachusetts was watching his 10-year-old son at a summer ice hockey practice. Concerned about aggressive play, he yelled at coach Michael Costin of Lynnfield, Massachusetts. A fight ensued, spilling into the hallway. Junta, who was 100-pounds heavier, repeatedly punched Costin in the face, while holding him down with a knee to the chest. Junta's sons begged him to stop and another adult broke up the fight, but Costin died. Junta was later handed a six-to-10-year sentence for manslaughter.

Ritual violence

High school, college, and even professional sports teams often include initiation ceremonies (known as hazing in the USA) as a rite of passage. A 1999 study by Alfred University and the NCAA found that approximately four out of five college US athletes (250,000 per year) experienced hazing. Half were required to take part in alcohol-related initiations, while two-thirds were subjected to humiliation rituals.

The most notable event in sport-related violence was the Heysel Stadium disaster, when 39 people died when a wall collapsed under pressure of Juventus supporters fleeing from 'football hooligans' supporting Liverpool F.C..

Prevention

Specialists in preventing sports violence have recommended emphasizing sportsmanship among young players, promoting positive sports role models, banning alcohol, and imposing tougher penalties for athletes. Some critics suggest that sports psychology professionals could also counsel athletes, but coaches, parents and athletes may balk at accusations of emotional damage.

In most sports, officials or referees impose penalties when ahtletes step outside the bounds of normal competitive play. Formal sporting organizations, such as the NHL, NBA, UEFA, sometimes impose suspensions, explusions or fines.

Hooliganism

Hooliganism is unruly and destructive behaviour, usually by gangs of young men. It is frequently linked in the public mind with the game and support of football (soccer) clubs. The term has however been widely used since (at least) the 1990s to describe various street gangs of youths behaving indecorously. Hooligans have also attached themselves to other sports, such as rugby and even of recent times cricket.

Violence in sports is probably as old as civilisation. In the 6th century, rivalry between supporters of the Blue and Green chariot-racing teams in Constantinople, led to 30,000 deaths in the week of the Nika riots in 532. The game of football has long been associated with violence since its beginnings in 13th century England. Medieval football matches involved hundreds of players, and were essentially pitched battles between the young men of rival villages. Only two periods in British history have been relatively free of football-related violence: the inter-war years and the decade following the Second World War.

The behaviour now known as 'football hooliganism' originated in England in the early 1960s. In other European countries, similar patterns of behaviour emerged about 10 years later, in the early 1970s. Italian fans created a particularly fanatical brand of football support known as Ultra. Ultras are now a major force in the Italian game and are prevelant in most European countries.

5

Psychological Factors Affecting Physical Performance

Some psychological factors associated with performance enhancement in serious athletes are discussed. Those factors are delimited to what occurs during a competitive performance. Four mental skills:

1. segmenting,
2. task-relevant thought content,
3. positive self-talk, and
4. mood words are reviewed.

Typical thinking developed through sport participation, a very common control condition, is not conducive to optimal or maximal performance. The implementations of these mental skills produce athletic performance enhancements, even in elite athletes. Any extra effort or physiological cost does not accompany improvements. It is proposed that the teaching of these and similar skills must become part of an athlete's experience if performance standards are to be improved further. Psychology is the study of behavior, it being both covert and overt. It is relatively easy to investigate overt behaviors accurately and reliably and to employ independent verification of phenomena, but when it comes to covert behaviors, such as thoughts and emotional interpretations, the ability to verify phenomena independently is usually thwarted.

While it remains possible to manipulate external events and observe behavioral outcomes, functional relationships between environmental psychological factors and performances can be described. It is not scientifically appropriate to attribute outcomes to intermediary events such as thoughts and perceptions when they have not been directly observed. A position on that restriction has been described elsewhere. While talk is of thoughts and covert activities, it is the external stimulating events that influence them which are really the causal factors in the research works discussed.

Serious Competitive Settings

A serious competitive setting is where the consequences of performance are most important and strongest for an athlete. Factors that affect an athlete's perception of this setting have been described in the *Sport Pressure Checklist*. Variations in these factors produce performance inconsistencies as well as suggest patterns that predispose excellent performances. In challenging and serious performance situations, it has been found that performance-oriented "strategies" (plans) of specific detail have notable effects on performance consistency and reliability. The need for specific preparations is now commonly recognized in several fields (e.g., business, performing arts) and its founding research so convincing that it is now rarely investigated. However, it is still being neglected in the majority of sporting situations by coaches and sport psychologists. Further, when strategies are formulated primarily by athletes they generally produce the following benefits:

1. reduction in uncertainty and interpretive distractions and the stress of negative situations,
2. enhanced performance consistency,
3. improved coping capacity for problems, and
4. minimized performance deteriorations. Research reports of the value of performance strategies in sports have been published.

1. Performance Segmenting

If an event is of long duration, it needs to be broken into segments. Partitions should be short enough for the athlete to totally concentrate on what needs to be thought of and done in that period. This assists focusing on the completion of successful competition elements. Structuring performances in this manner is called "segmenting." In the U.S. Navy, a similar approach to combat missions is known as "compartmentalizing" (e.g., TOP GUN). Segmenting originates from two sources. First, the goal-setting literature has shown that distant goals have less effect on performance than do more proximal goals. Short-term performance goals that focus on the processes needed for successful behavior enhance performance.

Second, individuals faced with extensive tasks usually break them down into more manageable segments. Botterill noted successful young athletes spontaneously reconstructed an endurance strength-task into shorter performance segments, each having its own goal or goals. A skier overcame difficulties with traversing a slope when attention was shifted to progress by task parts that eventually lead to completion of the total run. World-champion target sportspersons have reported attempting to fire "one shot at a time" during extended shooting contests. Performing artists have intuitively divided long performances into stages (e.g., acts and scenes, movements) so that performance quality can be maintained. Thus, theory and practice support the notion of segmenting extensive tasks for improved performance outcomes.

Manges and Wahl both tested the segmented versus total performance goal-orientation in runners. Using intraparticipant research designs, the value of short-term process goals over terminal (distal) goals was conclusively demonstrated. Manges' three runners improved 2.0-2.7% while Wahl's ranged from 1.1-6.5% with one participant not improving (-0.9%). The performance differences could not be accounted for in terms of altered physiological functioning, a phenomenon noted long ago by Wilmore. The way segments are structured and their content is particularly individual. Differences in segmenting strategies and moderating factors need to be determined to understand this factor more clearly. The anecdotal and goal-theory literature at present is inadequate for fully explaining this phenomenon.

2. *Task-Relevant Thought Content*

Performance efficiency is reduced by distraction and enhanced by relevant concentration. There are some minor exceptions to this principle (e.g., cognitive interference), but in tasks performed under stressful circumstances, the focus of attention has to be on the processes for completing the performance to achieve the highest level of outcome. This is particularly true in sports. Cognitive concepts such as "attentional focus," "concentration," and "flow" are characterized by a singular task-orientation, although that orientation varies according to the stage and type of activity. "The focus on task-relevant information is intended to ensure that all resources available to an athlete in a competition are used fully and in the most efficient manner possible".

While task-relevant concentration might seem to be an obvious characteristic of performance control, it is surprising how few athletes develop it effectively through normal training experiences. Training seems to develop a form of habitual/practice thinking that does not transfer effective benefits to competitive settings. Intraparticipant alternating-treatments designs have been used to compare "normal/ habitual" thinking with sport-specific task-relevant thinking that has been individualized to the participant. The experimental variable in this paradigm is confounded between individuality and task-specificity. Some studies have introduced other unrelated thinking conditions for further comparisons. Group designs do not demonstrate effects as well as single-participant experiments. Task-relevant thinking appears more consistent in influence the higher the standard of the athlete:

— Canadian elite rowers (N = 5) improved an average of 3.5% on an ergometer task.

— Canadian national team cross-country skiers improved an average of 1.96% over a training track lap.

— Norwegian junior national team cross-country skiers improved an average of 2.5% using both skating and classical techniques over a training track lap.

A common feature of these studies was the opportunity for the athletes to individualize the content and nature of their thoughts after receiving instructions. That feature may be a very significant moderating variable. The normal/habitual thinking developed through training and coaching is far from optimal in its effect on performance. Even though coaches commonly claim to teach and stress "technique," it was only after instructions and practice to use self- and activity-specific detailed content that performances improved.

3. *Positive Self-Statements (Thinking)*

Positive thinking is *the covert utterance of positive self-statements.* Taylor's work showed that under a positive mental orientation, the body's physiology performs more efficiently than when under an aversive or negative mind-set. Positive self-talk is also related to factors associated with improved performance, such as coping, self-concept, and self-efficacy. Dalton, Maier, and Posavac reported the direct effect of negative thoughts on swimming performance. Among 24 junior tennis players during tournament matches it was found that negative self-talk was associated with losing, and players who used and reported believing in the utility of positive self-talk won more points than players who did not.

Positive self-talk was an important part of a game strategy for improving basketball performance, for learning compulsory figures in ice-skating, and for increasing the number of games won from deuce-point in a tennis player. Intraparticipant investigations on the effect of positive self-talk on performance in a variety of settings produced results similar to those of task-relevant thinking:

— Canadian rowers improved from 1.21-2.20% on an evaluative ergometer task.

— A wide range of Norwegian cross-country skiers improved an average of 3.63% over a test distance.

— Superior Canadian age-group swimmers improved from 1.39-2.13% over two distances.

An emphasis on positive self-talk while performing a task enhances performance. This further supports the inadequacy of habitual sport thinking for provoking an optimal training or competitive response. Self-talk is an individual skill that needs to be practiced before it is evaluated for influence. The general level of effect is marginally less than that of task-relevant thinking, but that is not surprising considering it usually does not entertain direct effects on skill economy. Rather, it sets the "atmosphere" for efficient physiological functioning which then has to be translated into efficient movement patterns. There are certain characteristics of positive self-talk which are recommended for use in practical situations.

Positive self-statements should not be trivial, cheerleader-type expressions (e.g., "go, go, go," "let's do it now"). Four appropriate uses in competitions are:

1 encouraging oneself,

2. handling effort,

3. evaluating segment goals, and

4. general positive self-talk to maintain atmosphere.

It should be spread throughout a strategy. It could be most effective when second-person phrasing is used (e.g., "you," "your"), which produces a perception of control over oneself. The dynamics of positive self-talk in sport settings need to be delineated further.

4. Mood Words

Another form of covert vocabulary involves particular words that emote or energize the individual. Language has basic words which, when said or thought with appropriate feeling and emphasis, have some movement or emotional outcome. They cause a physical reaction in the body. Some languages/ cultures use these words more frequently (e.g., Italian, Arabic) than others (e.g., English). Performing artists frequently use simple words emoted in a particular way to promote a behavior that expresses a mood. Mood words require no translation. The expressive thinking of words should produce a feeling appropriate for some performance capacity. If a feeling does not occur, then the content is inappropriate and will be ineffectual. Mood words can reflect various performance capacities.

Typically, a list of monosyllabic synonyms for strength, power (force), speed, agility, balance, and endurance are presented to an athlete. The athlete selects from the lists, or augments personal words that have a similar meaning, the capacities and words that are meaningful to him or her. Those words are then inserted into a performance strategy at the time and during the appropriate task-relevant thoughts when they will be most effective. For example, a rower taking the catch in a stroke might think "BOOM" as a way of elevating the power of that part of the stroke. Rowers have reported that this does increase performance over thinking normally or imaging what is intended. That talk is more effective than imagery during performance has been reported.

Mood words of this type increase the effectiveness of thinking. When one wants to be powerful, thinking words that make one feel powerful will increase the actions of power. Rushall reported unpublished data on a grip-strength test with four Canadian rowers. Three thought-content conditions were used:

1. normal thought content as a control,
2. the utterance of a phrase that had the correct meaning

but was unrelated to the emotional state needed to be strong (e.g., the words "exert force"), and

3. the utterance of mood words, such as "crush," "grind," etc., of the athletes' choosing.

All athletes recorded the strongest grip under the emotive mood word condition. Mood words enhance performance marginally better than either task-relevant content or positive self-statements.

Closure

Task-relevant content, positive self-statements, and mood words presently are perceived to be the structures that should be employed as thought content during a segmented competitive performance. They should be integrated into a meaningful dialogue by each athlete, and practiced, performed, and evaluated for effect and possible improvement. Their inclusion in training programs is not difficult, and practice could constitute "sporting homework" in a fashion that is not possible with other performance factors. The magnitudes of the performance enhancements reported in controlled research settings with high-level athletes makes the use of thought-content skills an imperative for athletes wishing to maximize their performance and for coaches seeking to optimize their effectiveness.

These four psychological determinants of performance produced enhancements and alterations in a large number of the studies and participants considered. Performance improvements occurred without any notable extra perceived exertion, increase in direct measurements of physiological parameters, or other increased thought dynamics, such as the degree of concentration or "trying harder". These mental activities are a "painless" avenue for assisting athletes to improve. When athletes are exposed to these skills and evaluate their effects they are particularly enthusiastic about their value and use. Psychology offers many performance determinants, only a few being addressed here.

It needs to be recognized that psychology becomes more important, the higher the standard of competitor. It has been reported that psychological factors are better discriminators of high-level performance capacity than physiological measures. For example, Silva, Shultz, Haslam, Martin, and Murray found that psychological variables discriminated Olympic wrestling team qualifiers from nonqualifiers better than physiological variables. Psychology has a major role to play in determining the levels of performance achieved in competitive settings. Athletes should be appraised of the techniques and provided practice opportunities for their implementation as part of the evolving professions of coaching and sport psychology.

Psychological Factors

— *Intelligence*: Ability to interrelate perception of the environment into mental constructs, based on past experienceand education

— *Creativity*: Ability to establish new ways of doing things which are unexpected

— *Alertness*: Mental preparedness to adjust rapidly to changing situations

— *Motivation*: The ability to push the body towards a goal

— *Discipline*: Concentration to the exclusion of external and internal stimuli

Sport Psychologists

Sport Psychology is the study of behavioral factors that influence and are influenced by participation and performance in sport, exercise, and physical activity. Sport psychology professionals are interested in how participation in sport, exercise, and physical activity may enhance personal development and well-being throughout the life span. Have you ever heard a coach say that a sport is 50-90% mental? It is this mental side of sport that sport psychology professionals work with. Coaches often deal exclusively with the physical and strategic components of sport, whereas, sport psychology professionals seek to enhance the minds of athletes and exercisers to help them improve their performance by coming closer to reaching their potential in a competitive setting.

Among other things, sport psychology professionals help individuals who:

— lose focus during competition.

— lack confidence during games.

— get scared or anxious while competing.

— have trouble communicating with teammates.

— choke during important competitive events.

— have trouble motivating themselves in sport and exercise settings.

— get angry easily when they perform below their expectations.

Why do people contact sport psychology professionals?

— To improve performance. This is the most common reason for consulting a sport psychology professional. In general, performance may be enhanced through the teaching of mental strategies that either refine the practices of effective performers or help other performers overcome obstacles that prevent them from reaching their potential.

— To deal with the pressures of competition. Athletes at all levels seek help in dealing with the pressures of competition. Such pressures may stem from parental and/or coach expectations as well as the athlete's own expectations regarding performance.

— To enhance the experience of youth sport participants. Youth sport organizations may employ a sport psychology professional to educate coaches about how to increase the satisfaction and enjoyment of participants and about the coaches' role in promoting the development of healthy self- esteem.

— To get psychological assistance with injury rehabilitation. People with injuries may seek assistance with adjusting to non-participant status, adhering to physical therapy, tolerating pain, or other issues.

— To assist with an exercise program. People who want to exercise regularly may work with a sport psychology professional to increase their motivation and help with other issues related to exercise adherence.

— To receive guidance in dealing with life challenges. Concerns with personal problems can adversely affect exercise and athletic performance. People often find that counseling helps to put things in perspective and allows for greater satisfaction in life, career transition, and time management.

— To help make the transition out of sport participation more easily. People spend a lot of time in sport, and the transition to being a non-participant can be very difficult.

What services can a sport psychology professional provide?

Sport psychology professionals may provide a variety of services to individuals, groups, and organizations related to the psychological factors affecting sport, exercise, physical activity and team dynamics. The most common services focus on:

— assisting with exercise adherence, communication, teamwork, or program development and evaluation

— teaching participants specific mental, behavioral, psychosocial, and emotional control skills. They might, for example, focus on relaxation, concentration, self-talk, self-confidence, goal setting, aggression, burnout and/or the use of imagery

Sport psychology professionals who have special training or licensure in areas such as social work, counseling, counseling psychology or clinical psychology may also provide services such as diagnosis and treatment of psychological difficulties (e.g., depression, eating disorders, substance abuse), marital, family or group therapy, or the administration and interpretation of psychological tests in addition to those services listed above.

What roles may sport psychology professionals assume?

Sport psychology professionals may be trained primarily in the sport sciences with additional training in counseling or clinical psychology, or they may be trained primarily in psychology with supplemental training in the sport sciences. The activities of a particular sport psychology professional will vary based on the practitioner's specific interests and training. The three major roles of a sport psychology professional are teacher, researcher, and service provider/practitioner. Those individuals who focus mostly on teaching and research typically teach at colleges and universities.

In some cases, these individuals also work with athletes, coaches, or other athletic personnel. They provide education as well as develop and implement programs designed to maximize the overall well-being of sport, exercise, and physical activity participants. For the most part, their consultations will focus on enhancing the performance of individuals in these settings. Service providers/practitioners in sport psychology often use sport psychology concepts and principles to enhance sport, exercise, and physical activity performance or enjoyment. They spend the majority of their time working directly with individuals or groups who have asked for their help.

Individuals working in this are of sport psychology may consult with a broad range of clients and often serve in educational and/or counseling roles. Many of these practitioners may have additional training in counseling or clinical psychology.

We can't promise you that a sport psychologist will help you perform better. However, there is a lot of scientific evidence suggesting that sport psychology techniques help to enhance sport performance. Without boring you with these numbers, lets take a look at some evidence. During the last three decades sport psychology has received increased attention from elite and non-elite level athletes, coaches, parents, and the media. Consider, for example:

— A large number of elite, amateur, and professional athletes work with sport psychology professionals, and talk in the media about the benefits of this work.

— Coaches at the high school and university levels seek sport psychology professionals to work with their athletes and teams on game preparation, team cohesion, communication skills, and other areas that affect performance.

— Sport psychology professionals are put on staff at universities to work exclusively with athletic teams on issues such as life skills development and coping with the demands of being a student-athlete.

— Exercise specialists, athletic trainers, youth sport directors, corporations, and psychologists use sport psychology professionals and sport psychology techniques to improve exercise adherence, aid injury rehabilitation, educate coaches, build self-esteem, enhance group dynamics, and increase program effectiveness.

Who is considered a "qualified" sport psychology consultant?

Only those individuals with specialized training and appropriate certification and/or licensure may call themselves a sport psychologist. Anyone seeking the services of a sport psychology professional should ask about the professional's credentials, clientele, experience, and membership in professional organizations such as the Association for the Advancement of Applied Sport Psychology (AAASP) and/or the American Psychological Association (APA). A growing number of sport psychology professionals are certified by AAASP. These professionals—who earn the designation Certified Consultant, AAASP (or CC, AAASP)—have met a minimum standard of education and training in the sport sciences and in psychology. They have also undergone an extensive review process.

The AAASP certification process encourages sport psychology professionals to maintain high standards of professional and ethical conduct while giving service to others. Some sport psychology professionals may be listed on the U.S. Olympic Committee (USOC) Sport Psychology Registry, meaning that they are approved to work with Olympic athletes and national teams. To be on the Registry, a professional must be a CC, AAASP and a member of the American Psychological Association (APA). Some sport psychology professionals are also licensed psychologists. This means that they have met the minimum educational and training requirements by their state, and have passed a comprehensive test related to the practice of psychology. These are the only people who may call themselves "psychologists", and they would be qualified to help you with personal or clinical problems (e.g., eating disorders) in addition to problems of a purely performance nature.

Emotions

Emotions can be defined as brief positive or negative feelings occurring in response to meaningful or important situations, which can influence mood states. Basic emotions such as fear, anger, joy and surprise are commonly experienced in sport, although complex mixes of emotions are often evident. Positive emotions can help sustain motivation and enable us to approach events with enthusiasm and energy.

Negative emotions, by contrast, are linked to avoidance behaviours and withdrawal. Emotions in the sporting arena can be triggered by many things personal to an individual, including memories, conversations with other people, seeing the competition venue, weighing up the opposition etc. Researchers have studied emotions in order to determine why they occur and what impact they have on behaviour.

At first it was thought that emotions were simply the result of physiological changes, since physiological symptoms, such as increased heart rate, were commonly observed in such reactions. To test this theory, scientists injected volunteers with the so-called 'stress' hormone epinephrine (adrenaline) to see if emotions could be generated in the laboratory. A small minority of participants reported feeling genuine emotions (usually sadness) while most reported physiological changes (to be expected after administration of adrenaline) and 'as if' emotions - feelings closely associated with being happy, sad or angry, but not the 'real thing'.

Subsequent research demonstrated that emotions could be induced by directing participants' thoughts to emotional triggers, such as deceased relatives (sadness) or past achievements (pride). In summary, research in these areas has shown that both physiological arousal and the cognitive interpretation of that arousal are important in determining the emotional response. During the lead-up to an important competition, the body starts to prepare for the demands to come by releasing hormones such as epinephrine into the bloodstream, setting in motion the physiological changes associated with increased arousal (sometimes referred to as the 'fight or flight' response).

In addition, changes occur in the attentional system, as athletes become more focussed and alert, with increasingly active minds. This overall increase in arousal can be your best friend or your worst enemy: and the key to achieving an appropriate mind-set is to analyse the changes in a rational manner and channel your emotions in a positive direction.

Many elite athletes associate increased arousal with excitement as the body readies itself for competition, and use it as a cue to focus on pre-planned routines. This positive interpretation of the arousal response usually leads to more positive emotions and optimistic outlooks. Conversely, some athletes interpret physiological changes like an increased heart rate as anxiety, worry and apprehension , with a negative impact on emotions that is not conducive to good performance. The most important thing to remember is that your interpretation of physiological changes directs your emotional response. However, the relationship between thoughts and emotions works in both directions: although emotions are the result of cognitive interpretations, they can also impact on your thoughts, giving rise to a vicious circle of negative thoughts and emotions.

The good news for athletes who experience unhelpful emotions before competition is that you can gain more control by altering your focus of attention. The next time you feel these unwanted changes occurring try going through the following psychological routine:

— Tell yourself 'this is my body preparing me to perform well', and repeat the affirmation as necessary;

— Try to recall an image of yourself either winning or performing well, and connect this with the feelings you experienced at the time.

You will need to practise this routine on a regular basis in order to establish it as a habitual response that will help you feel more composed and energised before competitions. If negative images jump into your mind during this time, try to visualise the most successful athlete in your sport and the way he or she runs, competes, enjoys performing - in short every positive thing about them; Then visualise yourself with similar positive attributes. Even experienced athletes get nervous and irritable before competing, and a little tension (as long as it is controlled) is often necessary to inspire maximal performance.

The techniques outlined above will not remove all the tension, but they should help you to channel your emotions more positively, which is what top athletes have to learn to do. The difference between winners and losers often boils down to coping skills, in that some athletes have learned to cope with competitive situations better than others. It is important to challenge the belief of some athletes that emotions and mood states are simply reactions to external events; in fact, the athlete has considerable capacity for control in this area. A recent study by Stevens and Lane identified a number of strategies employed by athletes to regulate their moods.

Although unique strategies were employed for specific mood dimensions, results indicated that 'changing location' and 'listening to music' were among the most commonly used strategies. Various research studies have demonstrated the ability of music to impact on emotions and mood by either calming or stimulating the individual as required - although careful consideration is needed in the selection of appropriate music. Listening to music or engaging in a mentally active process, such as a crossword, can help to stop the mind wandering in the hours leading up to competition, although immediately beforehand athletes need to be completely focused on the task in hand.

Having worked with sportsmen and women who have experienced emotional disturbance prior to competing, it is clear to me that mental preparation needs are highly. The common approach that we have found successful is to develop with each athlete a coping response that becomes automated and can be consistently applied in changing circumstances. Such a coping response puts the athlete in control by creating a familiar psychological comfort zone regardless of whatever is going on in the external environment.

One of the biggest triggers for anxiety is uncertainty, which is, of course, inherent in all sporting events. The key principle for the athlete is to control the things you can control but not to waste energy on things you can't control. Many top athletes have found, to their cost, that giving attention to how opponents might perform or how technically good others were in the warm-up has a negative impact on their focus.

The one thing you can control is your own preparation, so that should have your full focus. By developing consistent routines and ways of coping with distractions, uncertainty can be reduced and you are less likely to be negatively affected by external factors. Because athletes have varying requirements, it is impossible to standardise the pre-competition preparation. However, you may wish to adopt some of the ideas below in creating your own pre-performance strategy to achieve the desired emotional state. These ideas are all designed to be put into practice in the hour before competition, although the principles can be adapted for other times.

Physical Preparation

The warm-up period can be an important psychological aid as well as preparing the body for the rigors of competition and helping to prevent injury. Remember the comfort zone? By developing a relatively stable warm-up routine, including mobility work, stretching and increasing deep muscle temperature, uncertainty can be reduced and the athlete's attention directed to appropriate cues, such as quality technique and body awareness. The development of routines in sport has consistently been shown to be important in directing attentional focus to important cues, so aiding performance.

Although during last summer's major athletic events it was impossible to observe what was going on inside the minds of the sprinters, you could clearly observe the regularity of the warm-up routines and the intense concentration written on athletes' faces prior to taking their marks. These routines are not haphazard, but have been systematically designed to promote optimal functioning in the final few minutes before performance. Golfers have routines that allow them to prepare in the same way for each shot, as do some rugby place kickers, and tennis players before serving.

The key to any routine is that it provides the athlete with control and directs attention to the important cues. Coaches and athletes should work together in deciding the key attentional cues and the sequence in which these should occur. Such routines are the opposite of superstitious rituals that take control away from the performer, as with superstitions outcome is essentially believed to be controlled by sources other than the self.

Mental Preparation

The mental aspects prior to performance should involve focussing on what you are going to do during the event. This can include specific strategies, and the establishment of optimal attentional focus. Some athletes will like to use imagery to recall positive past experiences and generate a sense of confidence. Imagery is a very flexible method to employ prior to competition but it needs to be used correctly for maximum effect. Imagery is not just a form of visualisation, but moreover an all sensory experience that should involve the kinaesthetic sense, emotions and auditory experiences to increase the impact.

Many people use imagery to simply see themselves winning but it can be employed to imagine good technique, coping with difficult situations, recreating emotional feelings and rehearsing the up-coming event in the mind. Imagery is a powerful technique since the brain interprets the imagined scenarios very literally, so directly enhancing such psychological variables as confidence. Always keep imagery sessions short and simple just before competition.

Tailoring the imagery to the desired outcome is essential, so if you want to improve your mood, imagine a realistic scenario that makes you feel good. For more advice on incorporating imagery into your preparation, you may like to read a very practical book entitled In Pursuit of Excellence. Mental preparation can include the repeated use of positive self-statements (affirmations) such as 'we have trained hard, and am in great shape'.

The 'quick set' routine

Psychologist Jeff Simons has described one of the best ways to organise the last 20-30 seconds before competition in what has become known as the quick set routine. This three-phase routine is designed to provide a quick focus that can be used just before competition or as a means of refocusing quickly following a distraction. It is minimal in content, which appeals to many athletes, and involves a physical, emotional and focus cue. An example for a sprinter could be:

— Close eyes, clear your mind and maintain deep rhythmical breathing, in through your nose and out through your mouth (physical cue);

— Imagine a previous race win, see yourself crossing the line first and recreate those feelings (emotional cue);

— Return your focus to the sprint start, thinking of blasting off on the 'B' of the bang (focus cue).

However meticulous your planning, things often occur at the competition site that are out of your control. Such events have the potential to impact on your emotional state, distract you from your goals and push you out of your optimal state of preparedness. However, it is important to remember that things only become distractions if you let them. They do not have to negatively influence your mood if you can learn to let them go and refocus. Such distractions can by provided by your opponents. It is increasingly common for opponents to use psych-out strategies or mind games to try and break your concentration and consistency.

If you feel yourself attending to them, it is important to become aware that you have lost your optimal focus and need to refocus quickly. First, 'let go' of the distraction and put it out of your mind; say to yourself 'let it go', shake down your body, and refocus on your breathing. Some people might prefer to use their quick set routine to refocus in such circumstances. Remember that some opponents are actively seeking to unsettle you, and that by reacting to their comments or behaviours you are falling into their trap and allowing them the psychological edge. By engaging in this psychological duel you run the risk of disrupting your emotional state, becoming over-aroused and suffering a catastrophic decline in performance that is difficult to recover from quickly.

Reacting emotionally often means that you discard your carefully laid plans and operate a strategy of reprisal. Self-control is best regained by not reacting to provocation. This, in turn, can make your opponent worried or angry as it demonstrates that his or her attempts to undermine you have failed. Attempts to engage in such antics can, in any case, be a sign that your opponent is worried about you.

A classic example of how emotions can affect sport performers came in a famous boxing match between Sugar Ray Leonard and Roberto Duran. Leonard was considered the better boxer who was expected to outclass Duran with slick movements and long-range punching. However, before the fight Duran insulted Leonard in front of his family and this, to the dismay of Leonard's Trainer Angelo Dundee, sent Leonard into a rage, which completely altered the course of subsequent events. Instead of fighting to the pre-planned strategy devised with his trainer, Leonard let his emotions take over and decided he was going to 'beat-up' his opponent. Duran's actions amounted to a psychological masterstroke as Leonard ditched his boxing skills and opted for a brawl. It was exactly what Duran had hoped for, and he won a points decision.

There are many other potential distractions for the athlete, including the actions of friends or family, coaches or team mates, the environmental conditions, memories, delays and irrelevant thoughts. All of these can detract from your preparations, so be ready to clear your mind and refocus as necessary. Additionally/alternatively, remove yourself physically from the source of these distractions if possible. Learning any physical skill takes time, effort and practice.

Psychological skills are no different in this respect, so don't expect miraculous overnight changes in your performance. If you are a serious athlete, it is best to work with your coach to devise routines and mental plans. Once you are happy with these, they can be introduced first to practice situations and later to competition. Give yourself a few weeks to use these new techniques before re-evaluating them and adding or deleting parts as necessary. It is unlikely that the initial plans or routines will be perfect, so do not be afraid to develop them. It is also sensible to add distractions to your training sessions in order to simulate more realistic conditions.

This can include attempting to refocus while people are trying to distract you. You might even practice your refocusing skills using imagery, by envisaging potential distracting scenarios in your mind. Only when you are comfortable with your strategies should you start to use them in competitions. Remember to give it time, as improvements take time to show through. Emotions are an essential part of sport and competition, but if you don't gain control of them before competing they might control you and hinder your performance. While it is true that some people are more emotionally sensitive than others, taking mental charge by implementing psychological plans and routines can help all athletes to a more optimal state of readiness for performance.

Self-Awareness in Sport

How to get the best from yourself or an athlete you coach by effective questioning and attentive listening. Long and varied career is the power of asking effective open questions in a bid to improve performance. Each of the sample questions below relates to one of the following elements: thought, feeling, will and action.

— How clear are my thoughts about what I want to achieve?

— To what extent are my emotions aligned to that vision?

— How far am I committed to this aim?

— How advanced is my action plan for implementing it?

High achievers in every sphere of life are highly aware of what they want to achieve, of their own strengths and weaknesses, of the need to improve performances and of their opposition or the environment of competition. They also take full responsibility for doing all they can to achieve their aims.

Sports Psychology - Thought Control

When it comes to running - or any other endurance sport - your mind can be your biggest asset or your worst enemy. Enjoying your training and achieving your best performances is not simply down to physical conditioning: your mental states and, particularly, the thoughts that run through your mind can affect the way you feel during exercise.

In fact the nature and quality of your thoughts can make the difference between winning or losing, enjoying or hating your training, and may impact on your decision to stay with an exercise programme. Much of this scientific evidence comes from studies of marathon runners. Neuroscientists have shown that athlets have thousands of thoughts running through our minds each and every day. Athletes spend a large percentage of their time thinking sport-related thoughts, but most of these are unplanned and random. The first step towards becoming more organised and purposeful in your thinking is to become more aware of them.

Techniques for dissociation

— *Music* - This can generate positive thoughts, improve your mood state and distract you from the physical demands of your sport. But be careful not to get too distracted if you are running in a busy area;

— *Counting game* - Count the number of blue cars you see, or the number of dogs of post boxes. Be inventive;

— *Alphabet game* - Work through from A to Z for a chosen category, such as women's names or countries;

— *Rainbow game* - Try to notice as many colours as possible while you work out: aim for all the colours of the rainbow;

— *Active fantasy* - Imagine yourself as a lottery winner and decide how to spend your winnings.

Avoid thoughts relating to your work, jobs you have to do and anything problematic, as this can increase tension. Try to be creative and have fun with dissociation. It can help you relax and enjoy your sport even more.

Association and dissociation

Association involves focusing on bodily sensations and monitoring any changes - usually internal - that occur. Breathing rate and muscular sensations provide physiological cues that allow you to pace yourself with a view to avoiding or minimising pain. By contrast dissocation is about directing attention away from bodily sensations by a form of distraction designed to reduce the athlete's awareness of fatigue or effort. This can be achieved by many means, including music. However, more 'active' strategies like counting tasks or the alphabet game might be more effective.

When trying to decide which strategy might be best for you, it is important to consider your personal situation, preferences and goals. For example, most athletes perform training runs at a slower pace than they use in competition, making body monitoring less essential. A better goal for training might be to relieve boredom and monotony, in which case dissociation, with active mental processing, might be most beneficial. Dissociation may also benefit athletes who want to improve their endurance by running or exercising for longer at moderate intensities. However, because dissociation works by distracting the mind, it might work against an athlete setting an ideal pace for optimum performance. The reason why association appears so important in competition is that, by monitoring his bodily responses, an athlete can ride that thin line between pushing for maximum performance and overdoing it.

Association involves entering a more concentrated state when you can react to changes within your body. And focusing on internal states like rhythmical breathing can help you feel more relaxed during physical activity. But, on the down side, there is some evidence of a link between association and injury; some athletes, it appears, choose to associate with pain and fatigue-related symptoms and end up pushing themselves too hard.

Most successful elite marathon runners have been shown to combine associative and dissociative strategies when planning their thoughts. There are times, especially in races, when you need to be very aware of your own physical state and of events in the external environment. However, there are also times when you can plan to 'switch off' and give yourself a break from the mental demands of competition or training. The best thing is to construct a plan with your coach, exercise leader or even a more experienced fellow athlete. Try to decide between you what is the best approach for you, and plan what you will be thinking about during the race or training sessions. For a 30-minute training run you might decide on cyclic phases of thinking- e.g. 10 minutes of body monitoring, 10 minutes of alphabet game, then more body monitoring to the end. It's all perfectly logical once you get started: you wouldn't leave your physical preparations to chance, so why allow your thoughts to crop up in random fashion.

Techniques for associative body monitoring follow this three-stage plan:

— *Focus on your breathing:* controlled, relatively deep rhythmic breathing is the key to relaxation. When you breathe out, try to imagine the tension leaving your body;

— Try to remain relaxed while running (or cycling or swimming), but be aware of tension and fatigue in your muscles. It's often a good idea to start from the head and work down, giving each area or group of muscles your attention. If you notice tension, try to focus on a cue word, such as 'relax' or 'easy' and try to let the tension flow out of the muscles;

— Keep your pace in line with the information you gain from body monitoring. You might, for example, increase the pace if you feel very positive.

Repeat the monitoring constantly or, alternatively, take some time out for dissociation. You might also reinforce your mood by telling yourself how well you are doing and that you need to keep working hard and remain focused.

Self-talk

When running, cycling or swimming for long periods of time, the mind can wander freely, if you let it. When this happens, your natural internal dialogue - or self-talk - becomes important. If your concentration does stray or your body monitoring detects fatigue, it is vital that your self-talk remains positive. The best thing is to avoid over-emotional self-talk and focus on self-instructing, motivational content. To this end, you can plan and even rehearse what you are going to say to yourself beforehand, just like your might rehearse an important telephone call or lecture. The key is to stay positive even when the situation is less than ideal. This is not an easy feat to pull off and will take some time to master.

The first step in this process is to become more aware of your thoughts during training and competition. If you want to gain more control over your thoughts, try to formulate a simple plan and try it out over a number of weeks during training. If you notice any undesirable patterns in your thinking, such as negative self-talk or loss of focus, you can try to combat these by planning more positive alternative thoughts. You can, for example, frame positive statements that you repeat to yourself regularly. Athletes often recall that their very best performances are accompanied by few thoughts, a feeling of complete control, effortless movements and a sense of being 'on automatic pilot'. Sport psychologists often refer to this as a 'state of flow'.

Suicide and Physical Activity

Physical activity especially vigorous aerobic exercise - has been shown to alleviate depression. Might it also reduce the risk of suicide, which is linked with depression? This is the hypothesis a pair of US scientists set out to test with a major questionnaire survey of nearly 5,000 college students, for whom suicide is the third leading cause of death. Students were classified according to whether or not they participated in any college sport teams. They were further grouped into five categories relating to their level of activity in the week preceding the survey, as follows:

— *Frequent vigorous activity* - exercise that made them sweat and breathe hard for 20 minutes or more on six or seven days;

— *Vigorous activity* - as above for three-five days;

— *Moderate activity* - a combined total of one or two days of vigorous activity and five or more days of walking or cycling for 30 minutes a day;

— *Low activity* - some activity but less than amounts typically recommended for health and fitness gains;

— *No activity* - the 'control' condition.

Students were characterised as suicidal if they indicated that during the past 12 months they had seriously thought about attempting suicide, made plans about how they would attempt suicide or actually attempted suicide. The results revealed distinct - and puzzling - gender differences in the association between activity and suicide, although the actual prevalence of suicidal behaviour among male and female students was similar. In terms of sports participation, there was a trend in favour of a protective effect, with male non-participants being

2.5 times more likely to report suicidal behaviour than participants and female non-participants 1.67 times more at risk - the latter finding being only of borderline statistical significance.

But when it came to activity levels the differences were more stark. For men, low activity was the only clearly protective level, with participants at almost half the risk of suicidal behaviour of those with no reported activity; the men in the three more active groups did not differ significantly in reported suicidal behaviour from the controls. Women, however, exhibited a completely different risk profile, with those reporting frequent vigorous activity having twice the risk of suicidal behaviour of the control group and moderately active women being 1.76 times more at risk. Women in the other two activity groups had slightly - but non-significantly - higher odds of suicidal behaviour than the controls.

These very different findings caused the researchers to engage in a great deal of head-scratching, having hypothesised at the outset that sedentary students of both sexes would run the highest risk of suicidal tendencies. They were especially puzzled by the finding that the association between physical activity and suicidal behaviour in women was independent of distorted weight perceptions that might drive them to exercise obsessively.

Future research should attempt to identify other factors that may be mediating an association between physical activity and suicidal tendencies among college-age women.' Meantime, they suggest that health professionals are in the best position to recommend increased physical activity when appropriate and to determine when such activity is being used excessively or inappropriately in order to mask problems that may require intervention.

Mental Stress affect your performances

Mental stress can hurt your performances in a variety of different ways. It can raise heart rate and oxygen consumption, harming your exercise efficiency and causing particular workout and race speeds to feel tougher than they actually should. It can increase muscle tension, reducing stride lengths (if you are a runner) and making your legs and arms considerably less 'springy' and powerful.

On a cognitive level, stress prevents you from 'mentally managing' your tough workouts and races; instead of relaxing and focusing on the task at hand, you are preoccupied with stressful thoughts and emotions, so the quality of your performance decreases. If you feel stressed-out before and during your competitions or hard training sessions, what can you do to control the stress, and thus increase your chances of performing at your highest-possible level?

Sport psychologists have proposed a number of different stress-managing techniques over the years, but one of the most successful has been something called 'stress-inoculation training'. Developed in the late 1970s and early 1980s by Donald Meichenbaum, a psychologist at the University of Waterloo in Canada, stress-inoculation training takes its name from the fact that it exposes individuals to stress in manageable but gradually increasing amounts, thereby enhancing 'immunity' to stress for the persons practising the technique. The key, however, to stress inoculation is not simply that stress levels are increased in a governable way during training; athletes also learn skills for coping with psychological stress and enhancing performance, including the development of productive thoughts and self-statements and the utilization of centring strategies.

There are usually three stages in the overall stress-inoculation process: A conceptualization phase, in which an athlete becomes more aware of how positive and negative thoughts, self-talk, and imagery influence performance, a rehearsal period, during which an athlete learns to use centring, positive self-statements, and other coping skills, and an application phase, in which the athlete actually practises his/her skills, first in low-stress situations and then in settings in which stress levels are gradually increased.

Banishing unsuitable 'headwork'

Stress-inoculation training was originally developed for the public-at-large, but psychologists quickly realized that it could be applied to sports settings. They knew that many athletes unwittingly respond to stress with maladaptive thoughts and images which greatly hinder performance. Once such athletes understand how their unsuitable 'headwork' is keeping them from reaching their potentials, they begin to eagerly construct new self-statements and images which can have a profoundly positive impact on their performances.

Scientific studies concerning the effects of stress-inoculation training on exercise capacity have generally been positive: In one study, two sessions of stress-inoculation training per week for 5.5 weeks improved the running economy of eight male collegiate cross-country runners. Stress-inoculation training has also been linked with improved performance during abseiling (descending mountain faces) and lower stress levels during squash competitions, and it has been particularly effective at boosting the performances of gymnasts. Not too surprisingly, a number of sport psychologists have examined the effects of stress-inoculation training on basketball players, particularly with regard to free-throw shooting, which is often a high-stress activity within the game.

Stress inoculation improved both free-throw and field-goal shooting, and a second investigation (carried out with just three players, however) determined that free-throw shooting accuracy increased from 50 to 88 per cent and self-statements changed from 86-per cent negative to 71-per cent positive after just 10 hours of stress-inoculation training. In practical terms, here's how stress inoculation works:

The conceptualization phase

If you are interested in managing your stress more effectively, you begin by keeping track of the things you say to yourself about your training and performances. You may want to write these things down, unless you are able to keep a fairly clear 'mental log' of your self-statements in your head. It's important to bear in mind that no statement you make about yourself and your running is 'too small' to record, and you should also make note of the emotional content of your self-statements. Do they make you feel somewhat hopeless and like a failure - or confident and strong? Here's a specific example of a common self-statement which endurance athletes make, along with an explanation of why they make it and what it does to their performances.

The self-statement, although temporarily relieving in a small way, is neither truthful nor realistic. The truth is that the individual is a good runner who performs well in other races, so she can do well in the marathon, too. The reality is that the individual is not doomed to a late-race slowdown; she can train to overcome the plunge in velocity over the final miles. The transiently relieving self-statement gives the runner the temporary 'warm-fuzzies' but actually works to block better performance and smooths the pathway to failure. In spite of the modest relief it provides, it needs to be completely jettisoned in favor of a positive and realistic statement which can push the individual toward better running.

There are many similar, transiently stress-relieving but emotively negative self-statements which endurance athletes commonly make. Try to gain an appreciation for the emotional content of your self-statements and understand how they might help or hinder your performances. Once you have gained a good understanding of how you have been talking to yourself and what your statements mean, you can move on to the next stage of stress management - rehearsal.

The rehearsal phase of stress inoculation

In the rehearsal stage, the negative self-statements are replaced with productive ones. For example, the runner who has been saying 'I just have to accept that fact the I am not a good racer' will put a halt to that kind of conceptualization, replacing it with something like 'I work really hard in my training and carry out my intense workouts very well. This hard work is going to pay off - I'm going to start having some breakthrough races.' Note that this new verbalization is no longer futile and helpless in tone; it is logical, positive, and optimistic. The runner is now 'inoculating' himself for success, not failure. He is giving himself a strong chance to perform up to his true capacity in his future competitions.

Also note, however, that the new self-statement, although positive and affirming, is not stress-relieving by itself. Negative self-statements tend to take stress away by touting the notion that nothing can be done to change things; positive self-statements proclaim that something can indeed be done, and thus the pressure (stress) is still squarely on the athlete's shoulders to perform. This stress is gradually reduced in the application phase of stress inoculation, when the athlete uses his self-affirming thoughts and statements, first in low-stress situations and then in gradually more anxiety-producing events.

The runner who has been saying to herself 'I just have to accept the fact that I will slow down a lot over the last six miles of the marathon' can replace that pessimistic phrase with 'I am going to train myself to hold my pace at the end of the race' and also 'The 20-mile mark is going to be my take-off point for a strong surge to the finish line.'

Once again, the new statements don't remove stress: The pressure is on the self-affirming runner to identify and carry out the proper pre-race training - and actually mount that late-race rally on marathon day. However, the new statements give her a real chance to perform at her highest-possible level, and the stress can be steadily reduced over time as pre-marathon workouts and races go well. In a similar vein, 'I don't have basic foot speed' can be replaced with 'I am carrying out strength and neural training to progressively develop my speed', 'I'm not much of a 40-K cyclist' should be cast out in favour of 'I'm going to upgrade my 5-K performances this year', and 'I have trouble with interval workouts' can sink into the cellar, replaced by 'I am really going to become proficient with my interval training over the summer.' Productive self-statements should carry a positive emotional tone and project a desired outcome.

Why rehearsal?

At this point, you might be wondering why this stage of stress inoculation is called the rehearsal phase, since one is primarily replacing negative self-statements with more positive ones and apparently not doing much rehearsing. The key is that once the new, stronger self-statements are formulated, one 'rehearses' them by repeating them on a daily basis; one also rehearses the basic act of monitoring self-statements and classifying them as negative or positive, as well as discarding the negatives in favor of productive verbalizations (many athletes have 'stream-of-consciousness' self-statements which flow through the mind throughout the day without being checked or adjusted).

An 'anti-stress' log book, in which one can - on a daily basis - write stress-producing self-statements (or negative self-statements produced in response to stress), can be helpful to many athletes. The idea is to jot down the negative self-statement as it experienced and then write alongside it the positive substitute. In addition, while one is developing more positive self-statements, it is productive to rehearse the strategies of centring and 'attentional control'. The concepts are related: centring simply means blocking out distractions, sensations, and thoughts which are irrelevant for good performance and turning one's attention inward in a productive way; some athletes use key words like 'go' or 'now' to relax and shut out external irritations and to begin focusing on their breathing and state of muscle tension.

Attentional control refers to keeping oneself focused on thoughts and movements which enhance performance, preventing one's mind from wandering or focusing on 'task-irrelevant' things (thoughts and feelings which can't help you perform well). Both of these strategies require rehearsal; in fact, once you begin to want to centre and control your attention, you will usually become aware of how non-centred and diverting your thoughts have been in the past. Note that stress-inoculation training takes into account the fact that stress is transactional. It is not simply a sticky blanket which drapes itself over one's shoulders and refuses to come off; it is something one can interact with and handle effectively by using various techniques.

In effect, you are having a conversation with your stress - on your own terms. There are times when you want to shut it out - when you centre and practise attentional control, but at other times you want to use the stress as a platform to make yourself a better athlete (as when you take the stress of 'I'll never be a good racer' and transform it into 'I'm going to focus on having some breakthrough races').

The application phase

Once you have developed positive self-statements and are better at centring and attentional control, you're ready to apply your new strategies in increasingly stressful situations - leading up to your big competitive event(s) of the year. Remember that stress-inoculation training doesn't initially relieve stress; in fact, in a study carried out with competitive gymnasts, the athletes performed better after going through stress-inoculation training, even though their anxiety levels were initially higher during competitions than they had been prior to the 'inoculation'. Don't be alarmed that the stress is not magically going away; in fact, you can use the 'somatic stress' (higher heart rate, higher breathing rate, greater muscle tension) which you might feel as a positive: when you experience it, simply say 'All right, my body is getting ready for a high level of performance.'

Cognitive anxiety (the mental stress you are feeling) will be relieved gradually over time, as your new strategies steadily enhance your ability to perform. For an athlete, there is no better antidote to stress than good performances. The athlete who is stressed out about racing is transiently relieved when he tells himself that he will never race well, but he is permanently and positively relieved when he begins to have solid races and set PBs. Basically, to apply your new stress-managing skills effectively, you would be wise to set up a moderate-length test race which you can carry out on your own.

Practise your positive self-statements, centring, and attentional control during the weeks leading up to this 'race', and then perform to the best of your ability. A few weeks later, enter a low-key contest outside your immediate geographical area, where you will know few of the other athletes (not knowing anyone makes attentional control easier), and use your skills again prior to this race. As the weeks go by, gradually enter more and more stressful races (i.e., races where you want to do fairly well, competitions in which you do know the other competitors, etc.).

Generally, your stress-managing skills will increase enough as time goes by so that you will be able to perform well at these races, in contrast to when you were not managing your stress. At your big event of the year, you will be in much better control of your mind and body - and ready to give yourself a chance to have a great race. If your problem is not the stress of racing itself but a within-race problem such as losing speed in the last portion of a marathon, the positive self-talk, centring, and attentional control will also work, and you'll need to use them leading up to and during a workout which duplicates the stress of marathon day.

A training session in which you run moderately for 20 miles or so and then 'take off' at marathon pace for three to four miles will be helpful, and so will all training sessions which require you to run at goal marathon pace while tired. If you use stress-inoculation training correctly along with your regular training, you can 'inoculate' yourself with the positive focus and self-statements which will make it possible for you to perform at your highest-possible level.

Any look at "*Sports science for the millennium*" must consider the fact that by its nature, there are no major breakthroughs in sports science, such as vaccines and antibiotics in medicine, or the genetic code in biology, or atomic theory in physics, or the big-bang in cosmology. Sports science in general consists of constant refinements or improvements across a broad front; a front that includes training, tactics, techniques, skills, equipment, biomechanics, psychology, chronobiology, nutrition, management and physiology - as well as all the medical aspects.

It was a special event. The attack on the world 10,000m record had been publicised worldwide, and the satellite sports channels had unique coverage. Steve Coe, the challenger, - grandson of a famous father, whose own world 800m record had lasted for almost as many years as Steve had been alive - had put in three periodised sessions daily for the past 24 months under his coach Harry Anderson, specifically to prepare for this attempt to be the first to run under 24 minutes for the distance. Luckily, or he would not have been attempting what he was about to do, Steve had been conceived with a genetic advantage in terms of his response to training. Athletes, otherwise equally endowed physiologically, may respond differently to the same training, because, as Professor Bouchard and colleagues discovered at Laval University, Quebec, some are genetically programmed to produce a better response to the same stimulus.

Good sleep was considered important for maximising the natural growth hormone training-response, and the sex itself for raising androgen levels. Both sets of hormones had an anabolic effect in helping to optimise the muscle response to training stimuli. Breaks and short holidays were considered vital, as was reasonable intellectual stimulus in the form of music, drama, poetry and general conversation.

Coaching Interventions for Athletic Excellence

In coaching literature, Martens, Haslam and Bloom, Durand-Bush, Schinke and Salmela have noted that the relationship between coach and athlete is complex. There is extensive literature outlining the challenging interpersonal dynamic between coaches and athletes. Martens and Wishnietsky and

Felder noted that coaches are often unable to reach their athletes due to personal shortcomings in communication such as impatience and the lack of understanding. Adding to the complexity of the dyad's relationship, Seligman and Rettew and Reivich have noted that athletes also vary in terms of how they perceive and subsequently respond to coach criticism based on their personal interpretation patterns.

Though coaches and athletes alike might not consider the root of such difficulties in the heat of the teaching - learning moment, there are reasons why their relationship is so complex, and in some instances, trying. Some of the factors that underlie the behavioral exchange between coach and athlete reside in the moment. However, there are also other historical factors that underpin the perceptual screens of coaches and athletes alike. Seligman has noted that peoples' perceptions and subsequent explanatory patterns are acquired based on what was learned in childhood from parents and teachers.

Schinke and da Costa recognized that formative interactions with earlier coaches also influence the athletic expectations of sport performers. It seems conceivable that momentary perceptions and responses in the present have their basis in past experiences and interactions. Thus, it is essential for coaches and mental training consultants to understand the current and historical aspects underlying the communication exchange between coach and athlete. In so doing, it is argued herein that coaching and mental training consultants can foster improved interpersonal dynamics and the increased likelihood for personal and athletic growth. Regardless of whether readers are mental training consultants or coaches, the consideration here is to understand how to work through interpersonal dynamics and develop athletes as performers while concurrently mentoring them on a more general level.

Imago Therapy

Imago Therapy is a process of communication developed by

Hendrix. Its underlying assumption is that the challenges people experience when interacting with one another are linked to how each has been hurt or oppressed in childhood. Emphasis is placed on teaching individuals to sensitize others to the manner in which they were hurt, and then in collaboration, to create an environment of safety to explore these experiences. The exploration first takes place through a process termed the "conscious dialogue." The foundation of the skill rests with each person learning to mirror, validate and empathize with the other's experience. The crucial premise, and hence recipe for success, lies in one partner's understanding that it is essential to accept and therefore understand the other's reality. To communicate at their utmost potential, coaches must learn how to borrow the lens through which their athletes view the world, while also, remaining conscious of how they as coaches react to such perceived experiences. For the sake of clarification, this process has previously been called "reflectivity" by social psychologists including Parker and Bruner.

Using a feedback process that was built on the foundation of the dialogue derived from Imago Therapy, it will be shown how coaches and other sport practitioners can work optimally with athletes. There is a number of beliefs regarding why Imago Therapy can contribute to coaching practice and athletic performance. First, there is an underlying assumption that there is ample opportunity to exercise a conscious dialogue process for coaches with their athletes. Coaches spend a lot of time exchanging thoughts and experiences with their athletes. When the time is invested working on the athlete's personal and athletic development concurrently, then the result will be a synergistic form of growth in both areas.

Second, it is the belief, based on the work of Seligman, that the areas in which the coach and athlete experience strife with one another may be directly linked to the manner in which the athlete [and sometimes the coach] have been oppressed or hurt in their own lives. If, for example, the possibility is embraced that some athletes have chosen the path of performing in front of a large numbers of people due partially to an unmet need for recognition in childhood, such information is useful for a coach to be conscious of and active in addressing. Alternately, if an athlete's partial motivation to perform is based on an overwhelming need to compete with others, and this is a life theme for the athlete, that information could also be deemed useful in gaining a deeper understanding of the athlete and how to work with him or her.

Gaining developmental information about each athlete is important in order to improve understanding and pedagogical delivery. Ultimately, improved athlete awareness can help the coach to select a method of communication and feedback that will be more likely to be heard and integrated, within the context, and within general life for that matter, in a positive way.

Ahtlete's Struggle with Confidence

Hendrix elaborates on six major stages of childhood development, which he believes largely influence the person on an individual and relational level; attachment, exploration, identity, competence, concern and intimacy. The attachment stage addresses the extent that the individual experiences acceptance or rejection from parents during infancy (0-18 months). The exploration stage addresses the extent that the individual was encouraged by parents to explore aspects in his or her environment while a toddler (18-36 months). The identity stage uncovers whether people were encouraged by their parents to assert themselves in social contexts during their third and fourth years. The competence stage is depicted through the actual willingness to exert effort and ability within achievement settings, and its basis is contingent on the previous three stages of development.

Concern is the first developmental stage where people learn how to relate to others outside of their parents or caregivers. Intimacy, the final stage, addresses the individual's resulting long-term relational ability with a partner, and its basis is linked to previous experiences during earlier developmental stages. In terms of personal development, the competence stage occurs during the 4-8 year age span. The ability of individuals to feel masterful in their environment and their world is, according to Hendrix, directly linked to retrospective factors experienced during childhood. Taking this premise to sport, something that Seligman has already teased at, athletes who feel competent and powerful in a performance environment undoubtedly have received a parent or caregiver's value during their earliest achievements.

These athletes may have been noticed for their accomplishments received target specific praise for their successes in and out of sport. The adaptive-competent athlete most likely received unconditional love as a child for efforts, despite the mistakes made. In addition, a caregiver, whether a parent or early coach, who was conscious of nurturing competence in a youngster, may also have purposefully provided concrete efficacy information regarding how to correct mistakes. The underlying intervention was to ensure that explanations and subsequent understandings for performance variance were explained by potentially controllable and impermanent factors.

The aforementioned adaptive intervention is in contrast to methods that critically disempower the individual via permanent and personal explanations for sub-par performances, or basing acceptance largely on successful and impermanent performances. Hendrix maintains that the individual who receives selective praise from a caregiver who demands and only notices excellence internalizes the message "do not make mistakes." Such messages are often translated into a fear of failure. Hence, it can be assumed that this might be part of the reason why some athletes are scared to fail and cannot withstand the ego damage from sub-par experiences where others can. There is a second adaptation to wounding in the athlete's competence stage. If a parent withheld instruction or ignored the child who did not excel, the message internalized might well have been "do not be too powerful, there is only enough room here for one of us to win and it is not you."

According to Hendrix, such an individual may operate from a place of fear of assertion affecting their level of success in life, and so, in sport. We believe that these are the athletes who tend to perpetually find themselves one step behind the proverbial gold medal because winning was not internalized as part of what they were accepted for and identified with. For coaches and other central coaching staff working with such athletes, conscious healing means noticing and accepting the assertive aspects of the athletes in an effort to connect them with their personal power, or agency. This sort of intervention might seem complex, but there is a concise means of achieving it.

The application of Imago Therapy to coaching may be viewed as such: In a relationship where coach and athlete are connected, there exists a potential degree of safety for the athlete. With this sense of security athletes' unresolved issues can surface as they attempt to heal unresolved experiences. Situations and feelings, which remind athletes of previous experiences, will trigger positive and negative affect [feelings] in the present. Such feelings, already recognized by Seligman, will typically come from explanations of past experiences. Fear of failure originating from the parent-child relationship may resurface into feelings of inadequacy, threat, and guilt as athletes relate with their coaches.

If believed that such a preoccupation could detract energy from the athlete's potential, it can become one potential coaching role to remain sensitive and intentional in communication. With a view toward building trust, coaches, and even coaching staff, can consciously give their athletes what they are craving on an emotional level; target specific praise for achievement, unconditional acceptance despite performance glitches, concrete and personally uncritical information to correct mistakes, and thus, a promotion of the athlete's personal agency.

The concept of coach intervention and our personal adaptation of an interactive approach take into account the link between the athlete's mind, heart and body and coaching interaction as a complex and interconnected system. It is assumed that peoples' minds, souls and bodies are intertwined in a world with others, as many adherents of social learning theory including Bruner, Bandura and Seligman agree. Hence, the underlying Imago adage developed by Hendrix seems applicable; individuals are born in relationships, they are hurt in relationships, and they need to heal through relationships. It is this adage that underpins the philosophy and rationale for coaches intervening with the athletes that they aspire to mentor as part of their role.

Becoming the Conscious Interventionist

To this point, we have speculated on the implications of earlier formative experiences on the athlete's current state of competence. The main feedback techniques proposed herein include the use of athletes' images, feelings, and body reactions with the use of the coach's technical suggestions. To these informational sources, coaches and athletes can select from a wide array of athlete and coaching evaluation sheets including those of Orlick, Lynch and Albinson and Bull. Combined, these informational sources can provide the coach and athlete with a wealth of information to improve athlete competence.

If, during a practice, the athlete experiences difficulty, and pictures the situation getting worse, it will more likely effect the performance in an adverse way. With both instances, it is of importance that coaches elicit the nature of such images through a feedback sheet. Subsequently, it is imperative that athletes share their thoughts and images openly through conversation before and during training and before and after competition to encourage a heightened and more adaptive level of athlete understanding. Conversely, the negative performance image can undermine the physical capability of the promising athlete.

Imago Theory takes an understanding of negative images one step further by providing the reasons why they occur. When the promising and under confident athlete is placed under stress, all past feelings of inadequacy surface through images long before the possibility of performance excellence is abandoned. The coach's ability to forecast the pending abandonment of performance quality provides pathway to remedial discussions where the athlete can be provided with a combination of healthy perspective and confidence boosting information prior to the performance attempt. Herein lies a useful remedial tool that can be employed by the conscious and well skilled coach prior to the athlete's acquisition of additional negative personal experiences.

Understanding Body Responses

Another pathway to confidence-based information is via the athlete's somatic response to athletic challenge or adversity. As others, including Orlick and Lynch have already noted, it is worthwhile to ask athletes to consider and write down their observations about how their bodies are reacting to specific situations during practice, prior to, during and after competition. The athlete's conscious awareness and subsequent sharing of tension, relaxation, fatigue or anxiety experiences, allows the coach to draw the link between the athlete's mind, body and performance. In relation to coaching intervention, somatic understanding can also help coaches understand where and when things are going wrong.

In addition, somatic information can help the coach decide whether to direct the athlete toward relaxation techniques, activation techniques, or simply paying attention to the success of mind and body working in harmony. Once the athlete and coach are able to comprehend what seems to be happening to the athlete's body, they can reach for a well-suited compensatory strategy so that the athlete can learn how to gain or regain physiological control. Inevitably, as Bandura and Schinke have already noted, such mastery and coping measures could also improve affective and psychological cues, and garner a level of athletic confidence leading to improved athletic competence. Without a collaborative discussion on how the athlete's body is responding, conversely, the athlete, the coach, or both in collaboration, might select an inappropriate coping strategy such as an activation exercise including performance imagery to battle pre-competition nerves.

According to Bandura, such negative sources of somatic efficacy information, in turn would re-confirm past maladaptive coping techniques and a sustaining of prolonged athletic incompetence that otherwise could have been avoided. In essence, an incorrect coping response can entrench what Seligman depicts as a personally helpless pattern of behavior. One potential result might be the athlete believing that there is no relationship between personal strategic efforts and abilities, and resulting successful athletic achievements. When considering helplessness in lieu of Imago Therapy, a negative and despondent response to pressure can be associated with past unresolved difficulties, and its seems plausible that such difficulties might "restimulate" so long as the athlete confirms past maladaptive self-beliefs through inappropriate coping behaviors.

Understanding the Athlete's Feelings

One word, specific descriptions should be provided during the affect-based component of the performance review. An exchange of affect-based information allows the coach and athlete to understand the reasoning behind a specific reaction or create an opportunity for further exploration of emotions that are either detracting or enhancing from the athlete's competence. Conversely, a coach can use this opportunity to communicate to the athlete his or her sense of fatigue for example, so as to prevent a misconception that occasional temper or impatience was a personal issue aimed at the athlete. This point is increasingly crucial depending on the extent of earlier ego damage experienced by the athlete during childhood and other formative moments

Therefore, a collaborative discussion on feelings and responses can provide the coach with a better understanding of where and to what extent their athlete's insecurities reside. Open discussion can also provide coaches with an opportunity to explain what they meant in their instructional criticism so that it is not internalized (or attributed) as any form of permanent, personal or pervasive flaw on the part of the athlete. On both accounts, the improved dialogue between coach and athlete can only add to the coach's credibility and success via the athlete's confidence.

In addition to images, somatic responses and feelings, the acknowledgement of performance can become another source of useful confidence-building information. Athletes can list numerous positive, specific, and measurable things they like about their performance. This might be a challenge for elite and aspiring athletes providing they have been conditioned to be perfectionists, and as a result, they have learned to criticize themselves openly at will. In addition, when athletes have relished their performances, others might have previously discouraged them from "bragging." How can performers be expected to enjoy and duplicate success when they are not allowed to acknowledge with what is going well? This is a noteworthy point considering that Bandura has repeatedly confirmed that the primary source of confidence is the self-acknowledgement of past correct performances.

If the mandate is confidence building, it is necessary for athletes to go against what, for some, has been socially engrained, and acknowledge positive personal experiences. It is imperative for coaches to provide numerous positive, measurable, and specific examples of feedback to the athlete. Given the professional credibility of most coaches, verbal persuasion and even positive facial expressions can add to the competence of a confidence-depleted athlete. This, too, carries forward from Bandura's aforementioned research on self-efficacy. Part of the mandate of a conscious coach, then, is to ask athletes to mirror or paraphrase feedback so as to increase probability that confidence-building information has registered intellectually and emotionally as part of the self-referent thought process.

Technical Suggestions

Technical suggestions are an additional source of confidence intervention that can be given by coaches to their athletes, and by athletes to themselves. A technical suggestion is not an order, but merely a suggestion meant to decrease the traditional manner in which correction is associated with criticism. A technical suggestion implies athlete agency and should always be stated in the positive so as to minimize defensiveness. It should also be as specific as possible so as not to leave any room for misinterpretation. Words like more, less, and bigger register in the brain in an abstract manner and are less effective. A very effective technical suggestion should conjure up a mental image for the athlete.

The Growth Gift

A "growth gift" is the final competence building component that should be given by coaches to their athletes, and by athletes to themselves. The growth gift, much like all other forms of feedback, should be positive, measurable and specific. An effective growth gift captures the individual's essence while simultaneously encouraging the potential for personal growth. An example of a growth gift for athletes who have difficulty experiencing their success or digesting praise, may sound like this: " For the next month, every time you practice your sport and someone pays you a compliment, mirror the compliment back to him or her. Accept the praise and say thank you while feeling the joy of appreciation."

The growth gift encourages the athlete to acknowledge the correct elements in their performance. This form of cognition is provided as a substitute to the ongoing rumination and dissection that Schinke and Seligman have noted seems to be prevalent for many athletes as they strive for excellence. Schinke and Seligman have found that too much critical thinking about what is going wrong in performance serves as a contributory factor to helpless - despondent behavior. What the growth gift seems to contribute to the development of athletic competence is an ongoing awareness for the athlete of that which is right and worth persisting toward in sport. The coach's role in this regard is to ensure that a growth gift is provided to the athlete on a consistent basis so as to ensure that competence develops in a synergistic way over time.

Flow, Intrinsic Motivation, and 2nd Generation Cognitive Science

In psychology, decision making, whether it is initiated or motivated by a conscious or non conscious estimation of the contingencies of reinforcement (as behaviorists would see it), biological sensitivities (as sociobiologists would see it), or mentalistic agencies such as will, need, or desire (as pop or social psychologists would see it) is generally accounted for apart from the patterns of neural activation that are responsible for translating motivating events into behavior. The actual neural and somatic processes that activate behavior are generally not considered as having a significant influence on how behavior is decided. Decision making is thus 'disembodied', since a consideration of bodily influences would not increase the predictive power bestowed by the behavioral road map provided by environmental contingencies, biological sensitivities, or just good old common sense. In contrast to the fixation on of behavioral, social, genetic and otherwise disembodied motivating entities that comprise most of what we call the psychology of motivation, cognitive psychology is primarily concerned with the physiological, biochemical, and morphological content of mental states, and how those states are integrated to produce vision, perception, attention, awareness, etc.

In other words, cognitive science emphasizes how mental processes are activated, not why they are activated. This bifurcation of psychological perspective into a separate emphasis on motivation and activation variables has historically separated cognitive science from those disciplines in psychology such as analytic, social and behavioristic psychology that are concerned primarily with how behavior is instigated or motivated. Within the last twenty years however, a new generation of cognitive scientists has begun to regard this divide as artificial, and has recognized that motivation and activation are tightly bound, and that each informs and explains the other. This position, also called bio-behavioral or second generation cognitive science, has found elegant and forceful advocacy in the works of the psychologists John Donahoe and David Palmer, the philosopher Mark Johnson, the linguist George Lakoff, the neuro-psychologist Antonio Damasio, and the immunologist Gerald Edelman. Their general position is that language, behavior, and value itself it strongly rooted in sensori-motor or bodily processes, and that activation in itself does influence motivation.

Thus sensori-motor and neural activation patterns underlie basic processes of reinforcement, create the basis of language through metaphor, continually influence behavior as emotion, and provide the basis of value and consciousness. However, the complex activation patterns that underlie language, emotion, and value do not in themselves implicate how decision making at its most rudimentary is performed. And here is the critical point. If decision making, if reduced to its molecular correlate of activating attentional processes in itself adds value to behavior, then no behavior can be reliably predicted without a consideration of the activation processes that make behavior possible. Moreover, if this is true, then many of the long held concepts in social psychology, behaviorism, and sociobiology must be reconsidered, reinterpreted, or abandoned.

On a molecular (neural) level, the shifting of attention that occurs as initiated by a sudden change in an environment-behavior (perceptual) relationship is isomorphic with the liberation of the neurotransmitter dopamine in synaptic clefts between coactive pre- and post synaptic neurons. The functional role of dopamine is to stabilize active neural representations in the frontal cortex, to label stimuli with appetitive value (i.e. it feels good), and to provide advance reward information before behavior occurs. Finally, dopamine is released in response to perceived deviations from learned predictions in future reward, or is sensitive to the perceived salience of responses and their consequences (i.e. response contingencies).

In other words, dopamine acts to make thinking processes more efficient and is essential to the process of reinforcement. If these hypotheses are true, then specific response contingencies (particularly variable ratio or 'gambling' schedules of reinforcement) may be hypothesized to signal frequent and consistent deviations in reward prediction, and these deviations will correlate with the consistent and elevated release of dopamine and the felt experience of elation or pleasure. This prediction has been recently borne out by a recent experiment that demonstrated that the increased release of dopamine occurs during the performance of a goal directed motor task: a video game. This result is underscored by an extensive record of self reports that relate ecstatic states to environmental contingencies that require a rapid attentional shifting between salient cognitive precepts.

A specific response contingency (gambling or video game playing) demands a rapid shifting of attention, but multiple concurrent contingencies involving similar behavior that lead to different rewards may do the same thing. If activation patterns (attention) are specific to prediction error, then the continuous prediction errors that sustains attention and the corresponding release of dopamine are inherent in the stimulus context that creates that prediction error, and not in the stimulus itself. Thus extrinsic motivators (money, power, sex, etc.) always include an intrinsically motivating component (pleasurable alertness) that is critically dependent upon how those extrinsic events are arranged to follow behavior. Thus extrinsic and intrinsic motivation are not separate entities, but are individual aspects of the same motivating or learning process. This explains the favor we give to behaviors that have a great deal of unpredictability, such as sports, gambling, and perhaps play writing.

The leads to a critical hypothesis: Objects do not reinforce, but rather the perceptual relationships denoted by those objects. These relationships occur virtually, and always represent as-if relationships and their corresponding prediction errors. That is, an object does not have to be possessed, but be potentially possessed. Reinforcement theory, as defined through modern cognitive science, contrasts with theories informed by behaviorism, sociobiology, economics, and even social psychology that correlate happiness with physical objects. Humans do exist to maximize value, but if value is determined by potential rather than actual events, then value can only be maximized by engineering social environments that provide multiple concurrent rewards for differing aspects of behavior, and inculcating through education our ability to perceive those rewards.

In other words, perfectly engineered societies are merely the societies we admire anyway, such as the idealized models represented by ancient Greece, Renaissance Italy, and Shakespearean England. These societies provide the multi-modal reinforcement for any variety of endeavor, from art to music to sports, but as importantly, they provide the means whereby we may easily perceive the potential approval of the an audience, a girlfriend, posterity, or a Queen. And the Shakespeares of the world, as well as its musicians, artists and saints come about because they are well reinforced by what they do, and this because they can empathize about the world.

Squat Exercise Through Psychological Modeling

Squats, perhaps more than any other resistance exercise must be performed properly. The considerable amount of weight used, in such a multiple joint movement, can result in a variety of injuries to the knees and lower back. However most of these injuries occur when people squat with improper form and technique. Many misconceptions concerning the squat are brought about by ignorance and false information. Adaptations to squatting include but are not limited to the following:

1. Muscles are strengthened far beyond the norm, making injury less likely to occur.
2. Bone density and strength are increased; especially if the stress is applied longitudinally (This is accomplished best by following the outline on proper technique in the subsequent paragraph).
3. Ligaments, tendons, and connective tissues are increased in thickness, viscoelasticity, and tensile strength, making injury far less likely.

Since the squat is a full-body exercise, it elicits one of the highest hormonal responses provided by resistance exercises. Hormonal actions that influence the adaptations to the squat exercise include, but are not limited to, improved force production, stimulation of cartilage growth, and enhanced size. Performing the squat exercise with proper technique is crucial in order to benefit from these favorable adaptations.

Teaching proper form to a student requires visual demonstration by the instructor. The literature in the area of motor skill performance as it relates to or is affected by modeling primarily considers visual perception of the modeled information as a mediating variable on behavior, but what ensues between perception and behavior does not appear to be fully addressed. Apparently, a myriad of intermediary components is essential in transforming the patterns of movement demonstrated by the model into appropriate actions to be accomplished by the learner. These components will be discussed following a brief description of proper technique in executing the barbell squat exercise.

Squatting with proper technique ensures that the quadriceps, biceps femoris, gluteals, and erector spinae receive an overload stress appropriate for development of muscular strength and hypertrophy. The following list will serve as a guideline for the novice lifter:

1. Bar placement should be approximately 1-3 inches below the anterior deltoid. The lower the bar placement, the lower the center of gravity, and the easier the lift will be

as long as the bar is not placed exceedingly low on the shoulders, then it becomes difficult to keep the torso erect and puts undue stress on the shoulder joints.

2. Even a slight variation in foot spacing causes a significant change in muscle involvement and places the lifter at a biomechanical disadvantage. Generally, the feet should be slightly wider than shoulder width. This will increase the availability and usage of the larger and more powerful muscles. Also, this stance will enable the lifter to arrive at a parallel position much earlier than with a narrow stance, thus shortening the distance traveled and consequently doing less mechanical work.

3. The lifter should start the descent by leading with the hips rather than the knees. If the lifter should bend the knees before shifting the hips backwards, then the shins will not be perpendicular to the floor. Keeping the lower legs straight, which is one of the most difficult skills to master, minimizes the stress on the knees by keeping the knee joint directly over the foot which also keeps power centered under the bar.

4. Heels should be flat on the floor for the entire duration of the lift. Raising the heels up predisposes the knees to injury and shifts the lifters center of gravity forward which forces the lower back to compensate and places the lower back in a precarious position. The erector spinae should be the stabilizing muscle that keeps the torso erect; it should not become the primary mover in the squat. The legs, gluteals, and hips are more powerful than the lower back.

5. The lifter should have fully inhaled while starting the descent. The breath should be expelled when the "sticking point" is reached in the ascent, which is typically around thirty degrees of extension. This technique will increase interstitial leverage and aid in keeping the torso erect by forcing the chest out in front of the bar.

Modeling

Modeling is an effective means of conveying relevant information to facilitate an observer's motor skill acquisition. The literature in the area of modeling primarily considers visual perception as a mediating variable on behavior. Visual demonstrations of motor tasks are retained by the learner in the form of cognitive representations, which may be construed as "mental blueprints" providing an essential link between perception and action. The brain not only categorizes these non-language representations; it also builds successive layers of categories such as shape, movement, and sequence. In this way, the learner organizes visual information, events, and their relationships. The significance of the modeling process lies in its effect on the behavior of the observer.

Particular events and attributes are singled out for observing and describing what exactly ensues between perception and action. So, it is crucial to demonstrate proper technique to the observer in the most effective manner, especially when one considers the many people in various weight rooms that are using bad technique, thereby setting a bad example to those observers. It is evident that the observer somehow retains the modeled action and can later replicate what was seen in the absence of verbal instruction. When the trainer gives too many verbal cues, it causes the trainee to think about too many things. This may result in confusion and attenuate performance. Too many instructions make it difficult for the student to totally isolate one strategy from another.

In doing so, some of the information is lost. It may be that the student is using various combinations of strategies and cannot be focused into using the most effective one. Therefore, it is important that verbal instruction be as clear and parsimonious as possible. The trainer should demonstrate the squat exercise with the learner standing behind him or her. This type of visual modeling facilitates motor skill reproduction. Bandura suggests that behavior is mediated by exposure to the model and that repeated exposure to the model will improve the quality of the cognitive representation which will, in turn, facilitate performance.

The concept of modeling is presumed to be controlled by four sub-components: "Attention", a conjecture that people cannot learn much by observation unless they attend to, and perceive accurately the significant features of the modeled behavior. "Retention", where it is submitted that people cannot be influenced by observation if they do not remember it. "Motor reproduction process", which is the conversion of symbolic representations into appropriate actions. "Motivation" which proposes that people are more likely to adopt a modeled behavior if it results in rewarding consequences.

According to Martens, Burwitz, and Zuckerman, the successfulness of the modeling process is limited by the difficulty of the motor task. This relationship between modeling and performance is predicated on two circumstances: an accurate perception of what is to be accomplished by way of strategy or technique, and the ability of the learner to reproduce the demonstrated action. Why are some people better at solving math problems than others, and why are other people better at performing motor tasks the first time they attempt them? Owing to the disparity in motor performance among clients and trainees learning to use free-weights may be a result of certain individuals generating false assumptions from the way in which they process and record the modeled information. Imagery perceptions are as important in understanding modeling as non-imagery perceptions are for understanding mathematics. These perceptions give the student a reference point from which he or she can improve performance.

The instructor should give immediate visual feedback by demonstrating the movement with an emphasis on correcting existing mistakes or replaying videotape of the student's performance, thereby providing visual assessment of the motor task in a timely manner. According to Adams, this knowledge of results enables the observer to correct errors in movement technique. The greater the accuracy of the cognitive representation of the modeled action, the greater the skill acquisition will be in the subsequent reproductions of it. This is consistent with the schema theory proposed by Schmidt, which states that sensory consequences and actual outcomes, for a given set of initial conditions, could be related by the subject. This expected sensory consequence for an intended movement could be generated even if that expectation required interpolating among previous entries in order to perform a novel movement.

Visualization and Imagery

Imagery is a pervasive form of experience and is clearly important for all individuals interested in the acquisition of free-weight lifting skills. The effectiveness of imagery techniques has been demonstrated in studies regarding sport tasks of accuracy, concentration, and strength. The physiological and psychological benefits from practicing visualization improve athletic performance, and have a direct application to the increase of strength. Imagery rehearsal of the desired sequence of sensory-motor behavior units involved in a good performance has been used both by itself and as a part of multiple models. Although the data are somewhat mixed, the weight of the evidence favors mental practice as productively cultivating athletic performance.

An interesting point to consider is that individual differences in imagery ability can influence motor task performance. Subjects with greater imagery ability achieve higher scores in replicating movement patterns than do subjects of lesser imagery ability. Experimental research has indicated that "high imagers" exhibited significantly greater recall scores than "low imagers". Visual imagery facilitates the short-term retention of visually presented sequences of movement. Imagery may have a functional role in the free recall of movement information, especially when imagery techniques are introduced to subjects after they have had some practice in demonstrating the correct movement pattern of the motor skill.

Otherwise, imagery can have an adverse effect on performance. In other words, it is possible for a trainee to mentally rehearse the execution of proper technique and retain the image of the correct motor pattern. Likewise, it is possible for a trainee to mentally rehearse the execution of poor technique and retain the image of the incorrect motor pattern. Clearly, it has been demonstrated that mental practice enhances performance. However, there still exists the misconception that once mental practice is learned, it can be used in an appropriate situation with a reliable frequency. Teaching someone mental practice techniques is one thing, teaching them to be able to initiate those techniques in specific situations such as learning to perform the squat exercise requires a close examination of technique and appropriate feedback in order to correct mistakes.

Upon visiting almost any fitness center, at least two things will be evident. Either people do not perform the squat exercise at all, or many of those who do, perform it incorrectly. This is due to false information and improper instruction. Another problem is that people learn to squat while looking at their refection in a mirror. Although mirrors do provide a modicum of necessary feedback as to how one is progressing in terms of appearance, they are an inappropriate orientation for observing the execution of a motor task, especially one as complex as the squat exercise. You wouldn't teach someone how to approach a bowling lane while facing a mirror, or demonstrate a tennis serve while facing the learner. Learning to squat in front of a mirror is not consistent with the notion of acquiring a cognitive representation through observational learning. A cognitive representation has two basic functions.

One is to regulate movement production, and the other is to serve as a standard of corrections for the detection of error between the cognitive representation and response-produced feedback. While it may be possible to detect error in the movement of a reflection in a mirror, it is impossible to construct an accurate cognitive representation and correct the error through the immediate feedback from a mirror. The learner should be able to use his or her cognitive representation as a reference of correctness in order to form a hypothesis about how to perform the movement better. This is accomplished most effectively by modeling via visual demonstration from the instructor and/or implementing videotaped performance for assessing proper technique in the barbell squat.

The free-weight squat is an open-chain, multi-joint, full-body movement, with a higher level of complexity compared to resistance exercises on machines. Therefore, the additional demands on balance, control, and technique make the squat a very challenging skill to acquire and an even more challenging skill to teach. The four modeling processes "attention", "retention", "motor reproduction", and "motivation" outlined above, are necessary for the learner to acquire proper technique in the squat through observational learning. The learner must understand the purpose of a physical action such as squatting, practice organizing the sequential movements, and receive further demonstration of the same task in conjunction with mental rehearsal in order to enhance performance. The relevant aspects of proper technique are most effectively conveyed to the student by visual demonstration because it provides a complete symbolic representation of the kinematic information in the complex sequential components in the action pattern of the barbell.

A Psychological Perspective in Human Performance

Psychology is the study of behavior, it being both covert and overt. It is relatively easy to investigate overt behaviors accurately, reliably, and to employ independent verification of phenomena, but when it comes to covert behaviors, such as thoughts and emotional interpretations, the ability to independently verify phenomena is usually thwarted. However, it is still possible to affect covert behaviors without actually observing them. While it remains possible to manipulate external events and observe behavioral outcomes, functional relationships between environmental psychological factors and performances can be described. It is not scientifically appropriate to attribute outcomes to intermediary events such as thoughts and perceptions when they have not been directly observed.

Serious Competitive Settings

A serious competitive setting is where the consequences of performance are most important and strongest for an athlete. The pre-competition and competition ingredients are unusually complex with the performance characteristics supposedly reflecting the benefits of training. Factors that affect an athlete's perception of this setting have been described in the *Sport Pressure Checklist*. Variations in these factors produce performance inconsistencies as well as suggest patterns that predispose excellent performances. In challenging and serious performance situations, it has been found that performance-oriented *"strategies"* (plans) of specific detail have notable effects on performance consistency and reliability. The need for specific preparations is now commonly recognized in several fields (e.g., business, performing arts) and its founding research so convincing that it is now rarely investigated. However, it is still being neglected in the majority of sporting situations by coaches and sport psychologists.

Further, when strategies are formulated primarily by athletes they generally produce the following benefits:

1. uncertainty and interpretive distractions are reduced;
2. the stress of negative situations is reduced;
3. performance consistency is enhanced;
4. the coping capacity for problem situations is improved; and
5. performance deteriorations are minimized.

Research reports of the value of performance strategies in sports have been published. Thus, the preparation of what is to be done and thought of during a sporting contest has strong validity for enhancing athletic performance as it does in other human endeavors. It remains important to describe elements that constitute effective performance strategies when used in a competition.

If an event is of long duration, it needs to be broken into segments. Those partitions or segments should be short enough for the athlete to totally concentrate on what needs to be thought of and done in that period. This assists focusing on the completion of successful competition elements. Structuring performances in this manner is called "segmenting." In the US Navy, a similar approach to combat missions is known as "compartmentalizing" (e.g., TOP GUN). Segmenting originates from two sources. First, the goal-setting literature has shown that distant goals have less effect on performance than do more proximal goals.

Short-term performance goals that focus on the processes needed for successful behavior enhance performance. Second, individuals faced with extensive tasks usually break them down into more manageable segments. Botterill noted successful young athletes spontaneously reconstructing an endurance strength-task into shorter performance segments each having its own goal or goals. A skier overcame difficulties with traversing a slope when attention was shifted to progress by parts of the task that eventually lead to completion of the total run. World-champion target sportspersons have reported attempting to fire "one shot at a time" during extended shooting contests. Performing artists have intuitively divided long performances into stages (e.g., acts and scenes, movements) so that performance quality can be maintained.

Thus, theory and practice support the notion of segmenting extensive tasks for improved performance outcomes. Manges and Wahl both tested the segmented versus total performance goal-orientation in runners. Using intrasubject research designs, the value of short-term process goals over terminal or distal goals was conclusively demonstrated. The performance differences could not be accounted for in terms of altered physiological functioning, a phenomenon noted long ago by Wilmore. Segmenting performances is a recommended procedure for performance strategy construction. It has recently been hypothesized that segments need to be shorter, the more intense the activity. The way segments are structured and their content is particularly individual. Differences in segmenting strategies and moderating factors need to be determined to understand this factor more clearly. The anecdotal and goal-theory literature at present is inadequate for fully explaining this phenomenon.

The need to concentrate on task-relevant thought content to complete a task proficiently is no longer investigated. It is a tenet of psychology that performance efficiency is reduced by distraction and enhanced by relevant concentration. There are some minor exceptions to this principle (e.g., cognitive interference), but in tasks that are performed under stressful circumstances, the focus of attention has to be on the processes for completing the performance if the highest level of outcome is to be produced. This is particularly true in sports. Concepts such as attentional focus, concentration, and flow are characterized by a singular task-orientation although that orientation varies according to the stage and type of activity.

For sports, it is important that athletes learn to use task-specific information in their thought structures that will focus on the performance itself. "The focus on task-relevant information is intended to ensure that all resources available to an athlete in a competition are used fully and in the most efficient manner possible". While task-relevant concentration might seem to be an obvious characteristic of performance control, it is surprising how few athletes develop it effectively through training experiences. What seems to be developed is a form of habitual/practice thinking that does not transfer effective benefits to evaluative or competitive settings.

A common paradigm for assessing thought-content effectiveness is to perform an intrasubject alternating treatments design comparing "normal/habitual" thinking with sport-specific task-relevant thinking that has been individualized to the S. The experimental variable in this paradigm is confounded between individuality and task-specificity. Some studies have introduced other, unrelated thinking conditions for further comparisons. In the Crossman and Selkirk studies, group experimental designs were used. They provided no opportunity to develop the mental skill of using particular forms of thinking under the stress of maximal effort to exhaustion. It appears that the design did not allow effects to emerge.

Once intrasubject designs were employed, which allowed learning to occur, effects became quite prevalent. It also appears that task-relevant thinking is more consistent in its influence the higher the standard of the athlete. A common feature of this group of studies was the opportunity for the athletes to individualize the content and nature of their thoughts after receiving instructions. That feature may be a very significant moderating variable in these impressive results. The disturbing feature of obtaining such impressive performance changes through instructions to use a particular mental skill is that the normal/habitual thinking developed through training and coaching is far from optimal in its effect on performance. Even though coaches commonly claim to teach and stress "technique," it was only after instructions and practice to use self- and activity-specific detailed content that performances improved. One has to ponder what would be the eventual performance outcome if the nature of task-relevant thought content became a large part of habitual performance thinking.

Positive self-statements

The definition of positive thinking is the covert utterance of positive self-statements. There are two main theoretical bases for this advocacy. The first is quite general. It relies heavily on Taylor's work which showed that under a positive mental orientation, the body's physiology performs more efficiently than when under an aversive or negative mind-set. The direct effect of negative thoughts on swimming performance was reported by Dalton, Maier, and Posavac. The second basis surrounds the convincing work involving positive self-talk. An extensive compilation of abstracts on the World Wide Web related this activity and its performance benefits. Positive self-talk is also related to factors associated with improved performance, such as coping, self-concept Smit, 1992, and self-efficacy.

The effect of self-talk on performance of 24 junior tennis players (mean age 15.4 yr) during tournament matches was examined. It was found that negative self-talk was associated with losing and that players who used and reported believing in the utility of positive self-talk won more points than players who did not. Positive self-talk has been an important part of a game strategy for improving basketball performance, for learning compulsory figures in ice-skating, and increasing the number games won from deuce-point in a tennis player.

The results are similar to those of task-relevant thinking. An emphasis on positive self-talk while performing a task enhances performance. This further supports the inadequacy of habitual sport thinking for provoking an optimal training or competitive response. Self-talk is an individual skill that needs to be practiced before it is evaluated for influence. The general level of effect is marginally less than that of task-relevant thinking but that is not surprising considering it usually does not entertain direct effects on skill economy. Rather, it sets the "atmosphere" for efficient physiological functioning which then has to be translated into efficient movement patterns.

The value of positive self-talk is further substantiated by its association with factors related to enhanced performance. It is a skill that needs to be taught as part of a coaching program and integrated with task-relevant thinking. The not-so-subtle effect of engaging in positive self-talk is that it is intrinsically reinforcing to the user. Thus, once it is initiated as an important part of a training program, athletes are very willing to continue with its practice. There are certain characteristics of positive self-talk which are recommended for use in practical situations. Positive self-statements should not be trivial, cheerleader-type expressions (e.g., "go, go, go," "let's do it now"). Four appropriate uses in competitions are:

1. encouraging oneself,
2. handling effort,
3. evaluating segment goals, and
4. general positive self-talk to maintain atmosphere.

It should be spread throughout a strategy. It has been suggested that it is most effective when second person phrasing is used (e.g., "you," "your"). The use of second person appears to produce a perception of control over oneself. However, some athletes prefer first person expression. The dynamics of positive self-talk in sport settings need to be delineated further. There are theoretical, experimental, and practical reasons for employing positive self-talk in competitive performances.

Mood Words

A third form of covert vocabulary involves particular words that emote or energize the individual. Language has basic words which, when said or thought with appropriate feeling and emphasis, have some movement or emotional outcome. They cause a physical reaction in the body. Some languages/ cultures use these words more frequently (e.g., Italian, Arabic) than others (e.g., English). Performing artists frequently use simple words emoted in a particular way to promote a behavior that expresses a mood. Mood words require no translation. The expressive thinking of words should produce a feeling appropriate for some performance capacity. If a feeling does not occur, then the content is inappropriate and will be ineffectual.

Mood words can reflect various performance capacities. Typically, a list of monosyllabic synonyms for strength, power (force), speed, agility, balance, and endurance are presented to an athlete. The athlete selects from the lists, or augments personal words that have a similar meaning, the capacities and words that are meaningful to him/her. Those words are then interjected into a performance strategy at the time and during the appropriate task-relevant thoughts when they will be most effective. For example, a rower taking the catch in a stroke might think *"BOOM"* as a way of elevating the power of that part of the stroke. Rowers have reported that this does increase performance over thinking normally or imaging what is intended. That talk is more effective than imagery during performance has been reported.

Mood words of this type increase the effectiveness of thinking. When one wants to be powerful, thinking words that make one feel powerful will increase the actions of power. Rushall reported unpublished data on a grip-strength test with four Canadian rowers. Three thought content conditions were used:

(a) normal thought content as a control;

(b) the utterance of a phrase that had the correct meaning but was unrelated to the emotional state needed to be strong (e.g., the words "exert force"); and

(c) the utterance of mood words, such as "crush," "grind," etc., of the athletes' choosing. All athletes recorded the strongest grip under the emotive mood word condition.

Mood words enhance performance marginally better than either task-relevant content or positive self-statements. The success rate for Ss was notably high and the magnitude of individual or averaged effects the largest overall. This indicates that mood words is a thought-content dynamic that should be visited more often in research and practical settings. The use of mood words be investigated and promoted as a vehicle for enhancing competitive performance. It is the third of the thought-content variables that can and should be implemented as a psychological part of coaching. Teaching the skill of using mood words has been described. The role of mood words is twofold:

— they enhance the performance capacities that are used in a contest, and

— they make the language of a strategy more meaningful.

Task-relevant content, positive self-statements, and mood words presently are perceived to be the structures that should be employed as thought content during a competitive performance. They should be integrated into a meaningful dialogue by each athlete, practiced, performed, and evaluated for effect and possible improvement. They should be treated in a similar manner to the physiological and biomechanical components of performance. Their inclusion in training programs is not difficult and practice could constitute "sporting homework" in a fashion that is not possible with other performance factors. The magnitudes of the performance enhancements which have been independently verified and duplicated in controlled research settings with high-level athletes makes the use of thought content skills an imperative for athletes wishing to maximize their performance and for coaches seeking to optimize their effectiveness.

Coaches are often heard to call to athletes during a performance "concentrate." It is as if they sense that the athlete is allowing the quality of performance, particularly skill components, to slip. A decline is recognized but the control mechanism to halt the degradation and recover does not exist in the performance. A principal aim of strategy use is to maintain control throughout a contest. As a performance progresses there is the potential that an athlete's focus and concentration on relevant stimuli will diminish. As an athlete tires, the symptoms of various forms of physiological or psychological fatigue emerge as strong distractions. Thought intensification is proposed as a process to cope with internal and external distraction factors and maintain "concentration" or "adaptive task application" in the face of mounting competitive distractions, particularly fatigue.

A major pain theory suggests that while the mind is kept busy and totally focused on some activity, the brain will not recognize pain/fatigue. This implies that if an athlete can keep the central nervous system task-focused, then performance control will be maintained. As the pain or distraction stimuli increase in a contest, the intensity of contest-relevant (strategy) thinking also has to increase in order to sustain controlled performance. Psychological intensification is used to guard against incurring the detrimental effects of fatigue. It stops complacency, loss of control, and loss of focus by requiring thought content and the intensity of thinking to gradually increase as fatigue develops. In the early stages of a competition where there is no fatigue, or the effort level is in steady-state, an athlete does not have to think too intently.

With most athletes, there is a stage in a contest where it is realized that a definite increase in effort is needed to continue. Before or at that stage is where thought control needs to be intensified otherwise performance might deteriorate. The intensification process relies heavily on the athlete developing various and different methods of thinking. If one concentrated too long on a single item, a rhythmical form of thinking could develop. A lack of continual thought vitality is counter-productive to good competing. Frequently changing content and thought modes is important in the intensification process. As with other forms of competition thought content, the individualization of the process and its content is paramount. Suggestions for intensification strategies commonly include: thinking faster, changing the nature of the strategy content (e.g., switching from pacing to lower body technique), thinking harder, increasing the thought "sound" volume and emotionality, picturing the written strategy, muttering, and combining any or all of these.

Closure

The psychological determinants of performance produced enhancements and alterations in a large number of the studies and Ss considered. Performance improvements occurred without any notable extra perceived exertion, increase in direct measurements of physiological parameters, or other increased thought dynamics, such as the degree of concentration or "trying harder". These mental activities are a "painless" avenue for assisting athletes to improve. When athletes are exposed to these skills and evaluate their effects they are particularly enthusiastic about their value and use. Coaches have largely remained resistan/t to using mental skills training. They too readily fall back on physical conditioning, skill performance, and/or game strategies as the important emphases for training. It is not the trained state or level of skill that is displayed during practice that is the major issue for coaching, but rather, the teaching of the mental skills so that those factors can be displayed under the stress of competition.

To ignore mental skills training of the type discussed is a dereliction of a duty of coaching. Psychology offers many performance determinants, only a few being addressed here. It needs to be recognized that psychology becomes more important, the higher the standard of competitor. It has been reported that psychological factors are better discriminators of high-level performance capacity than physiological measures. For example, Silva, Shultz, Haslam, Martin, and Murray found that psychological variables discriminated Olympic wrestling team qualifiers from non-qualifiers better than physiological variables. Psychology has a major role to play in determining the levels of performance achieved in competitive settings. Athletes should be appraised of the techniques and provided practice opportunities for their implementation as part of the evolving professions of coaching and sport psychology.

Personality, Emotions, and Health

Psychological factors are involved in causing and in healing many ailments of the body. Some researchers are just discovering these connections scientifically, although Chinese medicine was based on this idea 3000 years ago. A public television series and a book by Bill Moyers, *Healing and The Mind*, document in an interesting way the new mind/body methods of treating pain, stress, cancer (at least the emotional aspects of having cancer), etc. The impact of our emotions on our physical health is called Mind-Body medicine. They are beginning to learn about emotions influencing our body, e.g. sexually abused women develop a smaller hippocampus (which is involved in memory). Psychotherapy and self-help, if effective, produce physical changes... we may not know where the changes are but there are no ghosts in the body.

What does "no ghosts in the body" mean? It means that real, physical events carry out or mediate these mind-body connections. Most scientists believe that no thought, no feeling, and no mental change ever occurs without something physical changing in the body. For example, when long-term stress weakens an organ in the body, like the heart, the stress is physically present for months in some form in the brain, in the general nervous system, and in the weakened organ. Likewise, when a discussion in therapy or use of a self-help method improves some physical condition, the change mechanism between talk (or method) and the illness takes place physically somewhere in the body—nerves associated with thoughts change in the brain, messages are sent in the nervous system, conditions of the muscles change, hormones flow, the immune system activates or shuts down, etc.

There is no mystical magic here. It may seem like magic to you when you are able to influence your thoughts, i.e. neuronal action, which in turn may affect our feelings, then your physical health, then your psychological health, etc. But every action has a physical component (no ghosts) and is lawful and potentially understandable. In case you are thinking that psychological factors are a minor part of "medicine" or health care as we currently know it, consider this: the seven top health risks are behavioral—smoking, over-eating, drinking & drugging, injuries, suicide, violence and sexually transmitted diseases. Seven of the nine leading causes of death, such as auto accidents, have important behavioral components. Health is a complex matter and the current professionals on both sides are ill prepared to understand both mental and physical health.

Changes are needed! Perhaps we need a new profession that understands both psychological/relationship problems and physical illnesses. Perhaps we need to automate the initial psychological/medical diagnostic evaluation, so that everyone can easily get an annual check up. Perhaps everyone also needs to educate themselves so that self-diagnosis and self-care is much more thorough and effective. A fascinating 1995 finding from the 1921 Terman study of 1,528 bright California children: going through your parents' divorce as a child (before 21) and/or going through a divorce yourself as an adult may shorten your life by perhaps as much as four years! In addition, certain personality traits, such as conscientiousness vs. irresponsibility, are also powerfully related to longevity.

Stress and personality factors influence how long we live as much as blood pressure, cholesterol level, or exercise-diet factors. These are not minor factors in your life. Likewise, a survey of 6,307 HMO patients found that 10% had anxiety that had not been treated (15% had been treated for anxiety). These untreated anxiety patients (80% also had untreated depression) had suffered marked reductions in general functioning, health, and well-being, resulting in their utilizing a high level of primary medical care. Science can't yet calculate how much the millions of untreated psychological disorders are costing us Current thinking is: if we can express our emotions, talking openly or acting out our feelings, we can sometimes improve our health.

If we can relax, meditate, let ourselves be touched by others, or establish warm, caring relationships with others, sometimes we get better or get worse more slowly. Heart disease has been reversed by diet, exercise, meditation, and a support group. Women with breast cancer meeting with a support group lived twice as long as similar women who were not in such a group. We need human contact, with it we live longer, e.g. married cancer patients survive longer than unmarried ones. Between 10% and 30% of patients diagnosed as having psychological disorders are later found to have a physical or neurological problem. This highlights the need for referrals by psychotherapists to medical specialists.

Likewise, physicians should refer many of their patients to psychological-psychiatric specialists. For decades family physicians have estimated that 2/3rds of all the illnesses they treat are psychogenic, i.e. caused by psychological factors or stress. A 1995 report said 75% of complaints brought to MD's were psychological. It has been found that stress contributes to heart disease, strokes, cancer, breathing problems, accidents, cirrhosis of the liver, suicide, and many other leading causes of death. So, why is the treatment of most illness, physical and mental, still in the hands of very expensive MD's who have little training in dealing with psychological factors? Because our old laws and health insurance companies have enabled doctors to continue to monopolize health care and because science, until recently, has shown relatively little interest in treating psychogenic disorders.

Physical complaints can be, of course, clues to physical disorders, but pain and fatigue can be clues to psychological problems too. The pain is just as severe, regardless of whether the cause is physical or psychological. In the sections above about sources and effects of stress, we observed the stress-health connection. It works both ways: stress causes physical problems and physical factors cause emotions, e.g. the hormones in PMS cause tension, irritability, sadness, etc. PMS can be reduced by psychological self-help and chemicals.

Hippocrates, 400 years before Christ, thought certain personal-emotional traits were related to specific diseases. Dependable and conscientious young people live as much as four years longer than impulsive, undependable, self-centered people. People more prone to cancer tend to be depressed and/or worriers; they suppress their anxiety and hostile feelings, avoid conflict, act unassertively (overly patient) and feel hopeless; they long for closeness but feel abandoned in important relationships or at work, and just don't handle stress well.

People prone to get heart disease tend to be angry, impatient, and aggressive but sometimes avoid expressing their anger openly; they have repeatedly been annoyed and upset with people opposing them or getting in their way, and they resent not having the power to remove such people; they are suspicious and cynically distrustful, feeling no one cares; they are often trying to get away from someone who has hurt or disappointed them. Both the cancer-prone and the heart disease-prone persons feel tense and fearful. Many bad, unhappy things have happened in their lives which they think they were unable to prevent.

A few simple questions about these traits can supposedly identify the cancer or the heart disease prone person. Moreover, Eysenck says that psychotherapy—and I'd add perhaps self-help—can change a person's personality enough that serious disease can be prevented! Wonderful! What are we waiting for? Eysenck and Ronald Grossarth-Maticek provided "treatment" designed to help these patients

1. express their feelings,
2. learn to relax and handle stress,
3. overcome their passive-dependent nature, and
4. gain greater self-control.

Both kinds of "at risk" patients were taught to relax and overcome their fears (via desensitization), to be more confidently assertive but less angry and aggressive, to see themselves as able and actually be more in control (less passive-dependent or helpless), to express and release pent up feelings, and to know how to handle difficulties in their lives. The individual therapy involved 30 hours, but groups and shortened therapy lasting only 6-8 hours were also tried. The results of this therapy were impressive—the death rates 13 years later in the untreated groups are twice as high as in the treated groups. *If* 6 to 30 hours spent learning psychotherapy or self-help methods can reduce stress and increase the happiness and length of life, then we had better develop world-wide training programs for everyone soon. There is accumulating evidence that optimistic-pessimistic thinking (attitude) is also related to health.

Pessimists explain a bad event, such as breast cancer, in different ways than optimists do, e.g. pessimists say the cancer is "probably incurable," "a sign of terrible future health, ruining all of my life," and "caused by my genes...smoking habit...hopeless attitude...." Optimists would say, the cancer "can be removed," "won't influence my future very much," and is "caused by X-rays at work...air pollution...a virus...." The pessimist's thinking is "the outcome will be bad," "everything else is going to hell too," and "I am at fault." The optimist's thinking is the opposite: "I can become healthy and strong" and "I can handle the pain."

Positive thinking, especially a belief in your ability to control an illness, is associated with good health and good performance in school and at work. Pessimists can learn to change their thinking; some will need professional help. For decades, the psychoanalysts have thought that complaining and psychological sickness were due to an excessive need for love and attention, stemming from feelings of neglect or criticism as a sensitive, needy child. Most psychodynamic therapists would try to uncover these old, still unsatisfied needs for love and bring them to the light of day, then they will go away (or can be handled better rationally).

Athlets and Personality Type

Is there a relationship between personality type and sport preference? How do people choose the sport they participate in? Would it be a matter of personality preference? Are certain personality types more attracted to certain sports, like in careers? Why some people prefer individual sports over team sports? What do basketball players have in common? In order to answer questions related to athletes' personality type, over five hundred athletes were tested and evaluated by this author. To examine the relationship between personality types, sport preferences and performance, team and individual athletes' personality profiles were designed.

Results indicated that teams exhibit a predictable personality profile and that by understanding the psyche of the athlete, performance and team productivity can be enhanced. Interpersonal communication amongst players and coaching staff can improve, players can take advantage of their personal preferences and strengths and work on developing other areas identified in the assessment process. Optimal communication and performance can be achieved by identifying the athletes preferred learning and personality styles. Personality types are attracted to and succeed in certain sports just like they do in certain occupations. The more athletes and coaches understand about their personalities and the team profile, the more productive they can be.

Benefits of understanding the personality profile of athletes are as follows:

1. Helps assess the fit between persons and sports and even positions on a team
2. Helps athletes and coaches value their strengths and become more aware of those areas in which development may be warranted
3. Helps coaches and athletes in a strained relationship analyze the source of the conflict and build a strategy to reduce it
4. Can lead to motivated and committed behavior
5. Useful for the athlete and sports professional in career and life planning, self-management (such as stress/time management) and interpersonal skills areas
6. Many applications in team building and management training

The Myers-Briggs Type Indicator is organized by using eight different personality preferences. The preferences are arranged by four functions and four attitudes. The four functions are composed of two kinds of perception, sensing (S) and intuition (N), and two kinds of judgment, thinking (T) and feeling (F). The four attitudes are composed of extraversion (E), introversion (I), judgment (J), and perception (P). The roles of the functions are as follows:

— Sensing (S) seeks the fullest possible experience of what is immediate and real.

— Intuition (I) seeks the furthest reaches of the possible and imaginative.

— Thinking (T) seeks rational order and plan according to impersonal logic.

— Feeling (F) seeks rational order according to harmony among subjective values.

The roles of the attitudes are as follows:

— Extroversion (E) draws energy from objects and people in society and the environment.

— Introversion (I) draws energy from an inner world of concepts and ideas.

— Judgment (J) seeks to make decisions, closure, plan operations, or organize activities.

— Perception (P) outer behavior is spontaneous, curious, and adaptive, open to new events and changes.

The MBTI can be applied to many different settings, such as, education, counseling, career guidance, athletics and teamwork, and communications.

— In education settings, the MBTI can help to analyze curricula, methods, media, and materials in light of the needs of different types.

— In counseling, it can help couples and families learn the value of both their differences and similarities.

— Using the MBTI in career guidance can help guide individuals in their choice of school majors, professions, occupations, and work settings.

— For athletics and teamwork, it can help select teams, and help team members grow in their own development as each learns from the skills of the other.

— In a communications setting, the MBTI can help to increase understanding by "talking the language" of different types in the group.

The investigation of athletes personality type and its relationship with individual and team performance is innovative; results of the work conducted with NBA players, Olympic athletes and high school athletes have been very positive. Coaches and parents can now better understand the behavior of athletes and teams. Athletes can better understand their preferences and utilize that information to maximize their performance in sport and in their second careers.

Index

EUCLIDEAN GEOMETRY